Bringing Books to the Ozarks

A Branson Adventure

by

**Kathleen Van Buskirk
and
Lorraine Humphrey**

1998

Taneyhills Community Library

Copyright © 1998
Kathleen Van Buskirk and Lorraine Humphrey
Branson, Missouri
ALL RIGHTS RESERVED

ISBN 0-934426-88-0
LCCN 98-75116

Available from:
Taneyhills Community Library
200 South 4th Street
Branson, MO 65616-2712

Price: $14.95
(Subject to Change)

Printed in The United States of America by:
Stewart Publishing & Printing Company
Route 4, Box 646
Marble Hill, MO 63764
(573) 238-4273

Publisher's Cataloging-in-Publication
(Provided by Quality Books, Inc.)

Van Buskirk, Kathleen. 1924 -
Bringing books to the Ozarks : a Branson adventure / Kathleen Van Buskirk and Lorraine Humphrey. -- 1st ed.
p. cm.
Includes bibliographical references and index.
Preassigned LCCN: 98-75116
ISBN 0-934426-88-0

1. Taneyhills Community Library--History. 2. Public libraries--Missouri--Branson--History. 3. Taney County (Mo.)--History. 4. Branson (Mo.)--History. I. Humphrey, Lorraine. II Title.

Z733.T36V36 1998   027.4778'797
                          QBI98-1416

Dedication

This book is dedicated to the hundreds of women and men who served their community through membership in the Taneyhills Library Club; and to all of the other citizens of Ozark Mountain Country who have established a library in their own particular locality.

Acknowledgments

THE HISTORICAL COMMITTEE
Kathleen Van Buskirk, Author/Statistician
Lorraine Humphrey, Co-Author/Editor
Lola Charleston, Chairman/Organizer
Bill Ellen Hall, Consultant/Advisor
India Austin, Membership Research
Grace Eckert, Membership Research

ASSISTING LIBRARY CLUB PRESIDENTS
Bill Ellen Hall
Juanita Thompson
Marie Gibson Tammay
Barbara Boone
Florene Stilwell
Ruth Benson

COVER ART
Bill Stilwell

Table of Contents

Dedication & Acknowledgments   v

Chapter I	Winding Roads & Railroad Tracks (Pre-1930)	1
Chapter II	Enter "Taneyhills" (1931-1933)	10
Chapter III	The Literary Invasion (1933)	26
Chapter IV	A Time of Growing & Sharing (1934)	39
Chapter V	Faraway Tales & Friends Nearby (1934-1935)	51
Chapter VI	Movers & Shakers (1935-1936)	67
Chapter VII	Oh, for a Book & a Quiet Nook (1936)	78
Chapter VIII	The Roll Keeps Changing (1936-1938)	92
Chapter IX	Battling the Powdery Scourge (1938-1940)	104
Chapter X	"The Shepherd" to the Rescue (1940-1941)	117
Chapter XI	Sisters in Adversity (1941-1944)	131

Table of Contents

Chapter XII	**The Name's the Game** (1944-1946)	146
Chapter XIII	**Decisions, Decisions** (1946-1947)	159
Chapter XIV	**Some Clear Definitions** (1947-1950)	174
Chapter XV	**Learning Together** (1950-1952)	187
Chapter XVI	**Books for a Developing Town** (1952-1959)	201
Chapter XVII	**Home Folks & Thriving Tourism** (1960-1969)	225
Chapter XVIII	**Growing Pains & Building Fever** (1969-1975)	240
Chapter XIX	**The Fever Mounts** (1975-1977)	257
Chapter XX	**Property Owners Anonymous** (1977-1992)	276
Chapter XXI	**Moving into the Computer Age** (1992-1998)	299
Bibliography		319
About the Authors		322
Index		324

Photographs & Maps

Map of Branson	x
Branson Presbyterian Church	2
Helen Fletcher	11
Poet John G. Neihardt	19
Sara Heath, 2nd Pres., Taneyhills Study Club	24
Ella Patton, Innkeeper	28
Branson Hotel in 1952	30
Albert Parnell Office Building	45
Marie Gibson, Short Story Contest Winner	55
Mary Elizabeth Mahnkey	58
Vitae Kite, Lepidopterist	63
Jim Owen and Digging Crew	75
Owen Theater	81
Rose O'Neill	84
The Branson-Hollister Flood of 1927	102
Don & Jill Gardner & Family	116
Harold Bell Wright, Author and Minister	123
Teenager at Work in Branson Library in 1942	135
Branson's Main Street Bridge	153
Elizabeth "Lizzie" McDaniel	166
Old Matt's Cabin, "Shepherd of the Hills"	168
Library Club Officers, 1947-48	175
Branson's Community Building	178

Photographs & Maps

Library Club Officers, 1954-55	211
Margaret Cram, Librarian	252
Norma Root, Marion Stark & Bill Ellen Hall	255
Library Matrons Admire Cornerstone, June 1976	268
The New Library Building is Completed in 1977	273
Funny Fashion Show, 1980	281
Library Club Officers, 1981-82	282
Golden Anniversary Tree: 1933-1983	284
Admiring the Proceeds of a Fund-Raiser	302
Library Club Officers, 1994-95	303
Ground-breaking Ceremony '94 Library Addition	308
Honorary Memberships Awarded, June 1995	316
Kathleen Van Buskirk	322
Lorraine Humphrey	323

Drawing of New Library by Bill Stilwell	front cover
Branson Hotel	back cover
Taneyhills Community Library	back cover

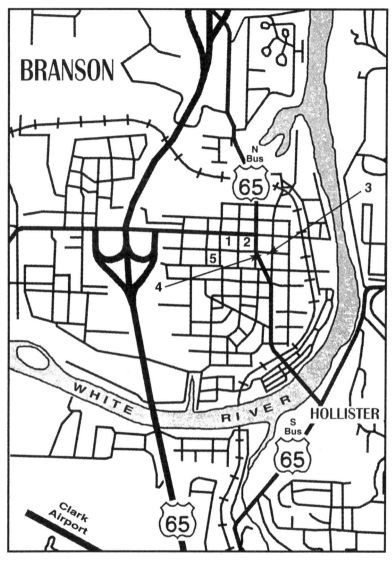

MAP OF BRANSON

1. Branson Hotel
2. Albert Parnell Office Bldg.
3. Civic League Building
4. Community Building
5. Taneyhills Community Library

CHAPTER I

WINDING ROADS AND RAILROAD TRACKS
(Pre -1930)

When I was a girl, books were scarce, but I grew up with the tattered remains of a grand old library....So I revered a book, and would walk miles to where folks lived who had books, thinking they would loan me one. One unseeing soul gave me a cabbage to carry home with me instead of a "blame book" and I never did like her, nor her folks.

These words, published in the *Country Home Magazine* in 1935, were repeated in front page stories all across the United States. They were spoken by Mary Elizabeth Mahnkey, a resident of Oasis, Missouri, population twenty-seven, while she was being feted in New York City as America's Country Correspondent of the Year.

Back home in the Southwest Missouri Ozarks, Mary Elizabeth's friends in the Taneyhills Study Club read her words in local news reports and nodded in understanding. There had been no public libraries in Taney County during the late 1800s, as she grew up,

Bringing Books to the Ozarks

taught school and married Charles P. Mahnkey; nor were there any in the early 1900s as she raised her family and, in spare moments, reported on the activities of her neighbors for county newspapers. Few families had even a half-dozen books in addition to the ever present Bible.

In 1935, however, thanks to efforts of the Taneyhills Study Club and to Mary Elizabeth herself, the western Taney County town of Branson, a dozen miles from Oasis, did have available a growing collection of books to read.

The Study Club, which was doing the collecting, began as an extension of the Maids and Matrons class of the First Presbyterian Church when class members grew conscious of the need

Branson Presbyterian Church.
When the Maids and Matrons Sunday School class of the Branson Presbyterian Church grew conscious of the need to expand their horizons, they went in search of books to study.

Winding Roads & Railroad Tracks

to expand their horizons beyond their little community of a thousand or so citizens. Interest in new ideas sent them in search of books and, as the women discussed information gleaned from what few books they could find, they also looked for ways to improve their supply of reading material.

Members of that Branson Sunday School class had no way of knowing that, in exploring new ideas, they were initiating a life-long journey--an adventure which would involve their daughters, granddaughters, neighbors and friends in the volunteer project of providing their community with books to feed the mind and spirit.

Their little town nestled in an alpine setting ten miles north of Arkansas on a sweeping bend of the White River, separated from the nearest larger population centers by miles and miles of steep hills, bluffs and narrow valleys.

In the early 1930s, area highways were twisting and narrow, keeping to the high ground whenever possible, descending over rocky outcroppings to cross creek bottoms which flooded with every heavy downpour. A few county roads were being graveled. The rest were scraped dirt trails, or twin paths worn by wagon and auto tires, teeth-jarring when dry and slick as ice or deep in mud whenever it rained.

Highway 65, the main road from Springfield through Branson and Hollister still was unpaved from Christian County to the Arkansas state line. Before the Depression brought paving projects to a halt, much of that road had been

Bringing Books to the Ozarks

cleared and leveled. Gravel piles dotted the right of way, waiting for the day when paving could resume. It would be a long time before blacktopping of that winding "major" highway was completed.

As this story begins, the town of Branson had been in existence less than thirty years. Taney County was formed in 1837, but prior to 1900 its population was concentrated along north-south trade routes further east, most passing through Forsyth, the county seat.

Already in 1900 there was, at the mouth of Roark Creek, a cotton gin, a saw and grist mill, a country school, a blacksmith shop, and a general store containing a post office bearing the name of its first postmaster, Reuben S. Branson. In 1901, for reasons which are obscure, the post office name was changed to Lucia.

Growth at Branson and across the White River at Hollister began shortly after the turn of the century, when the Missouri Pacific Railroad chose the valleys of Roark Creek rising north of the river and Turkey Creek flowing from the south as the best route for its White River Line. The completed railroad connected trade and industrial centers at Joplin, Carthage, and Springfield, Missouri, with central and eastern Arkansas.

When railroad construction began in 1903, on flat land in the river bend, the village of Branson suddenly had a business future. Enterprising men acquired farmland along what are now Main and Commercial Streets and laid

Winding Roads & Railroad Tracks

out the "Town of Branson." A rival group platted the "Town of Lucia" on adjacent land on the hillside near the store and post office. Within months, the post office was moved to the Branson townsite and changed back to its original name.

For a year or more, feeding railroad construction crews housed in tents was the main local industry. By 1904, several frame business buildings, including Henry and Mary Breeden's Hotel, appeared on the hillside that overlooked the not yet completed railroad.

Across the White River, a short distance up Turkey Creek, two or three buildings clustered about the new Hollister post office and general store. Upriver, on a high bluff known as Point Lookout, the "St. Louis Fishing and Hunting Club" was reassembling a great log lodge which had served as the Maine Building at the Louisiana Purchase Exposition held in St. Louis in 1904. Supervising that construction was the club's secretary, Willard P. Heath of St. Louis, who also was president of the Taney County Mining Company.

By the time a concrete railroad bridge across the White River connected the completed rail lines from the northwest and southeast in 1906, both Branson and Hollister were recognizable as towns. Ready access to markets encouraged farming for profit, and orchards, vineyards, and tomato patches soon began appearing on surrounding hills. Promising mineral discoveries, and plans for new factories and sawmill opera-

Bringing Books to the Ozarks

tions brought expectations of industrial development; and passenger trains began arriving, loaded with excited excursionists anxious to see the ruggedly beautiful but formerly inaccessible region.

The Branson Hotel, providing a large, gracious dining room and comfortable accommodations designed to attract traveling businessmen and vacationers, was in operation by January, 1905. The Bank of Branson opened for business in its newly completed brick building at Main and Commercial Streets in April, 1906.

The land along the railroad tracks was increasingly filled with logs and farm products awaiting shipment. Two blocks up the hill, on Commercial, several new business buildings appeared. A number of homes were built on the dusty streets which climbed the hillside.

In 1909, with considerable hope and faith in things not yet visible, the local Presbyterian congregation undertook to build a stone sanctuary and bell tower on the hill just above the Third Street business district. Before Branson's first church building was completed, however, most of the frame business buildings on Third had been moved down to Commercial and Main near the Bank of Branson.

Businessmen envisioned new potential for growth as construction began, in 1911, on a hydroelectric dam across the White River, downstream near Forsyth. The Ozark Power and Water Company's generators began operation in 1913, delivering electricity to distant cities. (It

Winding Roads & Railroad Tracks

was several more years before Branson businesses and residents received electric service.)

Upriver from Taneycomo's overflow dam, the backed-up water settled to a relatively predictable, navigable depth to and beyond Branson and Hollister, providing a normally stable, delightfully scenic water route to hotels and rustic resorts which immediately began developing along the shores to accommodate vacationers. Shortly after the lake was impounded, a steel bridge was built from the foot of Branson's Main Street to the narrow wagon road across the riverlike lake to the base of the Mount Branson bluff.

A sturdy concrete staircase built in 1914 allowed the occupants of the houses being built on top of the bluff easy access to Branson's many businesses. Any homes or resorts built on the shores of the lake were certain to be flooded, for the White River drains a wide section of rugged hills in southwest Missouri and northwest Arkansas, and frequently is subjected to very heavy rains.

In 1915, The School of the Ozarks, a Presbyterian boarding school which offered teenagers from isolated hill farms a high school education, was burned out of its quarters in Forsyth and found a new home in the then vacant lodge at Point Lookout. Residents of Branson and Hollister thus became close neighbors to succeeding generations of young people and to the educated men and women who came to teach them.

Each student at the school helped pay the

Bringing Books to the Ozarks

cost of his or her education by working at some campus job. Many of these hardworking young people decided to settle in Branson or Hollister after graduation, a decision usually encouraged by some local merchant. In Branson, many of those graduates gravitated to the Presbyterian Church up on the hill, for the faith of their mission-oriented teachers was strong and for several years the stone chapel remained the only church building in town. Graduates who settled in Hollister found another stone church on a hill above the railroad. It also was Presbyterian.

The bell in the Branson church tower was a familiar voice ringing across the valley. It summoned worshippers on Sunday and, in the early years, relayed the sad news of each local death. Those who were children in that long ago time cherished the memory that the bell tolled the years of the decedent's life, giving listeners at least a strong hint as to who had died.

The Presbyterian bell also was used to summon volunteer fire fighters (which included just about everyone in town) to each endangering fire. Twice in its early years Branson's existence hung in the balance as fire swept away familiar landmarks. On August 29, 1912, a blaze began in the Commercial Hotel at Commercial and Pacific Streets. Before the last flames died, twenty-one of the town's business buildings, almost all built of wood, were consumed by the fire.

Burned out buildings along Main and Commercial were rebuilt in fire resistant brick, cement and stone, but fourteen months later

Winding Roads & Railroad Tracks

flames again threatened the downtown section. This time, thanks to the "new, modern construction" and a better equipped and trained volunteer fire department, only six businesses were destroyed. Again, the fire loss was treated as an opportunity for civic improvement.

In 1930, there were several hotels within a few blocks of the train depot. Lumber yards, a pencil factory, and cottages of several vacation resorts stood in the areas near the lake. Hills around the business center were dotted with residences.

Still, the mountain town was a close and narrow world, or so it seemed to Fanny Dawes, who was teaching the Maids and Matrons class at the Presbyterian Church.

CHAPTER II

ENTER "TANEYHILLS"
(1931 - 1933)

There were twenty-nine women in the Maids and Matrons Sunday School class in 1931. The few still living in or near Branson in the early 1980s recalled that a girl joined the class when she became nineteen, or graduated from high school, or got married. Early club records indicate that there were members, too, who were considerably beyond their girlhood.

In amiable fellowship, the women spent long hours on money-raising projects for the church. Often they fixed meals for the men's group, bringing food prepared at home and charging twenty-five cents per person. The time involved was no less a donation than the food, for many of the women were employed, in addition to their family obligations.

Helen Fletcher, who started the Maids and Matrons class in the early 1920s, was one of those employed women. She and her husband, Rockwell, owned Branson's *White River Leader*. When Helen found the demands of operating the newspaper required that she give up teaching

Enter "Taneyhills"

Helen Fletcher Started the Maids and Matrons Class in the early 1920's.

the Sunday School class, leadership was assumed by Josephine Madry.

Josephine and her husband, Buford, moved to Branson from Aurora, Missouri, in 1925, shortly after their marriage. Buford operated the Madry Lumber Company on North Commercial Street, a block or two from their home on the Branson hill. In 1935, after the concrete bridge across Lake Taneycomo was completed, connecting Hollister's summer camps more closely with Branson's business community, diminutive, energetic Josephine Madry joined in partnership with Eula Whelchel Thornhill to develop Anchor Village, a picturesque resort and restaurant at the north end of the bridge.

Bringing Books to the Ozarks

Several years before Josephine became involved in the resort, however, she realized that teaching a women's Sunday School class was not something she enjoyed. When her close friend, Fanny Dawes, offered to take the class, Josephine turned over the leadership with a sigh of relief.

In the mid-1920s, Frank and Fanny Dawes left behind the educational, cultural and political world of Kansas City to settle in a large frame house several miles south of Branson. There they could provide a protected environment for their small son, Frank, Jr., who was a victim of hemophilia. Fanny's husband was a relative of Charles G. Dawes, the wealthy Chicago financier and active Republican who, from 1925 to 1929, served as Vice President of the United States with President Calvin Coolidge.

During those years, while many Dawes relatives participated in the excitement of having such a famous family connection, Frank Dawes and his brother, Herbert, developed the Oakmount Chicks Broiler Hatchery in Hollister. Fanny took care of her son and released her frustrations by single-handedly applying an intricate rock facing to her country home. When the boy's health was stabilized, however, a tutor was hired and the socially-minded mother turned her energies to community activities.

As teacher of the Maids and Matrons Sunday School class, Fanny quickly realized that many of the women she was teaching had little contact with the cultural world she knew so well.

Enter "Taneyhills"

Traveling four hours to Springfield and back over bumpy dirt roads to attend a play, lecture, or musical event seldom seemed practical. Nonetheless, the younger Maids and Matrons were, she decided, much in need of some mind-broadening activities.

The role that Fanny Dawes, then in her early thirties, assumed in leading the Maids and Matrons of Branson into closer contact with the world of art, music, and literature held some unique challenges. Josephine Madry later would recall that some of her Branson friends, not attuned to Fanny's organizational views and mistakenly feeling that she had usurped the leadership of the class, resented many of her suggestions.

It is a tribute to Fanny's discernment and patience that over a period of several years she succeeded in firing the group's enthusiasm for planning regular meetings, separate from the Sunday School class, for the enjoyment of music and literary discussion.

In 1932, class members voted to have study group meetings every other Saturday, alternating afternoon and evening sessions so as many members as possible could participate. Fanny planned the programs, opening doors to cultural opportunities in the vicinity of Branson that few of the women knew existed.

Gathering in different members' homes was an adventure in itself. Learning about music, art, and literature through guest speakers created unsuspected yearnings for social graces in the

Bringing Books to the Ozarks

participating women. Friends and neighbors who were not members of the Sunday School class began asking if they, too, could attend the programs.

From the earliest study meetings, the ladies came in their most fashionable clothes. Despite their apparent isolation, the women of Branson kept up surprisingly well with current fashions. The short, saucy hair styles and swishy above-the-knees skirts of Flapper days were giving way to longer, painstakingly marcelled hair and flowing mid-calf-length dresses. White gloves and feather-bedecked hats, often concocted by local milliners, were worn for these occasions.

Even in forming a study group, Branson women were following a nationwide "fashionable" movement. In the 1930s, lectures, and music and dance performances were being sponsored by women's clubs all across America. In cities such as Dallas, Chicago, St. Louis, and Kansas City, local speakers could be engaged on a myriad of subjects for a relatively modest fifty dollar fee. Nationally renowned lecturers could be arranged for two hundred to eight hundred dollars.

Fanny Dawes was well aware that such fees were beyond the means of the young women who were the focus of her concern. She began her campaign by calling on talented neighbors already known to many of the women.

The first reported study group meeting was held on November 24, 1932. The Maids and Matrons who gathered at young Kathleen Todd's

Enter "Taneyhills"

home on their "regular meeting day," were holding a remarkable combination of church circle meeting and cultural study session. After Lena Williams, wife of the Presbyterian minister, Rev. Glen A. Williams, lectured on material in a Presbyterian home-study book, all present took a test on what they had just learned, followed by an English quiz prepared by Pearl Denham.

In a short business meeting, the twenty women who crowded the Todd living room elected Fanny their teacher for another year.

Three months later, on a wintry Saturday in mid-February, 1933, the process of separating the Study Club from the Sunday School class began. Women from Branson and all over the surrounding hills gathered at Lonnie and Lee Allen's Allendale Resort on North Commercial Street for a luncheon-study meeting sponsored by the Maids and Matrons class of the Branson Presbyterian Church.

Lonnie greeted her forty-seven guests in the resort's new clubhouse. Allendale is still a familiar vacation spot near the mouth of Roark Creek in downtown Branson, though the trestle-like bridge which once carried all north-bound traffic past its doors was replaced in the 1930s by a higher concrete structure upstream.

Food for the luncheon that day came from the Maids' and Matrons' larders. The quarter paid by each woman who attended (including those who brought the food) went into the club's treasury.

Plans for luncheon-study programs at Allendale in March and April were outlined by

Bringing Books to the Ozarks

Fanny Dawes, with the promise of further activities on the second Saturdays of May and June. After a recess for July and August, the meetings would resume in September and, she concluded, "the fall programs will then be established and a year's programs adopted."

Josephine Madry was presiding. Still thinking of the meetings as an adjunct of the Sunday School class, she emphasized that the aim of the Maids and Matrons "is to create week-day activities in a mental capacity in connection with our work in the church. The primary purpose of the club is to study."

And study they did.

Maude Horine, a talented writer and businesswoman who lived south of Hollister, reviewed current events in a charming, whimsical style. Mrs. Bennett, the wife of Dean John Bennett of Springfield's Drury College, then adeptly led the women through a maze of authors and their books. She explained the writing styles of John Galsworthy, Sinclair Lewis, Sherwood Anderson, and several others, and pointed out the propaganda lines or unusual perspectives of each. Branson's seekers after mental food were not going to be fed milk toast.

Mrs. Bennett, and her husband as well, were to appear on many future Study Club programs. In payment, they received transportation costs and a free lunch.

Thirty women attended the March 11th Study Club luncheon. A full afternoon was planned. Jessie Gansz, wife of Phillip Gansz, a well-known

Enter "Taneyhills"

Missouri newspaper editor, spoke on "The advantage of using a definite outline in studying literature." Josephine Madry led a lively discussion of world events and Fanny Dawes reviewed the current bestseller *Magnificent Obsession* by Lloyd Douglas. The event was covered at length in the *White River Leader*.

At the April 8th luncheon, Mrs. Wilmer Thompson, another visitor from Springfield, explained to the thirty-six women present the relationship of art to home, garden, and dress. Again the women shared information on current events. No business was discussed, though the following year, and for all the years since, the club has celebrated its birthday on April 11th.

Actually, the club's anniversary date stems, not from that luncheon meeting, but from a dinner meeting of the sponsoring Maids and Matrons held the following Tuesday at the country home of Fanny Dawes. Before the latter session adjourned, members of the Maids and Matrons Study Group elected Pearl Denham their first president. Kathleen Todd was to be vice president; Bill Ellen Hall, secretary; and Helen Alexander, treasurer.

All of the new officers were women in their early twenties. Pearl and Ted Denham operated a restaurant on Commercial Street. Across the street and a bit further north in the same block, Helen Alexander, who had been a teacher in the Branson schools before her marriage, now worked side by side with her husband, Al, in their A. H. Alexander Drug Store. Bill Ellen Hall,

Bringing Books to the Ozarks

too, was a school teacher not currently under contract due to her marriage to Ted Hall the previous year. Kathleen Todd was keeping house for her brother, Stanley, and her father, Vernon Todd.

Through most of 1933, the Maids and Matrons Study Club members planned their monthly programs at separate business meetings.

The popularity of the Allendale luncheons reached a new peak in May, when sixty women responded to the introductory roll call by reciting their favorite verse of poetry. The day's program was devoted to poets, specifically to the life of poet Dr. John G. Neihardt.

Dr. Neihardt, in 1920, had moved his family from Nebraska to a stone house on Main Street beyond the west edge of Branson. There he reveled in the surrounding wooded hills, the clear waters of Roark Creek and nearby Lake Taneycomo, and far vistas of Ozarks plateaus and valleys. Daily he worked on his poetic "Cycle," a six-volume epic of the opening of the West and the struggle between Native Americans and westward moving pioneers. (His life and works are chronicled in *John G. Neihardt, A Critical Biography*, by Lucile Aly.)

Thanks to Dr. Neihardt, his wife Mona, their four talented children, and his mother Alice Neihardt, from the Maids and Matrons first tentative study meetings those present were led into the world of classical music, sculpting, drama, and poetry.

Enter "Taneyhills"

Poet John G. Neihardt and his Wife and Children
brought poetry, classical music and art into the lives
of Taney County women.

Mona Neihardt, an accomplished musician, charmed the women with several violin recitals. In the early 1930s, radio was a raucous and uncertain infant and there were few phonographs in Branson. Playing for women, many of whom had heard little music other than hymns and hill songs, she drew rapt attention as she performed the melodic works of the classical masters, interspersing the music with information about the composers' works and lives. At other meetings Mona Neihardt discussed her

Bringing Books to the Ozarks

own work as a sculptress, or reviewed her husband's writings.

In 1921 Dr. Neihardt, an intense, charismatic man, small in stature but spell-binding before audiences, had been acclaimed the poet laureate of Nebraska. By the 1930s, with his western fiction and poetry internationally famous, he was much in demand in lecture halls throughout the United States. For the Maids and Matrons he performed "readings" of his own poetry and explained the poet's craft, inspiring several to write poetry of their own. At one well-remembered session, held in the Neihardt home, he explained that "writing poetry is like having a baby. I get all the materials within myself and then all of a sudden I have a poem."

The younger women drank in his words, starry-eyed. Mothers with several children stifled smiles.

Mary Elizabeth Mahnkey was present that day, though neither she nor her husband drove. Thanks to Sara Heath, who provided Mary Elizabeth with a ride, she attended most of the 1933 programs. Sara, with her husband Willard, had moved from St. Louis to a country home south of Hollister in 1929. Other women attending, including a full carload from rural Ridgedale just north of the Arkansas state line, had moved to the physically isolated area because of their husbands' employment or to escape the pressures of city life. There also were several young teachers from the nearby School of the Ozarks. The response of these women to having such cul-

Enter "Taneyhills"

tural events available was like that of thirsty wanderers in a desert suddenly finding water.

When the Study Club met in May, Alice Neihardt gave a mother's view of Dr. Neihardt's life and career. Long a participant in similar study groups in Nebraska, the sweetly Victorian grandmother provided rare insights into her famous son's awakening to his literary gifts, his "inward urge that won't be silenced . . . a gift akin to inventive genius." Mona Neihardt also appeared on the program that day, performing on the violin accompanied at the piano by her daughter, Enid.

Finally, Pearl Denham was introduced as the president of the Maids and Matrons Study Club, and plans were revealed for the development of a permanent organization. The new group would need its own name, so a contest was to be held. Each member of the Maids and Matrons class and "those who are charter members of the club" could submit one entry.

The tremendous success of the May meeting, pleasing as it was, left the Maids and Matrons in a real quandary. The day marked the fourth time in as many months that they had brought food from home to serve the meal, then paid their twenty-five cents before sitting down to eat. The more popular their study programs became, the higher the personal cost to the class members.

The problem was very apparent to one of the supportive guests, a plain spoken woman of the hills, who pulled Bill Ellen Hall aside and cautioned, "Honey, you can't go on giving food for

Bringing Books to the Ozarks

the club. Electric bills are getting higher all the time, and it even costs money to flush the toilet these days."

Those words did not go unheeded. When the women met in June to hear osteopathic physician Dr. Charlotte Martin discuss "The importance of knowing and understanding one's own body," they met at the Branson Presbyterian Church. No luncheon was served.

Many pleas were voiced that day to continue the programs through July and August. When Sara Heath invited the group to meet in July at her home, Journey's End, that invitation was quickly accepted.

A newspaper comment on the planned continuation through the summer sounds familiar in today's Ozarks. "This is the season of the year when most civic and social organizations in this section suspend activities because of hot weather and summer tourist business."

Before the June meeting ended, Fanny Dawes promised that a constitution and bylaws would be presented in July. The Study Group president and secretary already were hard at work preparing such a document.

Pearl Booth Denham, the new president, had been brought to Branson as a small child, when her father was hired to build the Presbyterian church. In 1919, after she completed the sixth grade, her family moved to Baxter Springs, Kansas, where she finished high school. Ten years later she returned to Branson with her husband. As a member of the Maids and

Enter "Taneyhills"

Matrons class, Pearl's energy, ready wit, and speaking ability soon involved her deeply in church and study group activities.

Bill Ellen Riley Hall had come, as a 12-year-old child, from a farm north of Green Forest, Arkansas, to attend The School of the Ozarks. She graduated from high school there in 1928, and by 1930 had earned a two-year degree and teaching credential from Warrensburg State Teachers' College, and accepted a contract to teach in Branson.

In the Denhams' apartment behind the restaurant, Fanny Dawes instructed the two young women in preparation for their task, assuring them, "There's nothing to it." They soon discovered, however, that their organization did not fit any dimension described in *Robert's Rules of Order.*

Through the warm days of June, they spent hours with papers spread on the kitchen table, struggling with rules for writing constitutions and trying to organize the Study Club under the auspices of the sponsoring church group.

Frequently Pearl's attention was diverted by the needs of her year-old son. Both she and Bill Ellen felt the pressure to get their job finished. The Denham baby would soon be old enough for his mother to return to helping in the restaurant, and Bill Ellen and Ted Hall were completing plans to open a gift shop in downtown Branson.

Repeated searches have failed to unearth any copies of that first constitution. Its authors recalled, in later years, that it tied active mem-

Bringing Books to the Ozarks

In 1934 Sara Heath (left) Became the Second President of the Taneyhills Study Club. In 1933, her daughter Dorothy Heath Jaenicke (right) was named the group's first Honorary Member for suggesting the name "Taneyhills Study Club."
(Photo courtesy of Paul Jaenicke)

bership, the right to vote and hold office, directly to membership in the Maids and Matrons Sunday School class. Other interested women could be accepted as non-voting, non-office-holding associates. Provision also was made for awarding honorary memberships to "such person or persons, not already members of the club, who have rendered very distinctive and outstanding services to the club and community."

The constitution apparently was presented, as planned, at the July meeting, having first been approved by the sponsoring Maids and

Enter "Taneyhills"

Matrons. Were there some unhappy "associates" among the forty-nine women who gathered at Sara Heath's home on that hot Saturday afternoon? Undoubtedly. The meeting concentrated, however, on the results of the club-naming contest.

Hereafter the group would be known as the "Taneyhills Study Club." The committee making that selection included Lyta Davis Good, an instructor at The School of the Ozarks and wife of its president, Robert M. Good; Louise Cahill, also a teacher at The School of the Ozarks, and Miss Zamah Bigelow, a visitor from New York. The winning name came from Dorothy Jaenicke, daughter of the Heaths. She and her husband Arthur had only recently moved to the Ozarks from St. Louis.

Dorothy's reward was "a lifetime membership in the club." She also received a ten-dollar bill, which she promptly returned to the group's treasurer.

Without question, the club was the big winner that day, for the attractive young mother earned what was immediately recognized as an Honorary Membership many times over in the next fifteen years.

CHAPTER III

THE LITERARY INVASION
(1933)

How can we study without any books?" one woman complained, when the Study Club met in August at the Branson Hotel to discuss current events.

"We could share what we have. Each of us bring a book or two from home," another offered.

Bill Ellen Hall declared, "I'm going to give my *Pollyanna* book, and my copy of Harold Bell Wright's *The Shepherd of the Hills.*

Taking their cue from Bill Ellen's eager promise, the women began delivering their loans and donations to the Halls' small rented house, across Main Street from the Branson Hotel.

Delighted, Bill Ellen, Ted, and their close friends immediately began reading. "We had read half the books before a library shelf was found to hold them," Bill Ellen recalled years later.

A second book collection began growing in the garage of Claude and Gwen Binkley's home. Claude owned the local Chevrolet dealership. Gwen was not a member of the Sunday School class or the Study Club. However, having lis-

The Literary Invasion

tened to reports of the project and donated books from her own collection, she wrote enthusiastically to her sister in Galesburg, Illinois, telling of the club which was trying to start a library. By return mail, Gwen received a box of books, with the promise of more if the study club could pay for postage. The Binkleys had friends all over the Ozarks, and after each social visit the stack of books grew larger. Their garage began taking on the appearance of a warehouse.

The Halls stacked boxes filled with books on their front porch, for there was little extra space inside their house. One evening in late August the young couple went across the street to the Branson Hotel for dinner. Ella Patton, remembering the discussion at the recent Study Club meeting, asked if the growing collection of books was beginning to be a problem.

Without waiting for an answer, the elderly innkeeper then announced, "There's space in the back of the hotel hall you can use to start your library."

At the September Study Club meeting, held at the nearby home of Josephine Madry, a committee was appointed to set up library rules, and members volunteered to prepare the books for checkout and locate some bookshelves.

The next edition of the *White River Leader* boasted, "Club Fosters Public Library." Through the next eleven years, the collection of books which the women of the Taneyhills Study Club worked very hard to support and enlarge was the "Taney County Public Library." Changing the

Bringing Books to the Ozarks

Ella Patton, Innkeeper, Found Space for the Books
in the Branson Hotel's back hall.

The Literary Invasion

name in later years did not alter local feelings on the subject. Though, to this date, no library taxes have been levied in Taney County, club members agree that the community's loyalty toward its "public library" has made the fund-raising efforts in support of the library much easier.

In the fall of 1933, while Katherine Ellison, Dorothy Jaenicke, Mabel Richardson and Edna Rhoads carded donated books for lending, club officers put together the Study Club's first yearbook.

The covers were folded sheets of yellow construction paper. For every copy of the three dozen booklets, Fanny Dawes typed out the new constitution, a list of club officers and the schedule of monthly programs. The club has used the same "Collect," or opening prayer, since its inaugural meeting in February, 1933, and it also may have been in that first yearbook.

Half a century later Bill Ellen recalled, "When the yearbooks were all typed, Fanny, Pearl and I assembled and stapled them. The club paid two dollars for a ream of typing paper."

The following year, and again in 1935, yearbooks were typed and put together by hand. Since 1936 they have been printed, or at least mechanically copied. None of those handmade yearbooks have been seen for many years.

The yearbooks were distributed on October 14th, when a sparkling literary occasion took place at The School of the Ozarks, bringing together a number of area writers, the mothers of

Bringing Books to the Ozarks

The Branson Hotel in 1952

three writers, and a very enthusiastic group of local women. The president and secretary sent handwritten invitations to at least twenty Missouri writers. Several declined the invitation, some failed to answer, but enough accepted to make it truly a day to remember.

Alice O'Neill, whose daughter Rose was a world famous writer, artist, and creator of the beloved Kewpie characters and dolls, was one of those who accepted. She was born Asenath Cecilia Smith in Bloomsberg, Pennsylvania. When she met and married tall, courtly William Patrick O'Neill on his return from naval service

The Literary Invasion

in the Civil War, Alice was a lovely diminutive eighteen-year-old with a flair for the dramatic and an excellent musical education. In the mid-1870s, William, drawn by the wide open spaces, left a successful publishing business in his native Wilkes-Barre, Pennsylvania, and moved his growing family to Nebraska.

By 1893, however, Omaha had become too populated to suit the reclusive Irishman. He sought out a bluff-bound glade on Bear Creek in northern Taney County and moved his wife and family into a two-room log cabin there. In later years, his daughter, Rose, built a fourteen-room manor house around the log cabin. From a nearby hillside spring, water was piped to the house, and by railroad the "first bathtub in Taney County" was transported from back east to Springfield and hauled by wagon south to Bonniebrook, the O'Neills' Ozark hideaway. Even in the 1930s, the long, narrow tub with its Queen Anne style claw feet continued to be the subject of much local comment.

In October, 1933, Josephine Madry, familiar with the way to the Bonniebrook, was asked to pick up Alice, who was to speak at the Study Club meeting but did not drive. The small valley which contained the big country house is reached today by a ten-mile drive north on Highway 65, and a short stretch on a hard-surfaced road beside Bear Creek.

Mrs. Madry drove over the ridge tops for twenty-three winding miles, then turned right off of Highway 65. Let's follow author Maude Horine's

Bringing Books to the Ozarks

directions in *Memories of Rose O'Neill:*

> . . . Down Highway 76 [now 160] until just in sight of Bear Creek Bridge where we "took out" on a one way bluff bound road . . . . The trail seemed to narrow as it progressed until the hill fairly crowded . . . the [car] over the creek bank . . . a tricky ford was facing us farther on . . . . Of the four or five roads used [according to weather and washouts] to reach the O'Neill homestead, all converged at the Fairy Tree. [Because of a combination of hill, rock and stream, the sharp turn onto the narrow lane to the house could only be made by circling the tree.]

Waiting for Josephine at the end of the country lane was a tiny woman dressed in a black silk skirt, and a matching shirtwaist with a high neckline. Alice settled herself in the passenger's seat, her round face wreathed in a warm smile. Josephine, on learning that it had been several weeks since her passenger had been to town and thinking that she might need groceries, asked if she would like to stop at a store. Josephine found her eighty-four-year-old passenger's reply both startling and amusing.

"Yes, I'd like to get a fiddle string for Uncle Joe."

At The School of the Ozarks, the two women, along with forty-eight other members and guests, enjoyed a luncheon prepared and served by students under the direction of their work supervisor. Then Maude Horine, program chairman of the day, began introducing the speakers.

The Literary Invasion

Alice O'Neill told of the life and work of her famous daughter. Alice Neihardt related the events which led her son to settle in the Ozarks. Mrs. W. E. McCanse, mother of writer, poet and professor Ralph Allen McCanse, explained that her son had come home to Springfield to convalesce from an illness, and while there had written *Road to Hollister*, a successful book of poetry. Adelaide Wayland, Dean of Women at the College of Eureka Springs, in Arkansas, delighted her listeners with readings of her own poetry.

The women then listened with rapt attention to readings from or discussions of the works of twenty-four other famous Missouri writers and "would have heard more, but the afternoon was almost gone."

It is difficult today to comprehend the hunger for literature, art and music that kept fifty women attentive through such a long program.

Among the honored guests at that literary afternoon was Mary Elizabeth Mahnkey. Though she asked to be excused from speaking, those present enjoyed hearing one of her poems read by Fanny Dawes.

The "country correspondent from Oasis" was short and plump, with flawless pink and white skin and lovely thick white hair. She had begun writing a weekly column of neighborhood notes for Forsyth's *Taney County Republican* in 1891, when she was fourteen years old. Through forty-two years her lilting reports of the daily lives and the joys, triumphs and sorrows of her neighbors and friends had attracted a host of admirers all

Bringing Books to the Ozarks

over the region. In the *Republican*, and later in the *White River Leader*, her readers also frequently found poetically phrased accounts of the tragedies of life in Taney County, reports which served to embark sinner as well as saint into the next life with the concerned best wishes and understanding of their neighbors.

At the Study Club's November luncheon, Mary Elizabeth Mahnkey provided a rousing "defense of the authenticity of Vance Randolph's book *Ozark Mountain Folk*." This meeting, held at the home of Opal Parnell, was neither as long nor as celebrity-laden as the October gala. However, members were intrigued by the informative descriptions of Marble (Marvel) Cave, provided by Professor S. Fred Prince. Prince was the geologist who, prior to 1900, surveyed for the United States government many extensive caverns, including Marvel Cave, which today is a popular feature of Silver Dollar City, twelve miles west of Branson's library.

Lyta Good concluded the scheduled program with an appeal to the women "to recognize their own needs, to be tolerant of others, more helpful in cooperation, more loving in the rendering of Christian service to humanity."

Mrs. Good, the daughter of missionaries to China, had been a member of the faculty of The School of the Ozarks since before its move to Point Lookout in 1915. Her role at the school, particularly after she married its director in the 1920s, was that of teacher, parent and character guide to the hundred or more students and role

The Literary Invasion

model to the young women who came there to teach. She would address the Study Club over and over again through the ensuing years. Many of the women on The School of the Ozarks staff joined the club and supported its activities. However, Mrs. Good never became a member, feeling that her responsibilities to "her young ones" must take precedence over any social activities.

An air of sadness pervaded that November meeting, for Peggy Thompson, an enthusiastic member of the Maids and Matrons class and the Study Club, had been killed in an automobile accident. The bell in the Presbyterian steeple no longer tolled the death of Branson citizens, but the club members, that day, memorialized their friend by rededicating their energies to the library which she had wanted very much to see established.

A few weeks later, at 2 p.m., on Saturday, December 2, 1933, the "Taney County Public Library" began operation. One hundred and fifty books were catalogued and ready to loan to the general public. These included a generous contribution of modern fiction from Dr. Neihardt who, as literary editor for the *St. Louis Post Dispatch* between 1926 and 1938, received a continuing supply of the most recent new books for review.

Ella Patton had joined enthusiastically in fitting the books with card pockets and circulation cards. Etta Mann loaned a bookcase and additional shelves were made by volunteers. Files to

Bringing Books to the Ozarks

hold magazines, and special equipment for a children's section, would soon be ready for use.

Books on child care and education, religion, economics, poetry, classical literature, and modern fiction were now available at the library, which would be open three hours each Wednesday and Saturday afternoon.

However, initial checkout policies seemed to belie the name Taney County Public Library. Members of the Taneyhills Study Club could borrow books after payment of an initial ten cent fee for a borrower's card. Non-club members must have their registration card signed by a property owner in Taney County, and then must pay a rental fee of five cents per book per week. Persons who did not qualify for a card could check out books on payment of a returnable one dollar deposit. Late return would bring a fine of two cents a day per book.

On the day the library opened, a "ledger of acquisitions" was begun. Six decades later those lists are still on file, confirming that, in December, 1933, Fanny Dawes donated fifty-two books and loaned twenty more, Dr. Neihardt gave forty-one, and fifty-nine came from the Heaths.

The practice of charging a general rental fee was discontinued almost immediately. Such charges just didn't seem reasonable when the supply of donated books kept increasing, Dorothy Jaenicke was serving as a volunteer librarian, and no rent was being paid for the library's space in the hotel.

While the library was in the hotel, quite a few

The Literary Invasion

guests took advantage of the visitor's deposit rule. After diners had enjoyed the family-style meal served in Ella Patton's elegant dining room, she ushered them into the back hall to see the library and encouraged those staying several days to enjoy a good book during their visit. Some guests who accepted that offer later sent books to be added to the library shelves.

Many a visitor's evening was spent reading *The Shepherd of the Hills*, drawn to that book because part of their day had been filled with a heart-warming and sometimes hair-raising ride through Shepherd of the Hills country, chauffeured by Branson's colorful taxi driver, Pearl "Sparky" Spurlock.

Pearl and her husband, G. F. Spurlock, came to the Ozarks in 1918 and knew immediately they had found a home. It didn't take Pearl long to discover that she was born to be an Ozarks taxi driver. She delighted in driving visitors to the headwaters of Roark Creek northwest of Branson, giving their nerves a good jangling as the taxi bumped its way up the rocky unpaved goat trail on the steep slopes of Dewey Bald, then slid and skidded over the winding, grassy path through Mutton Hollow, following the legendary "trail nobody knows how old."

The theatrical cab driver costumed herself like a mountain granny, in a long calico dress and flowered bonnet. Usually puffing and chewing on a corncob pipe, she punctuated the wild ride with episodes from the old book, pointing out each site involved in Harold Bell Wright's

Bringing Books to the Ozarks

story. While regaling her passengers with tales of make-believe mingled with homespun truth, Sparky halted at Marble Cave and nearby Fairy Cave (presently known as Talking Rocks Cave) so sightseers could descend to hike by torchlight among the domes and awe-inspiring draperies and columns.

In the course of every trip, Branson's cabby encouraged her passengers to read *The Shepherd of the Hills* for themselves, and while the library was located in the Branson Hotel they could do so that very night, providing the book was not already checked out.

CHAPTER IV

A TIME OF GROWING AND SHARING (1934)

When the Taney County Public Library first opened its doors, on December 2, 1933, the ruling elders of the Branson Presbyterian Church realized they were in an impossible situation.

A Sunday School class might conduct a special study group, even sponsor a series of lectures open to the public, but the church should not accept responsibility for a "public" library being supported and operated for community-wide use. Clearly, the Taneyhills Study Club would have to be removed from its church related status, and soon.

The Maids and Matrons had been making donations to the church from the Study Club treasury for more than a year. The last of those donations was made in February, 1934. The only business discussed at the January and February meetings had to do with changes needed to establish the Study Club as an independent organization. When new officers were elected at the March meeting, full membership was open to

Bringing Books to the Ozarks

all interested Taney County women.

For Sara Heath, Opal Parnell, Maude Horine and the many other participating women who had enjoyed no voice or vote in the decision making through the past year, the change brought deeper involvement and commitment. The Sunday School class members who had so eagerly sponsored the popular programs through 1933 continued to be active, some for a year or two, several for the rest of their lives.

On the other hand some Maids and Matrons, feeling that families, church, and jobs were their main priorities, dropped from the club's roll between November, 1933, and February, 1934.

In the revised constitution, the library was not mentioned. Dues, to begin for all members on April 1, 1934, were ten cents a month or a dollar per year. The only "associates" would be those who wished to belong but found it impossible to engage in active membership. Two meetings were to be held each month, alternating afternoons and evenings. Club leaders scheduled a luncheon or tea on the first Saturday of each month and special interest meetings on each third Saturday.

The women who gathered at the Branson Hotel for the March 3rd luncheon were seated at a long table covered with spotless white linen and set with fine china, glistening crystal glassware and linen napkins. Their luncheon cost twenty-five cents in addition to their dues.

Ella Patton, their warmhearted hostess, was acclaimed the Study Club's second Honorary

A Time of Growing and Sharing

Member that day. Through the following months, as she stumbled around boxes of books which had overflowed the library shelves and were stored in the hotel pantry, Ella could take comfort in reminding herself that her generosity was much appreciated by the women who ran the club and by those who borrowed books from the library.

Pearl Denham was not on hand to conduct the 1934 election. She, her husband and little son had moved to Kansas the preceding month. The nominating committee presented a double slate of candidates from which leaders were elected for the coming year.

New officers were installed in April at the club's first anniversary luncheon. President Sara Heath, vice president Edna Rhoads, treasurer Ethel Evans, and parliamentarian Alice Neihardt were former associates. Recording secretary Gay Miser, corresponding secretary Josephine Madry and press reporter Bill Ellen Hall were Maids and Matrons.

Two accounts of the event were published. Bill Ellen noted in the Branson paper that fifty women enjoyed John Neihardt's discussion of world conditions, a talk by a visiting foreign missionary, and news that several dozen books from the St. Louis Public Library would soon be available on the library shelves in the hotel hall.

Mary Elizabeth Mahnkey's report of the meeting appeared in the *Springfield News-Leader*. Her warmly interesting stories of the club's activities were read all over Southwest Missouri, develop-

Bringing Books to the Ozarks

ing for the Taney County Library and its sponsors a regional rooting section. Almost every mail brought more books to stock the library shelves.

Of the new club president, who continued to make sure that her friend in Oasis got to the club meetings, Mary Elizabeth wrote:

> She has a sense of humor,
> But does not act the clown.
> This sparkling, sweet, gay whimsy
> Means more than costly crown.

Sara Heath, whose matronly appearance belied her many years experience in education, business, and club work in St. Louis, would be needing that sense of humor.

When monthly reports were heard at that first anniversary meeting, the nine dollars and twenty-seven cents in the treasury sounded acceptably familiar to the Maids and Matrons present. Seldom during the past year had their funds exceeded ten dollars and, thus far, the five-month-old library had brought little increase in expenses.

To the new president, however, that report raised several questions about the responsibilities she was assuming. In a matter of weeks, she would find herself employing all her wit and knowledge to keep the library open.

Meantime, she presided at the May luncheon and basked in a little glory. The guest speaker was the president of the Sixth District of Federated Clubs of Missouri, who surprised and

A Time of Growing and Sharing

delighted her listeners by declaring, "Perhaps no other similar organization has at hand such a wealth of talent." It was a memorable compliment for women who had so short a time before felt isolated and culturally deprived.

Second on the program was Louise Cahill, who had been hired to establish and direct an art department at The School of the Ozarks. She spoke on "How to Study Pictures."

After the meeting, many members took time to look over the growing collection of books behind the hotel stairs. In the spring of 1934, the little library was, like its sponsoring club, experiencing a remarkable popularity. Each added bookcase was filled as soon as it was in place and the only thing preventing total overflow was that so much of the donated reading material was being enjoyed in Taney County homes.

Dorothy Jaenicke, whose golden hair and friendly smile brightened the windowless, book-filled hall, enjoyed the company of Ella Patton. However, the volunteer librarian soon became uncomfortably aware that having readers of all ages trailing through the hotel lobby in all kinds of weather was causing many problems for the library's hostess. Ella Patton's warm friendliness never failed, but she was seventy-eight years old and increasingly frail. Preparing for the hotel dinner hour on the days when the library was open was taxing her sense of humor.

Concerned, Dorothy told Sara Heath, "Mother, we've got to find a library room downtown before the summer visitors fill the hotel."

Bringing Books to the Ozarks

Encouraged by her mother and the other club officers, Dorothy arranged with Branson's mayor, B. Albert Parnell, for the library to operate in a small rear office at 104 West Main Street. To get money to pay the six dollars per month rent, club officers canvassed Branson businessmen for contributions.

However, the town's only bank was struggling to reorganize under new leadership after having failed in 1933, and local businesses faced severe financial problems. In 1934, donations toward the library's rent were made in quarters and dimes more often than in dollar bills.

Fanny Dawes, recognizing the region-wide popularity of Mary Elizabeth Mahnkey's poems, had been encouraging her to put several dozen of them together in a small book. With the help of friends the selection had been made, but Mary Elizabeth had no way of paying for its printing or distribution. Many of her readers did seem interested in such a book, however. So Fanny suggested that if the Study Club could arrange for publication, advance the costs, and help with sales, Mrs. Mahnkey would probably be willing to share the profits from her *Ozark Lyrics* in support of the library.

Despite their near empty treasury, the club board accepted the challenge. Quickly the word went out that the four-hundred-copy first edition of *Ozark Lyrics* would be in print by early July. Before the June meeting ended, the club members had enough orders to assure publication costs. (The first three editions of the poetry book

A Time of Growing and Sharing

Albert Parnell Owned this building on Main Street
where the library was moved in June 1934.
Downtown merchants helped pay the rent.

bore the title *Ozark Lyrics*. A reprint issued by The School of the Ozarks Press in 1972, and subsequent reissues, are titled *Ozarks Lyrics*.)

Sara Heath and her fellow officers were greatly relieved! Typesetters and printers could not afford the gamble of doing the work before they were assured of being paid, and the club had no reserve funds to meet such bills, or even to pay the two dollar copyright fee.

Mary Elizabeth's book of poems proved a continuing joy to readers and a tremendous asset to the library and Study Club. In June, 1934, however, the project was not far enough along even to pay its own expenses, and the new library

Bringing Books to the Ozarks

room needed a lot of work.

No rent payment was made for June but, with five dollars and fifty-five cents worth of lumber and paint, volunteers constructed shelves and made needed alterations to the small office in the Parnell Building. Two large, sturdy bookcases were donated by a new associate member, Dorothy Worman. A wealthy young St. Louis matron who both donated and borrowed books at the Branson library, Dorothy often stayed at the family's lodge at Devil's Pool, in the cedar-laden hills up the creek just east of the Mahnkey store and home in Oasis.

Preparations for moving the library books were just beginning when the Study Club held its June, 1934, luncheon at the Hollister Presbyterian Church. That afternoon the women watched in fascination as Mona Neihardt, who before her marriage had studied sculpting in the Paris studio of Auguste Rodin, sculpted the face of fellow member Helen Stratte, the librarian at The School of the Ozarks.

Later that month, club volunteers joined in a transformation project of their own--dismantling the library in the Branson Hotel, boxing up the five hundred books, and carrying them to the new location a block away. The distance seemed to increase with each load of books.

The women who had been seeking donations to cover the library's rent reported at the July 7th meeting that their collections had reached sixteen dollars. Mr. Parnell would be paid three months' rent before the library opened in its new

A Time of Growing and Sharing

location the following Tuesday. When the rent came due again, Parnell lowered it to five dollars a month.

Club members were sharing lunch that Saturday in the "English Garden" setting of the Blue Lantern Tea Room in Hollister. The speaker was Mrs. Wilmer Thompson. Drawing on her own artistic background and on knowledge acquired through her architect husband, she discussed American architectural development. Her listeners remembered with pride her observation that—

> . . . in copying England's half-timbered structures built on fieldstone foundations, the builders of Hollister's Downing Street truly had used the stone and timber that abound in the area in a way which fit beautifully and snugly in the Ozark hills.

At a sunny table near the front windows, Mary Elizabeth Mahnkey wore out her hand that day signing copy after copy of *Ozark Lyrics*. The thirty-two page booklet, which sold for a quarter, contained fifty poems, a mere sampling of the hundreds of lyrical writings created at the poet's kitchen table over the preceding four decades.

Those autographed books, which included a "Forward" written by John Neihardt, were collectors' items from the day they were sold. Few are to be found today. Several Branson women later reported ruefully that their copy had long since disappeared, loaned to some friend and never returned.

Bringing Books to the Ozarks

The sixteen dollars and fifty cents collected from book sales at the July meeting enabled the treasurer to pay A. A. Ball Company fifteen dollars for preparing the book for printing. And, belatedly, application was made for the poet's copyright.

By the end of July, sales of the poetry books enabled payment of the twenty-five dollars due the Sunshine Press of Springfield for printing and binding.

The first edition cleared fifty-eight dollars. Today the amount seems an insignificant sum raised through a heavy investment of talent and energy. However, the Study Club's share of forty-three dollars paid half the library's rent and expenses that year, together with membership dues and businessmen's contributions covering the one hundred and five dollar annual expenses of the library and club.

Mary Elizabeth Mahnkey's greatest rewards were seeing her book in print and knowing she had helped the library. She had written her weekly column for years with no payment other than an occasional supply of stationery and stamps. Her writing, like the running of the little library, was a "not for profit" endeavor. Nonetheless, in an economy notably short of cash, the fifteen dollars she received in royalties undoubtedly were very welcome.

The club's treasurer carefully recorded all the expenses and receipts from *Ozark Lyrics*. Each entry, even for speakers' travel and Mary Elizabeth's royalties, has the added notation,

A Time of Growing and Sharing

"+2c tax." Those notations are poignant reminders of the club's first encounter with government rules and regulations.

After several years of bankruptcies and tax defaults, in 1934 Missouri lawmakers, desperate for cash to put jobless citizens to work and get much needed road paving done, adopted a one-half of one per cent sales tax. Merchants were to collect one half cent on the dollar, or one mill on each twenty cents. Cardboard discs the size of milk bottle caps were distributed at ten mills for a penny. (Plastic mills, distributed in the 1940s, were abandoned in favor of pennies when the tax was increased to one per cent.)

There was much confusion in the cities where the cardboard coins were first distributed. In isolated places such as Branson, it was months before the mills appeared. Learning to handle a tax which was supposed to be paid with coins one had never seen created shopping and bookkeeping nightmares in Ozark towns and villages.

Later in 1934, when the full regulations finally became available, the exasperated Study Club treasurer found the tax didn't apply to most of the club's transactions anyway.

As Sara Heath and the other club officers groped for understanding of the Study Club's legal responsibilities, they also learned that their popular library was going to require more volunteer workers.

Meantime, with the club's treasury chronically almost empty, most of the thirty-five enrolled members happily involved themselves in reading

Bringing Books to the Ozarks

books and enjoying the monthly meetings, while a few volunteers struggled to keep the programs and books available.

CHAPTER V

FARAWAY TALES AND FRIENDS NEARBY
(1934 - 1935)

Through 1934, talented Ozark neighbors schooled in the arts or world affairs challenged members of the Study Club with thought provoking performances or information at every monthly program. One day Grace Palmer, the librarian of the State Teachers College in Springfield, shared her experiences as a visitor in Russia, and Jewell Phillips, a young teacher at The School of the Ozarks, told of the knowledge and understanding she had gained as a delegate to the International Collegiate Council at Geneva, Switzerland.

Another day, the women listened eagerly to Mae Stafford Hilburn, a Taney County poet and writer whose weekly literary programs were broadcast from Jefferson City on the statewide radio network. Few in the audience had heard Mae Hilburn on the air. In the White River hills, at that time, most radio reception was terrible to non-existent.

That same day, Dr. E. E. Corlis, a local physician who also was serving as county agricultural

Bringing Books to the Ozarks

agent, reported on industries then supporting Taney Countians; and Study Club member Hazel Vaughn, a teacher in the Taney County schools, discussed and read the lovely poetry of fellow member Vitae Kite.

From Vitae herself, whom many of the club members knew as the mother of Hollister's druggist, Rolland B. Kite, Jr., the group heard exciting recollections of girlhood in Eureka Springs, Arkansas, during that town's booming infancy as a health spa in the 1880s and 90s.

"The power of classical literature to lift the human spirit" was explored for eager listeners in November by Dr. T. W. Nadal, the president of Drury College. His address was followed by a lively panel discussion on the values of high school literary contests. Before the meeting ended, Prof. Vernon James of the Branson schools, along with educators from Hollister, Reeds Spring, Blue Eye, and The School of the Ozarks, helped the Study Club set up plans to sponsor such a contest.

Josephine Madry made the arrangements for the last meeting of 1934. In celebration of Christmas, vocal and instrumental soloists and choruses from Drury and the State Teachers College were bussed from Springfield to The School of the Ozarks to join with students and teachers there in presenting a musical afternoon. The public was invited, for a charge of fifteen cents for adults, a nickel for children. Lyta Good was also on the program, telling of the history and significance of many Christmas carols.

Faraway Tales & Friends Nearby

The auditorium was full, and the audience was very appreciative, but by the time transportation costs were paid for the many guest participants, the club barely broke even.

The library which Josephine had hoped to benefit continued to operate on a very tight budget. Dorothy Jaenicke's domain was a warm and friendly nook reached by first going through a business office. Donated rugs and furniture provided an attractive atmosphere, and three dollars and eighty cents had bought a small wood-burning stove which chased away the winter chill.

The book collection continued to grow. Dr. Neihardt brought in sixty more classics and new bestsellers. Fifty-two books were received from Sara Heath's sister-in-law, Minnie Todd, forty from Dorothy Worman and twenty-five from Mrs. W. F. Dewey. The shelves, however, were far from full, since most of the books usually were being enjoyed by one or another of the two hundred cardholders.

In early 1935, as Sara Heath neared the end of her term as president, the library was an obvious success, the study programs enjoyed tremendous popularity, and the club treasury was ending the year with eighteen dollars, not a comfortable backlog, but twice the balance of the year before. Taneyhills Study Club members obviously were pleased with their leadership. In March the group re-elected their president and most of her fellow officers for a second term.

The office of parliamentarian, which had been held by seventy-seven-year-old Alice Neihardt,

Bringing Books to the Ozarks

was left vacant in that election. The elder Mrs. Neihardt had died in early January, 1935, after a short illness. Her warmhearted support had been available for virtually every undertaking of the club and library through 1933 and 1934. She would be missed.

For that election meeting, the Study Club gathered at the Branson Hotel. It had been six months since the women last met for luncheon at the hospitable inn on Main Street, and nine months since the library was moved. Ella Patton was noticeably more frail, but she greeted her friends warmly and mentioned having missed all the activity surrounding the library.

Among the guests were the winners of the literary contest. The judges had been Mrs. John N. Bennett and Mona Neihardt, who found the quality of the four best entries, all short stories, so nearly equal that they were unable to reach a decision and called on Dr. Neihardt to assist. Ultimately, the judges agreed that each of the top contenders--Weldon DeBoard, Robert Hart, Mary Hoyt and Marie Gibson--should receive a first place prize of two dollars. All three local high schools, Branson, Hollister and The School of the Ozarks, were represented among the winners.

Marie Gibson Tammay remembers that her knees were shaking as she stood before the club to read her story that Saturday. The audience didn't know about the knocking knees, but it was noted that the petite girl's brown eyes seemed to grow as she read her sensitive story of a troubled marriage.

Faraway Tales & Friends Nearby

Marie Gibson, one of Four Area High School Students
who shared first place in the library club sponsored
short story contest in 1934.

After a career that took her to the business world of New York City, Marie Tammay returned to Hollister and in the year of the club's golden anniversary became president of the organization which had given recognition to her writing talent forty-eight years before.

Today she recalls that the clubwomen expressed amazement at the insight displayed in her story. That insight, she notes, improved considerably when she followed the suggestion of her sponsor, Hollister School Superintendent Jay Talley, to change an unhappy ending to a pleasant one.

When the meeting was over, with the contest prizes awarded, the board members rechecked their bank balance and quickly planned a fund-

Bringing Books to the Ozarks

raising event so the library rent could be paid for the next three months. The only remaining memory of that project is a nine dollar entry in the treasury book labeled "cash received ticket sale Treasure Island." It was an important deposit, whatever its source. When the women were joined by their husbands for a gala second anniversary dinner at the quaint Hollister hotel known as Ye English Inn, the rent money due on April 10th was in the treasury.

Mary Elizabeth Mahnkey had promised to be present that night to receive an Honorary Membership. Though stormy weather kept her at home, Sara Heath announced the award, and promised to deliver the membership card in person within a few days.

Among the guests at the dinner was Rose Wilder Lane, a well known author from Mansfield, Missouri who was staying at the inn and had been invited to speak. Today Rose Wilder Lane's fame has been eclipsed by that of her mother, Laura Ingalls Wilder, whose *Little House on the Prairie* books have gained renewed fame in recent years through a television series. In 1935, *Little House on the Prairie* was just being released and its author had only one previous book to her credit. Rose Wilder Lane, on the other hand, was the author of four bestselling novels, co-author of a fifth, and her newest novel was at the printer. No one was thinking of her as "Laura Ingalls Wilder's daughter" when she spoke at the Taneyhills Study Club anniversary dinner. In fact, reporters of her visit to Ye English

Faraway Tales & Friends Nearby

Inn complained of difficulty in obtaining copies of her very popular books.

A few days after the dinner, Rose Wilder Lane's activities in Taney County made local and Springfield headlines:

> Prompt action of neighbors and of a distinguished guest who was being entertained by the W.P. Heath family Sunday, prevented the burning of the lovely country home, Journey's End, on highway 65 near Hollister.
>
> Mrs. Rose Wilder Lane, novelist of Mansfield, was guest at Journey's End for a pleasant, old-fashioned country dinner. About 1:30 p.m. the brooder house, in which were 100 baby chicks, caught fire. Apparently a kerosene stove had exploded. The big barn, tool shed and hen house quickly were swept by flames. The garage also burned, but the automobile was moved in time to save it.
>
> Neighbors, seeing the flames, rushed to assist in fighting the fire. Mrs. Lane pumped water steadily and valiantly. If it had not been for the efficient fire-fighting, the home would have been lost.

By the time Rose Wilder Lane's stay at Ye English Inn was over, she was near the top of the local women's list of most admired writers and poets.

Poetry was a popular topic among the Study Club members in the spring of 1935. A "poetry division," guided by Dr. Neihardt, held reading and study sessions each month. For the May

Bringing Books to the Ozarks

Mary Elizabeth Mahnkey was Feted in New York City
as "Country Correspondent of the Year" in 1935

Faraway Tales & Friends Nearby

luncheon meeting, "Why We Should Read Poetry" was the subject of the day and Dr. Neihardt was the principal speaker.

Also discussed were plans for a second printing of *Ozark Lyrics*. The clubwomen were not aware of it, but they were about to receive a tremendous boost for the sale of those books.

The Crowell Publishing Company recently had conducted, through its magazine *The Country Home*, a nationwide competition to discover America's "best country journalist." Mary Elizabeth Mahnkey's many admirers and friends tried very hard to get her to submit an entry in the contest, but for some time she refused to consider it. How could she ever choose the required few columns from the more than two thousand she had written in the past forty-four years?

Finally, after the editor of the *Taney County Republican* offered to make the choice for her, she capitulated.

What none of Mary Elizabeth's friends knew, what those who judged the contest entries did not know, was that Taney County's beloved column writer was the person who had suggested the contest to the Crowell Publishing Company. She agreed to send in her entry only after she was assured that the final judging would be completely "blind." The judges would have no names before them when they read the more than four hundred and fifty entries involving some fifteen hundred columns.

There was great celebration among her

Bringing Books to the Ozarks

friends and neighbors when Mary Elizabeth's entry won first place in the country journalist contest. Initially she was awarded a fifty dollar prize. Then the magazine editors decided that the world should meet the winner of such a prestigious award.

The white-haired grandmotherly writer, who had never owned an automobile, traveled by train to New York City to receive due recognition. Her traveling wardrobe was in a suitcase loaned by Rose Wilder Lane, who hurried to Taney County to offer it as soon as she heard of the impending trip. And Mary Elizabeth carried a new, large handbag purchased by her friends in the Taneyhills Study Club. Ella McHaffie, a long time friend and the mother of Opal Parnell, went along to share the adventure.

Half the pages of the club's 1930s scrapbook are filled with clippings from newspapers far and near, detailing Mary Elizabeth Mahnkey's reception in New York City and Washington, D.C. She enjoyed a week of sightseeing and shopping, met New York's Mayor Fiorello La Guardia and Governor Al Smith, and was interviewed, photographed, discussed, and sometimes picked apart. She enjoyed emotion-packed visits to Edgar Allen Poe's home, the nation's capital and Mount Vernon. She was not, however, willing to "bother" President Franklin Roosevelt with taking time to meet her.

In New York, the gentle country correspondent also was interviewed on a nationwide radio broadcast. Few Taney Countians heard her.

Faraway Tales & Friends Nearby

Local radios could not pick up that program either.

By the time she returned to the Ozarks, the whole country had become acquainted with Mary Elizabeth Mahnkey's remarkable writing gifts, her down-to-earth philosophy and the reverence she held for good books.

The members of the Taneyhills Study Club basked in their friend's recognition. Shortly before her departure for New York, she had been guest of honor at the July meeting. By that time enough orders had been received to proceed with the printing of the second edition of *Ozark Lyrics*. The School of the Ozarks was to print the books, which would be available at the August meeting. Mary Elizabeth nodded pleasantly when asked if she could be present to sign each copy.

The August meeting was held at the home of Vitae Kite, on the Hollister shore where Turkey Creek enters Lake Taneycomo. Members were promised that there would be time to stroll through the gardens which filled the level ground south of the Kite home, time for admiring the flower-laden plants and the colorful butterflies that clustered on the blossoms.

Vitae Kite was a self-educated lepidopterist, whose retirement hobby of collecting, classifying and mounting butterflies and moths had brought her widespread recognition in the scientific world. In the course of her work, the slender, regal grandmother had identified a number of species not previously known to be in the Ozarks, and she engaged in worldwide corre-

Bringing Books to the Ozarks

spondence and specimen exchange with other butterfly collectors.

She also created many framed hangings using the fragile, winged creatures that she cultivated in her garden just as she cultivated flowers.

After a relaxed picnic lunch, the Study Club members listened intently as Vitae told of her moths and butterflies. Then they walked along the bank and enjoyed the rare view of the Missouri Pacific Railroad bridge looming upstream, the new Highway 65 bridge not far downstream, and canoes and excursion boats gliding up Turkey Creek to the landing several hundred feet away, as such boats had been doing through the twenty-two years since Lake Taneycomo's impoundment.

In the 1930s, the Sammy Lane Boat Line ferried vacationers, as well as local residents and the United States mail, to and from the downstream resort communities at Rockaway Beach, Powersite and Forsyth. Two mail boats and a double decker "dance boat," all named to remind visitors of the area's close connection with Wright's *The Shepherd of the Hills*, offered a sometimes faster and much more enjoyable trip than did the rough roads of that era.

The second edition of *Ozark Lyrics* was on hand that day at Vitae Kite's, but Mary Elizabeth, still exhausted from her trip and all the attention it had brought, sent her regrets and the promise that she would attend in September. During the business meeting, announcement was made that all the second edition had been

Faraway Tales & Friends Nearby

Club Member Vitae Kite, a Lepidopterist,
was credited with identifying several hitherto unrecognized varieties of butterflies in the Ozarks.

Bringing Books to the Ozarks

spoken for, but a third printing would be ready shortly. A few more poems were being added, the author's picture and a few notes about her life would be included, and each book was to be autographed.

By September, the Springfield newspaper had selected Mary Elizabeth Mahnkey as their "Poet Laureate of the Hills." Again invitations were sent to regional writers and club leaders to attend a literary banquet. This time Sara Heath was confident that most of the invitations would be accepted. Members and guests who were invited to dine at the Grandview Hotel, atop the high bluff called Presbyterian Hill across Lake Taneycomo from Branson, would be honoring the area's latest celebrity.

As the club officers prepared the invitations, however, they were more than a little concerned about meeting the food bill for the two hundred diners, half of whom would not be expected to pay for their meal. Despite the success of the second edition of *Ozark Lyrics*, few of the four hundred books had been delivered and paid for and, on September 2nd, the day the printing bill was paid, the club treasury was reduced to twenty-five dollars.

Fanny Dawes offered a solution. Whether it was welcomed or not was a matter of opinion. She and Frank would provide fifty pounds of chicken at cost, eight dollars and thirty cents, if the club members would pluck and clean them.

On a hot September morning, several of the women drove to the Dawes' home prepared for

Faraway Tales & Friends Nearby

action. Some had cleaned chickens before and already knew they were not going to enjoy the job. Some had never plucked a feather. No one was prepared for the size of the task. The story has been repeated endlessly through the years-- it has grown with the telling.

One squeamish lady cried, "I'll wash them, but not clean or pluck!" and, true to her word, she bent over the big tub of water until every chicken was washed. When the final bird was parted from its last pin feather, Fanny Dawes invited her "guest help" to share the delicious lunch she had spent the morning preparing.

It was a "brilliant gathering," that night at the Grandview Hotel when the Taneyhills Study Club saluted the nation's "Country Journalist of the Year." Mae Stafford Hilburn, as toastmistress, provided warmly humorous introductions for the many notables so that they could offer their own congratulations. Mary Elizabeth accepted all the accolades with quiet simplicity. She told about her adventures in New York, and noted that she had tried to remember "that she was an ambassador from her own hills."

The members and guests were then entertained by Etta Mann, who gave a vivid account of her recent explorations of London's narrow alleys and the byways of rural England and Ireland.

Sara Heath proudly reported to members and guests that the three-year-old library now had eight hundred books to offer local readers.

Also among the guests applauding Mary Elizabeth were Dean and Mrs. John N. Bennett,

Bringing Books to the Ozarks

of Drury College. However, the dean had recently retired. The couple now had a new Hollister address and Mrs. Bennett was an active member of the Study Club.

Mary Elizabeth and Preston Mahnkey also had recently moved because, she told New York reporters, "Oasis is going to be submerged" by Table Rock Dam. Since before the building of Powersite Dam, the citizens of Taney County had been bombarded with plans and rumors of plans for a giant hydroelectric dam at the high bluff several miles upstream from Branson. With each new proposal, the location and height of the planned structure changed, but the predicted results almost always included the inundation of the Long Creek village of Oasis.

Early in the summer of 1935, with newspapers again full of such speculation, the Mahnkeys sold their house and store at Oasis. They moved first to Forsyth, then to Mincy several miles south of the county seat. Neither place was more than a dozen miles from Branson. However, they now were closer to their family and to neighbors of earlier times. In the future, friends in the Study Club could not expect to see as much of Mrs. Mahnkey as they had in recent years. She would, however, continue to be much in the women's minds.

CHAPTER VI

MOVERS AND SHAKERS
(1935 - 1936)

Through the closing months of 1935, the Taneyhills Study Club reaped the profits of the second printing of Mary Elizabeth Mahnkey's poems. In November they took delivery of the third printing, another four hundred copies of *Ozark Lyrics* from The School of the Ozarks Press.

By the time those books were received, however, virtually every household in western Taney County already possessed a copy, and sales were suddenly very slow. Thankfully, an admiring donor had defrayed much of the expenses of the banquet, so there was money in the treasury to pay the printing bills. Mary Elizabeth received her royalties on the third edition in early 1936, but the last copies from that printing were not sold until five years later. The women who had a volunteer contract to support the Taney County Public Library soon realized they needed to develop some new sources of income.

There was no slowdown in the growth of the two-year-old book collection at the library. The

Bringing Books to the Ozarks

librarian reported, at year's end, that the three hundred and eighty-one card holders now had available a thousand and forty-three volumes, an increase of well over two hundred since September. She added that, for the first time, six of the library books were planned purchases, paid for with library funds.

Dorothy Jaenicke had a second appraisal of the condition of the library, one not mentioned in her year-end report. The office which had seemed so gracious and comfortable eighteen months before was now more than a little crowded. In the weeks just before Christmas, volunteers had built, installed and immediately filled another bookcase.

Faced with a growing gap in the library's finances, Study Club members sold subscriptions to magazines and to the *White River Leader*. The December meeting, held at The School of the Ozarks, was a fund-raising "silver tea," for which the school's music students, directed by Edith Carter, entertained with old English Christmas carols. The tea netted a dollar and twenty cents. After several months of selling subscriptions, that project was found to have raised a bit less than thirteen dollars.

Despite the disappointing results of those fund-raisers, the Taneyhills Study Club members were very enthusiastic about their community library in the early days of 1936. They were spearheading a county-wide effort to get a library in operation in every town which could possibly support one. Branson's Public Library was not

Movers & Shakers

going to appear bogged down in problems.

Their organizing ventures seemed to be going very well. In late 1935, a library opened in Forsyth under the sponsorship of another study group, the Yanet Club. One of the women involved in the organization was Annabelle McMasters, who had been a member of the Maids and Matrons Sunday School class, but had moved away before the beginning of 1933.

At Rockaway Beach, two civic-minded citizens donated a hundred and fifty books to begin a library collection which would be housed in the Flint Hill School, with the teacher acting as librarian. Across the lake from Branson, members of a Bible class at the Hollister Presbyterian Church announced that their "public library" would be open for three hours each Wednesday afternoon. Mrs. C. E. Hathaway, as volunteer librarian, would have available in the basement of the church some two hundred books, to be augmented by loans from the Taney County Public Library.

On Saturday, January 26, with four libraries operating in the county, the executive board of the Taneyhills Study Club met with representatives of various clubs and civic-minded persons to set up a county library association, "to continue the development of the library movement beyond the limits possible by local management."

In the mid-1930s, after seven years of overwhelming economic problems, there was no suggestion of working toward a tax-supported

Bringing Books to the Ozarks

library system. The county government was struggling to meet a host of truly pressing needs, and too many Taney County residents already had lost their land, homes or businesses because they couldn't pay property taxes.

The fact that volunteers could get those libraries into operation in 1936 was truly a heartening development. Encouraging, as well, were the many signs of local business growth in response to recovery programs instituted by the federal, state and county governments.

Road building, which headed the list of public projects, did much to stimulate local business. The paving of Highway 65 had been completed through Branson. Plans were underway to hard surface that major road on south through Hollister to the Arkansas border, a move publicly hailed by School of the Ozarks president Dr. Good as "even more important to the development of the School than a new building on campus."

A number of county roads were being graveled. Grading on Sparky Spurlock's goat trail over Dewey Bald had already begun. Initially designated State Highway 78 (now 76), it proceeded, then as now, west from Branson over Dewey Bald and through the Shepherd of the Hills country to Highway 13 in Stone County. There were several pauses in the road work when county funds temporarily ran out, but the improved highway inspired Branson businessmen to develop an airport a few miles west of town. The grass landing strip was welcomed by

Movers & Shakers

one and all as a magic carpet to the future.

With Dewey Bald Road being made passable, the State of Missouri saw an opportunity to give the area's tourism a boost. In 1926, Miss Lizzie McDaniel, daughter of a well-known Springfield banking family, had bought the farm made famous by Harold Bell Wright's *The Shepherd of the Hills* and refurbished and refurnished the log house which had provided the setting for much of the novel's action. In the mid-1930s, she offered the state a fifty-year lease on Inspiration Point, the author's old camping spot just west of the cabin, for development as a state park. Soon a statue of Wright was erected there.

The way of life depicted in *The Shepherd of the Hills* was fast disappearing from the Ozarks by the time Dewey Bald Road was graveled. Agricultural and home extension agents encouraged modernization of Taney County farm homes. Profits to be made from tomatoes were turning subsistence farmers with but tiny acreage into producers of cash crops, and canneries were operating in almost every town and village.

Members of the Taneyhills Study Club found, in the early months of 1936, that their library increasingly was involved with the reviving business community, with local government, and with the Branson Civic League.

To understand that involvement requires a look back to the summer following the first disastrous fire which threatened Branson's existence in 1912. When local businessmen and

Bringing Books to the Ozarks

their families gathered for a community picnic on the Fourth of July, 1913, the men proudly discussed their successful rebuilding program. The women's conversation turned to their town's many needs and problems which were receiving little attention from the men.

As a result of the latter discussion, the women of Branson, including Ella Patton, formed a Civic League and began finding ways to finance and carry out projects which would make life better in their town. Countless civic improvements were funded through the efforts of the Civic League members. Two of their major achievements strongly influenced the history of the Taneyhills Study Club and its library.

In the 1920s, some local businessmen, wanting to bring a radical publication to Branson, had gone into debt to lease and improve the first floor of the McGill building, which had been built on land at the southwest corner of Commercial and Pacific after the 1912 fire. The Masonic Order, under a separate contract, had reconstructed the second floor of the large brick structure. The publication stayed in Branson only briefly. At the time of the nationwide "crash" in 1929, the lower floor was being used as a community hall and occasionally as a motion picture theater.

The businessmen, with a bank loan of nine hundred dollars on their portion of the building, could see no hope of paying that debt. Defaulting would have undermined the already embattled local economy. The Civic League, then under the

Movers & Shakers

leadership of Gwen Binkley, agreed to take over the loan, the lease, and responsibility for the first floor of "the Community Hall." Between 1929 and 1933, the businesswomen and the wives of the businessmen of Branson developed a well-orchestrated program of projects to meet those loan payments. When the Bank of Branson failed in 1933, the women still owed approximately five hundred dollars. Their payments never faltered.

Civic League members were not displeased, however, when a young entrepreneur named Jim Owen contracted, in October, 1933, to rent their hall for a full-time movie theater.

Jim Owen had come to Branson in 1932, when his father, John B. Owen, purchased what had been the J. T. Duckworth Drug Store across Pacific from the Community Hall.

To turn the Civic League's building into a "state of the art" theater, a sloping floor, theater seats and a permanent movie screen were installed, and inside walls were given a "theatrical appearance." The latest movie equipment with "sound on film" promised Branson citizens "a type of entertainment equal to that provided by the larger cities." A ticket office was built by the entrance, under a stylish new awning, and glass-covered frames were hung on the brick exterior to hold advertisements of present and future attractions.

Meanwhile, in the one-story addition on the west end of the building, the old kitchen was cleared for a Civic League clubroom, and a storeroom became a compact kitchen.

Bringing Books to the Ozarks

In 1933, with Owen's rent making the payments on the building loan, members of the Civic League were free, for the first time in years, to enjoy some relaxed social life. Many chose, instead, to join the Study Club and help sponsor a community library. Others, including Ella Patton and Gwen Binkley, did not join the new group, but supported their younger friends with donations of books and much encouragement.

Jim Owen was not satisfied for long with simply showing movies in a rented hall. By 1935, he also was operating the Owen Boat Company, providing equipment and guides for White River float trips. On wintry days, when ice choked the lakeside docks and snow filled Branson streets, Owen would hitch a sled to his truck and haul laughing, shouting young people down the white-blanketed Main Street hill, across the bridge or the solidly frozen river, and over the winding road to Kirbyville. That year, too, he waged a successful campaign for election as Branson's mayor.

The enthusiastic young businessman announced, in early 1936, that building would begin immediately on an up-to-date movie house south of the Civic League Building on Commercial Street.

Members of the Civic League, long accustomed to recognizing opportunity in each new turn of events, sought a new tenant for their big hall. And again they rearranged their club rooms, this time to make space for the library.

Plans to move the library to the Civic League

Movers & Shakers

Jim Owen and Digging Crew Break Ground in 1936
for Branson's up-to-date movie theater on Commercial Street.

rooms may have been underway as early as January, for despite the fact that there was sixty dollars in the Study Club treasury, the three months' rent due at the first of the year was not paid to Albert Parnell until March. Before the library could be moved, however, events occurred which altered both the Civic League's and the Study Club's vision of where the library should be housed.

On Friday, February 28, ground was broken for a new community building in the city park beside Lake Taneycomo. The Federal Government would pay the construction workers' wages under the Work Projects Administration (WPA), and the cost of materials was being underwritten by the local American Legion Post.

Bringing Books to the Ozarks

That winter morning when workmen started excavating a few yards from the lake, the women of Branson reacted with dismay and disbelief. Just the previous March the land now being prepared for a much needed public building had been under many feet of water when the White River, backed up to form Lake Taneycomo by the hydroelectric spillover dam near Forsyth, but otherwise unimpeded during heavy rains, crested at fifty-five feet.

The Civic League members, realizing that the planned new civic building would be continually imperiled beside the lake, gasped, "Oh, No!" and went into action. Within hours they arranged to purchase, from Albert Parnell, the large corner lot just west of their club rooms, a site facing on the new Highway 65 and well above any danger from flooding. They had no cash to pay for the land. For seven years every penny the women could raise had been used to reduce the principal and interest on the Civic League Building. However, in February, 1936, that loan was close to being paid off, and the group's credit was excellent. When Civic League officers, with no collateral to offer, asked businessman A.A. Jones to loan them the needed six hundred dollars, he did so immediately.

His confidence was well placed. Within a year the hardworking women finished paying the loan on the Civic League Building, and kept at the task of meeting their payments until the unsecured loan on the Community Building lot was paid in full.

Movers & Shakers

The WPA workmen did not begin a second day of digging in the lakeside park. Early Saturday morning, February 29, 1936, the women deeded the lot at the corner of Pacific and Highway 65 to the City of Branson "for park purposes" and the WPA approved the switch to the new building site. For the second day in a row, ground was broken for the new Branson Community Building. Responsibility for hauling the building materials to the new location and filling in the lakeside excavation fell to the local businessmen.

By the time the Community Building was completed the following November, control of its upper floor had been allotted to the American Legion. Responsibility for the lower or ground floor was given to the Civic League.

CHAPTER VII

OH, FOR A BOOK AND A QUIET NOOK
(1936)

The changes downtown had just begun to develop in April, 1936, when a whole new group of officers took over leadership of the Taneyhills Study Club. The challenges they faced differed markedly from those Sara Heath had faced two years before.

Annual expenses of the library and club still barely exceeded a hundred dollars and the year-end treasury balance was less than thirty-six dollars. The collection of dues on a monthly basis had been changed to an annual payment of one dollar; fifty cents for those joining late in the club year. The volunteer library staff was now in charge of over twelve hundred books, including some of the finest literature in the western world and fiction and non-fiction by many popular modern writers, all crammed into the small rented office on Main Street.

Monthly programs continued to reflect a lively interest in literature, artistic endeavors and world affairs. All three were usually included at each meeting. However, the rapidly growing

Oh, For a Book & a Quiet Nook

library, the "state of the art" motion picture theater, and the discovery of so many neighbors with talents and experiences to be shared, had opened many paths to cultural enrichment. The fervent excitement that marked the early meetings now was somewhat muted.

The new president, Sybil James, had been active in the Study Club since its organizational meeting. She understood the responsibilities she was assuming. She also was well aware of the work the members faced in moving the library to the somewhat larger room being made available by the Civic League, and hoped the women's enthusiasm would carry them through a second move when the Community Building across the alley was completed.

Sybil had a keen interest in the development of the library, for she was employed in the dual role of principal and teacher at the Branson Grade School and her husband, Dr. Vernon James, was superintendent of the Branson schools.

The new officers were installed at the April birthday party, held again at Ye English Inn. Before the evening ended, Etta Mann and Mary Wilbur, who had agreed to chair the new library committee, asked for volunteers to help transfer the books to the Civic League Building.

Sybil, who delighted in recounting hilarious tales of her classroom experiences, certainly added to her collection of anecdotes in April and May of 1936. For the big move, the women borrowed a wheeled baker's tier. Over and over

Bringing Books to the Ozarks

again they pushed the tall cart, precariously stacked with books, down Main Street, along Commercial, and up Pacific Street while other volunteers hurried ahead with the shelves so they would be in place to receive the books again.

Apparently no volumes were lost in the journey, but for a while finding wanted books was quite a challenge.

When Dorothy Jaenicke reopened the library to its patrons on May 9th, she already was grateful that the new location, for which the Study Club was paying three dollars a month, was only temporary.

Much effort had always been made to keep the book room a warm and friendly place. No "Quiet" signs inhibited conversations. However, with the Civic League clubroom on one side and its kitchen on the other, visitors still could not reach the library directly from the street, and it was hard to sustain a cheery atmosphere in a crowded room with little available daylight.

Through three Saturdays, the line of youngsters waiting to buy tickets to the matinee stretched past the outside door which led to the library. If that distraction did not disappear entirely when the new Owen Theater opened its doors, at least the line did have to be longer before it caused a problem.

The last movie was shown in the Civic League Building on Saturday night, May 23. Before the audience had left the building, League members and their husbands were at work with crowbars and hammers. The seats, the slanting wooden

Oh, For a Book & a Quiet Nook

Owen Theater Opened in Late May of 1936.

floors, the old movie screen and other theater trappings being abandoned in favor of more modern equipment had to be removed quickly so the heavy presses of the *White River Leader* could be installed there "between editions."

Through the following two weeks there was much dust and very little quiet in the Taney County Public Library. On May 29, the *White River Leader* was printed in the old plant two blocks away at Main and Highway 65 for the last time. Five days later, Forrest and Evelyn Runyon, owners of the paper since the previous September, had their presses in operation beyond the wall of the library.

Branson's weekly paper proved a very noisy neighbor for the library. On the other hand, the Study Club received much welcome news cover-

Bringing Books to the Ozarks

age as a result of that proximity, and the fact that Evelyn Runyon was by then an active library supporter.

After the club met in June at The School of the Ozarks, however, it was the banner headline story in the *Taney County Republican* over in Forsyth which was saved in the club's scrapbook. Rose O'Neill had been the speaker of the day. Her mother, niece, and sister Callista also were guests. The event was reported in colorful prose:

> Clad in a red velvet gown, cut in simple, flowing, graceful lines and with sandals on her feet, with luminous eyes and a flashing smile that caught and held the heart of each listener, Rose O'Neill was a striking figure. In seeing Miss O'Neill and listening to her, one gets a clearer understanding of her writing, the individuality, the illusive charm of her characters, the subtlety, the wit that runs through her stories.

The "mother" of the Kewpies concluded her talk with a description of the home she owned on the Isle of Capri. The Villa Narcissus, relic of a three-hundred-year-old convent, contained marble from the gardens of Emperors Augustus and Tiberius, and was served by sewers built two thousand years ago.

Following Rose O'Neill's appearance, in recognition of her continuing interest in and contributions to the Branson area, the women voted to make her the fourth Honorary Member of the Taneyhills Study Club.

Oh, For a Book & a Quiet Nook

On the day the O'Neills were present, the club members made a serious decision about their own obligations to the library. For two and a half years, Dorothy Jaenicke had served as volunteer librarian, contributing her time, talent and energy to maintain regular library hours and keep the books in good order. The club was in no position to vote her a regular salary, but surely it could at least pay the extra personal expenses she was incurring through her service.

A motion was approved to pay Dorothy ten dollars a month. The aftermath of that vote might seem strange today. The librarian did not refuse the stipend, but did ask that it be reduced to eight dollars a month. After all, there really must be money available to keep the books in good condition.

In agreeing to pay the librarian, the Study Club members were embarking on a new and demanding adventure. That ninety dollars a year would double the cost of maintaining the library. If no ways and means committee had existed before, it surely came into being in the summer of 1936. Efforts to fund the librarian's "salary" were underway before the month was out.

The following week a newspaper headline announced, "Taney County Library Will Present Play." The story reported that

> A dramatization of the book "The Shepherd of the Hills" will be presented at the high school auditorium tonight by Walter C. Gran . . . The proceeds of the entertainment will be used for the support of the library.

Bringing Books to the Ozarks

Rose O'Neill

Oh, For a Book & a Quiet Nook

The drama of that June night was heightened by the fact that the 43-year-old monologist had been blind since he was seventeen years old. His performance drew laughter and tears, sparking a renewed interest in Harold Bell Wright's book and netting two dollars and forty cents for the library.

The club's informal breakfast meeting, held in August at the home of Etta Mann, proved to be a better fund raiser than Gran's monologue. Sybil James and Etta provided the food and the ten dollars and fifteen cents paid by the members went into the treasury.

Etta lived in a comfortable house beside the highway connecting Hollister and Branson. In the flatland across the road were the cottages of a resort which she and her husband had developed when Lake Taneycomo was new. By 1920 her son-in-law, Dr. Harry Evans, had moved to the area to practice medicine. He and his wife, Etta's daughter Edna, built a rock house next door to the Mann home. Both women's names were on the Study Club's "charter associates" list. In 1936 Edna Evans was serving as treasurer.

From time to time Etta Mann delighted the group with fascinating inside stories about the motion picture industry. Her son, Ned Mann, was internationally known in the movie world as "the Miracle Man of special effects." Branson news reports about him noted that producers in Hollywood and London vied for the services of "one of our own sons" and frequently held up completion of important films until this "local

Bringing Books to the Ozarks

boy" was available to help create needed segments.

When the club women gathered at the Mann home for breakfast, they were anticipating moving the library next door to the new community building within a few weeks. However, their countdown to moving day came to a halt before the end of August. The WPA ran out of funds to pay the work crew.

The number of books in the library continued to increase, a fact which delighted Branson readers and both pleased and frustrated the librarian. The *Reader's Digest* magazine, paid for by Stella Owen, had begun arriving each month. During August and September, over two hundred donations of modern novels, classics, mysteries and children's books were received from club members, local supporters, and friends in St. Louis. Dr. Neihardt again brought in an accumulation of books he had recently reviewed. Shelf space was found for the popular new additions by packing seldom-called-for volumes in boxes which were stacked along the library walls.

In early October, the WPA called the Community Building construction crew back to work, announcing that it had discovered additional payroll funds. Study Club members monitored the workers' progress anxiously, for the expected completion date was in November.

The club's October meeting was held at the Anchor Tavern, a restaurant which Josephine Madry and Eula Thornhill had just opened in

Oh, For a Book & a Quiet Nook

their resort. Some of the older members who had, in the past, faced long drives from their rural homes to get to the club meetings, walked to the luncheon that day. The picturesque Anchor Village tourist cottages beside Lake Taneycomo were becoming a popular retirement alternative.

Monthly reports spoke of the club's "first fund-raising season," then in progress. A jitney dinner held in September cleared twenty-five dollars and fifty cents. For that community event, every able-bodied member of the club prepared food, dished up individual servings and kept the "cafeteria" table stocked. Diners paid five cents for each portion, whether meat, vegetable, bread or dessert.

Participation was urged in the upcoming bake sale, an event which netted fifteen dollars and fifty cents. By November, with another moving day in the offing, the club treasury had a sixty-seven dollar balance.

In later years, when the ways and means committee was struggling to cover an annual budget of several thousand dollars, Josephine Madry, who was much involved in the money-raising efforts of the 1930s, quite firmly voiced the opinion that those early annual expenses of one or two hundred dollars had been much harder to meet.

The event which all of Branson had been looking forward to, the opening of the new Community Building, arrived with considerable fanfare on Sunday, November 22, 1936. The ded-

Bringing Books to the Ozarks

ication ceremonies became a regional celebration when the local Pemberton-Jennings American Legion Post invited the Legion's 17th District to hold its convention in the Branson-Hollister area that weekend. The Community Hall was the scene of a gala ball on Saturday night, and Sunday's ceremonies began with a parade from the Hollister train depot, across Lake Taneycomo on the Highway 65 bridge, to the new building.

The Community Building was dubbed a civic monument by the *White River Leader:*

> Facing west on Highway 65 . . . the huge structure of native stone and timber . . . is designed with two wings . . . . The south entrance into the auditorium and main part of the building . . . leads into the large room from a low porch.....constructed of native oak and cedar timber. An arbor is to be built at the north entrance into the wing at the end of the building. The main entrance, when finished, will be on the ground level and will lead both into the basement and up to the auditorium, through a lobby.
>
> The auditorium [with a stage and dressing rooms at the south end] will seat 700 persons. A huge fireplace on the west wall gives the room an air of coziness, and for the time being, with a stove at the extreme north of the room, will supply heat for the auditorium.

Lloyd Eiserman, the architect, was promising that the building would soon be air-conditioned, a new technology just beginning to appear in public buildings in the Midwest.

Oh, For a Book & a Quiet Nook

The dining room on the ground floor is the same [size] as the great room above and the wings at each end contain the necessary smaller rooms.

In the south wing, at the west, is the ladies' dressing and rest room, next on the east is the pantry and kitchen. Separating this part is a hall leading from an outside entrance to the dining room and on the east is the men's dressing and rest rooms.

Sharing responsibility with the Civic League and American Legion on the board controlling the new Community Building were the City Council, Park Board, Taney County Public Library, Spanish American War Veterans and the Chamber of Commerce.

On the day of the dedication, a few essentials of the building were yet to be completed. In addition to the unfinished entrances, no plumbing had been installed on the ground floor. The "Civic Monument" story made no mention of any space earmarked for the library, but the Study Club had been promised the northwest corner of the lower floor, which would permit an outside entrance and allow the library two rooms.

Though the last rent payment to the Civic League was delivered November 12, 1936, it was to be several weeks before the move to the new building could be made. Meantime, the librarian surveyed her cramped domain, tried to ignore the clatter and roar of printing presses, and prayed for dry weather. As construction of the

Bringing Books to the Ozarks

Community Building progressed, each heavy rain had brought an increase in the runoff funneled through the alley between the two buildings and down the sidewalk past the entrance to the Civic League rooms. The low door sill provided no real barrier to the rushing water. Resulting wet conditions were disastrous for the books, particularly those in boxes.

December was very rainy. In early January, with the soggy books beginning to mildew, emergency arrangements were made to move to a single room "under the stairs" of the north entrance to the Community Hall. There would be no rent to pay, since the Civic League had included the library in its lease arrangements with the city.

The allotted space was too small to allow shelving of all the books. At least a third would have to be stored in boxes.

Nonetheless, with the prospect of the second room and a library entrance from the street, Dorothy Jaenicke put together a year-end report filled with indications of growth. In the past twelve months, the book collection had grown by five hundred and forty-one; all but six had been donated. From the fifteen hundred available volumes, twenty-three hundred adult books and almost two thousand juveniles were loaned. On average, every book had been checked out two or three times. The librarian's report concluded that though five hundred and fourteen user's cards were on file, only two hundred and thirty-six cardholders actually borrowed books that year--so, also on average, each reader had

Oh, For a Book & a Quiet Nook

checked out eighteen.

The two-room library on the ground floor of the Community Building never materialized. Later that spring, an adjoining area was furnished as a reading room, which lessened crowding a little. However, other groups used the reading room except during Wednesday and Saturday afternoons, when the library was open.

CHAPTER VIII

THE ROLL KEEPS CHANGING
(1937 - Summer 1938)

In early January, 1937, as the women worked to establish the books in yet another new home, they mourned the death of eighty-year-old Ella Patton. For a quarter of a century the grandmotherly innkeeper epitomized Branson's hospitality to tourists and travelers. Many a troubled neighbor leaned on her strengthening counsel, and she gave of her time and energy in support of countless community undertakings. In February, remembering the many times she had helped the library and Study Club, the club members approved a resolution in her honor.

Two months later, with the library move complete and the printing of the Patton resolution paid for, the club treasury had again fallen below thirty dollars. To bolster the shrinking funds, Ellie Mitchell planned a jitney supper for January 30. That event was "postponed indefinitely," however, when Dr. and Mrs. Guy Mitchell's twenty-year-old daughter, Betty, became very ill. On February 12, Betty's life was claimed by an infection for which, in 1937, no

The Roll Keeps Changing

"miracle drug" existed. The supper, rescheduled for mid-March, made over seventeen dollars, though other volunteers carried out the chairman's plans. Soon, however, Ellie Mitchell was working harder than before in support of the club and library.

Yet another sorrow marked the early months of 1937. In mid-March eighty-six-year-old Alice O'Neill died. Her funeral notice reminded that, in the 1880s and 1890s, this gentle unassuming woman traveled on horseback over the hills giving music lessons to the farm children of western Taney County. Many Study Club members read of Alice O'Neill's intellectual accomplishments and her widely recognized writings, and pondered the loving acceptance with which she had lived in the shadow of her famous daughter and tolerated her husband's long absences.

For the election that March, a luncheon was held at the Branson High School. Five chickens, donated by Fanny Dawes, were prepared by the club members and served for thirty-five cents a plate.

Sybil James congratulated her successor, Edna Rhoads, and entertained visions of taking a rest, but needs of the club and library called her to another task. When the committee leaders were announced for the coming year, the retiring president had accepted the work of raising funds.

As ways and means chair, Sybil faced a formidable task. Anticipated club expenses and the librarian's salary totaled a hundred and twenty-five dollars. With an expected forty dollars in

Bringing Books to the Ozarks

dues and the hope of perhaps twenty dollars from sales of *Ozark Lyrics*, the gap which must be filled before any further improvements could be made in the library was all too apparent.

Monetary problems and sad thoughts were pushed out of mind on the April evening when ninety members and guests gathered at Ye English Inn to celebrate the club's birthday with a three-course dinner. Dorothy Jaenicke proudly reported that between the hours of 1:00 and 5:00 p.m. that day, ninety-one loans had been made, a record for the library.

The librarian made no mention of renewed "moisture problems." Later events and some painful memories indicate that when the spring rains came, the women in charge of Branson's books in the new Community Building found water flowing from the wall against the hillside and spreading in sheets across the library floor.

No such report marred the April dinner. Club members performed in an impromptu playlet, entitled "The Chigger Hollow Sewing Circle," in which members and guests alike came in for a share of jesting. "The characters were dressed in old-fashioned costumes, with hairdress in keeping," the newspaper noted. Hilarity ruled the evening, and the unwritten script went home with the players, which was, from all reports, just as well.

The frivolous nature of the anniversary dinner set the tone for the year's programs, which explored such subjects as travel, sports, wild flowers and food. In November, club members

The Roll Keeps Changing

traveled by car to Springfield for lunch in the tea room at Heer's Department Store and an interesting lecture on antique glass collecting.

The number of members answering roll call at those monthly meetings seldom exceeded twenty-five, a fact which did not disturb club leaders. Most dining facilities in the area were crowded even with that number. In the Study Club that year, and through the rest of the 1930s, membership usually was less than forty.

There were, however, many changes in the names on the roster. Mary Wilbur, after helping relocate all the books twice during her year on the library committee, moved away in August, 1937, when her husband had a change of jobs. She was not gone for long, however. In a pattern which many members would repeat in future years, Mary was back on the rolls by 1939, when the yearbook for the first time carried a roster of members.

Mrs. H. R. Masure, a charter member, in 1937 moved with her husband to Cotter, Arkansas. Recently widowed Edith Carter, whose School of the Ozarks music students had performed for the Study Club several times, departed for Texas. Mrs. J. S. Flautt and her husband moved to Oklahoma.

On the other hand, Ruskin C. Boehm arrived in Hollister that year to assume management of Ye English Inn, and eighteen months later his new bride, Virginia, became a member of the Study Club.

Another newcomer was Ethel Paramore, a

Bringing Books to the Ozarks

Chicago secretary who came to Branson to visit her mother and sister in 1937 and returned to stay after her retirement at the end of that year. Both Miss Paramore and her sister, Mrs. Jessie Parks, became strong supporters of the Taney County Public Library.

In the 1930s, the Study Club had among its members several women whose husbands were local ministers. Margaret Bell was the wife of George F. Bell, who was associated with The School of the Ozarks and also pastor of the Hollister Presbyterian Church. Lena Williams' husband, Glen, was pastor of the Branson Presbyterian Church. When Reverend Williams moved away in 1937, Rev. R. Waller Blain was called to fill that pulpit and Winnie Blain became a member of the Study Club. All three women were given complimentary memberships because their participation was prized by the clubwomen.

Helen Fletcher, as wife of the owner-editor of the *White River Leader*, also was carried as a free-dues member, and when the paper changed hands in late 1935, that designation passed to Evelyn Runyon. Until well into the 1950s, there usually were three or four such "free dues" members on the club roll.

Another lively and constantly changing dimension was added to the club by the talented and enthusiastic young women who taught in the Branson and Hollister schools and at The School of the Ozarks. Many stayed only a few years before moving on to better, more challenging, or simply different jobs. Charter member

The Roll Keeps Changing

Hazel Vaughn, a local girl, accepted a missionary position in Venezuela and, in 1937, news came that she had married. That year, also, Helen Stratte, until recently the librarian at The School of the Ozarks, was reported to be working in Minnesota.

Several of the young teachers married local men, with a subsequent name change on the club rolls. By the late 1930s, these newly married women no longer faced automatic unemployment, and many who in earlier years had endured such discrimination had been rehired. Bill Ellen Hall was, in 1937, teaching in a nearby rural school and in the early 1940s returned to a Branson classroom.

Despite the Study Club's constantly changing membership, the women easily kept track of current members. Through almost forty years, meetings always included a roll call. Records of attendance are maintained even today, as members pay for their luncheon or dessert. Despite the loss of club minutes and membership rolls from the 1930s, it has been possible, in the past decade, to reconstruct a master roll, including dates of membership and offices held, of more than a thousand women who have helped to keep the Taneyhills Library in operation since 1933.

Some of the early members whose dates of joining are unknown made important contributions to the club and library. One such was Caroline Ballentine. Though she had moved to Branson in the 1920s, and probably joined in the club's first year, her name appears in the records

Bringing Books to the Ozarks

for the first time in 1937.

A successful and strong-willed professional woman, Caroline had settled in a house on the Roark Creek bluff in Branson, seeking a quiet life in which to recuperate from a serious illness. In 1932, she was an active member of the Civic League and the Presbyterian Church, and is remembered as a hard worker in the Study Club from its beginning. In 1937 and again in 1939, she was called on to tell of her travels in California and Hawaii.

To the delight of Taney County readers, in February, 1937, Caroline purchased a dozen best selling fiction and non-fiction books to set up a rental shelf in the library. For such currently popular novels as Margaret Mitchell's *Gone With the Wind*, library patrons signed on a waiting list and willingly paid the ten cents a week rental fee. The following fall and again and again until the project became self-supporting, Caroline donated whole shelf-loads of the latest, most popular books, to be rented to library patrons.

The library also was lending much new reading material without charge. Only two dollars and twenty-five cents was spent on books that year, but Dr. Guy Mitchell contributed twelve new mysteries, and Dorothy Worman brought in a boxful of her own latest favorites, as did club member Dorothy Garner. From the public library at Galesburg, Illinois, came eight boxes of used books, sent with the understanding that the Study Club would pay the five dollar freight

The Roll Keeps Changing

charge. The association with Gwen Binkley's sister in Galesburg was paying off handsomely for Branson's library!

Dorothy Jaenicke and the current library committee members, Ella McHaffie and Reva Ford, spent hours preparing the new books for shelving. As the women sorted the donations, they also were making room for them on the shelves by removing those which were worn out or seldom read. At year's end, despite the addition of more than ten boxes of books, the library was offering for loan only sixteen hundred volumes, a mere handful more than the year before.

While library workers toiled over the books, Sybil James was involving the rest of the club members in meeting budgeted expenses. For the rummage sale on June 26, attics and closets all over western Taney County were turned inside out. The sale was held in Hollister's Egner Shoe Store, then occupying a building which had begun life as a bank and served for years as the local post office. The event netted sixteen dollars and some lively memories.

Years later, Bill Ellen Hall laughingly recalled that the women all donated their "old hats," then bought a "new chapeau," a community trade-off which caused many giggles and snickers in Branson and Hollister churches the following Sunday.

Early that September, the women raised almost twenty-three dollars with a highly successful cakewalk, and later the same month they put on yet another jitney dinner. The profit from

Bringing Books to the Ozarks

the latter event was fourteen dollars. Obviously, jitney dinners were going to need a new format to make the work involved worthwhile.

Sometime after the June meeting, but before the yearbooks were distributed in September, Edna Rhoads resigned her position as president, and Etta Mann assumed leadership of the club, with Ellie Mitchell taking the office of vice president. Mrs. Rhoads was moving to Springfield, but she continued her membership in the Study Club for several years.

Sybil James rounded out her year of fundraising with a turkey raffle in November, clearing sixteen dollars and forty cents and bringing her committee's total profits for the year to sixty-eight dollars. Her commitment to the library was strong. The following year she accepted the fundraising post again.

Meantime, Caroline Ballentine distributed some of the remaining supply of *Ozark Lyrics* for sale through nearby resorts and gift shops, a move which, by year's end, had added another thirty dollars and fifty-five cents to the club funds. Finally the treasury balance was staying comfortably ahead of expenses.

As members of the Taneyhills Study Club greeted 1938, the four-year-old library was growing in popularity. During the year just ended, six hundred and sixty-five cardholders had borrowed five thousand one hundred and sixty-seven books.

Branson's citizens were looking forward to the new year with much optimism. Local doctors,

The Roll Keeps Changing

responding to the area's growth, opened a hospital in the Mount Branson Lodge. The Civic League finished equipping the kitchen of the Community Building and turned it over to the city. Mayor Jim Owen, the town's popular young mayor opened a roller-skating rink, to the joy of the local teenagers. Last, but far from least, after several winters of heavy snow and bitter cold, the winter of 1937-38 had thus far produced no snow and little rain.

By February, however, the women of the Study Club realized that 1938 was not going to be a perfect year. Their president, Etta Mann, was in St. Louis undergoing surgery; and the mild winter everyone had longed for was now producing rain, rain, and more rain. The river was in flood and so was the library floor. Dorothy Jaenicke and her committee, recently augmented by Ethel Paramore, were spending much time and energy encouraging the water on through that outside door.

The club members did enjoy some nice moments that January and February: a thought-provoking book review, a fascinating look at midwestern art, and the wedding of popular young Bobby Saad to Majelly Jabara. The excitement of the wedding over, Bobby and Majelly departed for New York City where the groom was now employed.

When the March Study Club meeting was held, Etta Mann still was recuperating. Ellie Mitchell presided over her own election as president, and there was little change in the executive board.

Bringing Books to the Ozarks

Branson-Hollister Flood of 1927 Inundated Everything
East of Sycamore Street in Branson,
including the approach to the Main Street bridge.
Between 1925 and 1945 flooding of downtown Hollister and
the Branson waterfront became progressively worse.

The election meeting was preceded by a public announcement which never before had been made. The Taneyhills Study Club was having a membership drive.

Branson shared a problem which troubled all of Missouri in the late 1930s. Rural and small town young people were moving to big cities in search of jobs. The results were shrinking school enrollments and diminishing community leadership. In the Study Club, there was a marked drop in the number of members willing to accept offices, and a handful of women were simply rotating positions. Nominating two candidates for each office fast became impossible.

The Roll Keeps Changing

Perhaps Mrs. John Bennett, the new program chairman, had the problems of shifting population in mind when she embarked the women on a new course of study in 1938 and 1939. Each month, in addition to the guest speaker, someone was assigned to seek out information about one of Missouri's cities and report her findings to the club.

The guest speakers, whether club members or visitors from distant communities, continued to receive a free lunch, but payments for travel expenses were no longer offered.

For the June meeting, members lunched at the Table Rock Inn, then adjourned to Maude Horine's home where they shared recollections of visits to historic shrines of America and heard Rose O'Neill read from her own poetry.

In August, the women drove to Ozark Beach. After a delightful luncheon in view of the dam which forms Lake Taneycomo, Vitae Kite, program leader for the day, introduced Mable Cluggston who gave a report on the history of St. Joseph, Missouri. Then Dr. Florence Boehmer, a psychologist and the Dean of Women at Drury College, directed the club members' attention to "Budgeting Time, and the Wise Use of Leisure."

Dr. Boehmer's subject may have earned some inward groans from the women who were running the library and those who were working to support it. In the summer of 1938 they were enjoying little spare time.

CHAPTER IX

BATTLING THE POWDERY SCOURGE
(Summer 1938 - early 1940)

Dorothy Jaenicke, her new unpaid assistant, Ethel Paramore, and Caroline Ballentine, Dorothy Garner and anyone else who would volunteer spent many tedious hours, in the summer of 1938, "cleaning the books." The long rainy season had saturated the soil and filled underlying cracks and hollows of the hillside above the Community Building. Until that "spring water" drained out of the hill, moisture continued to seep through the western wall. Again, dampness penetrated everything in the library. The women kept careful watch on which books were being borrowed. Any that stayed on the shelves for several days were sure to develop green-tinged covers, black-speckled pages and the musty odor of mildew.

Despite those problems, the library committee launched a summer story hour in 1938. Little folk of all ages were invited to gather in the room above the library on July 9, when Misses Jane Mitchell and Georgia Cantwell told stories, and played nursery songs on a victrola.

Battling the Powdery Scourge

In support of the library, sisters Ethel Paramore and Jessie Parks served an elaborate benefit breakfast in June, at their Pacific Street home a block above the Presbyterian Church. Those were the last peaceful moments enjoyed by Branson's library supporters that summer.

The Study Club was going to produce "a play in the park," and the help of the entire community would be needed to make it all happen. President Ellie Mitchell coordinated the event. A professional singer, director and playwright, Miss Margaret Merle, was imported from Kansas City to produce the show. She arrived in Branson on Sunday evening, July 30, bringing her original script for "Coast-to-Coast."

By midweek Miss Merle had enlisted several choruses and the Branson Community Band. Auditions were scheduled to select seventy-five actors and "amateurs" to perform in her play, which was patterned after the popular radio show "Major Bowes' Amateur Hour."

Rehearsals went on almost non-stop through ten hectic days, continuing right up to curtain time for the first performance. While the production took shape, Study Club members were collecting prizes from sponsoring merchants and registering boys and girls, ranging in age from six years down to eighteen months, for the "Beaux and Belles of 1950" contest. (The "1950" indicated the year that the tiny charmers would be reaching "dating age.")

Margaret Merle's clever comedy-musical was performed on Friday and Saturday nights,

Bringing Books to the Ozarks

August 11th and 12th, on a stage constructed for the occasion in the City Park beside the lake. With so many of the town's young hopefuls involved, every parent, grandparent, brother, sister and neighbor in western Taney County was offered tickets, which were sold at twenty-five cents for adults, ten cents for children.

There are no figures on the total receipts. After the sometimes frightened but always adorable Beaux and Belles were awarded their prizes, Margaret Merle was paid as promised, and the cosponsoring Park Board and Community Building received their agreed percentages, the Taneyhills Study Club was left with over seventy-four dollars "to enlarge the Taney County Library."

To enlarge the Taney County Library?

That short phrase in the midst of a column-long news account of the play and its participants was the first visible hint that the Study Club's footloose books soon would be moving again.

Through the fall, Sybil James industriously continued her campaign to fund the project. A cakewalk, bake sale, and silver teas in the homes of Maude Horine, Ellie Mitchell and Clara Bushnell brought in fifty-two dollars.

By January the Study Club members may have been ready to take a vacation from fundraising, but Sybil was not. A set of gold-finished flatware had been given the club by Dorothy Worman and there was only one practical way to decide who would be the proud new owner of all

Battling the Powdery Scourge

those gorgeous knives, forks and spoons. Raffle tickets were sold at fifty cents a piece. Several members invested all they could spare on the chances, but when the lucky ticket was drawn, it belonged, not to a member of the club but to a neighbor in nearby Kirbyville.

Though some surely took one final longing peek at the golden table service, the women of the Taneyhills Study Club had every reason to be pleased with their money-raising prowess. Including the money from the raffle, the year's receipts totaled two hundred and seventy-two dollars. Of course, after all the year's bills were paid, the treasury was back to less than eighty dollars. Virtually every penny spent that year had gone to support the library.

Day after day through the last half of 1938, while club members raised money and the librarians and their faithful helpers worked frantically to save the books from the powdery scourge of mildew, the din of hammer and saw drowned out all conversation in the damp room under the stairs. Willing husbands and friends, using materials donated or provided at cost by the Madry Lumber Company and Whelchel's Hardware Store, were completing a cheerful, larger (and dry) library room on the floor above.

Early in January, 1939, Dorothy Jaenicke, Ethel Paramore and Ellie Mitchell took the library's share of the play receipts from the previous summer and drove to Springfield to buy book shelves and some needed furniture. The following month, the *White River Leader* was

Bringing Books to the Ozarks

directing readers to the relocated library which was entered through a new door on the second level, at the north end of the Community Building:

> The room, . . . is large enough to allow adequate shelf-space and to accommodate a reading table and the librarian's desk. The room is attractive, with north window light and stained wood walls. Built in the shape of an L, it provides more than the usual amount of wall space.

The vast amount of work that went into that move is only hinted at in the newspaper. Today there are memories to indicate that before each book could be placed on an upstairs shelf the cover and every page had to be carefully inspected, freed of mildew, and thoroughly dried.

On March 4th, when the tired but jubilant women met at the Grandview Hotel to elect officers for the coming year, either the club members were very satisfied with their leadership or the newer members were too intimidated by all the work to accept an office. Edna Evans accepted the presidency. Every member of her board had held office in the club before. The retiring president, Ellie Mitchell, was taking on the leadership of the ways and means committee.

Year-end reports received that day were very satisfying. With ample room to shelve all the books, library use was increasing. The rental section was a great success, and the ten dollars received from rentals and fines had been used to

Battling the Powdery Scourge

buy additional bestsellers to rent.

The pleasant glow lasted one week.

On Monday afternoon, March 11, 1939, a chimney fire destroyed "Journey's End," the Heaths' home south of Hollister. Sara Heath, who had been making doughnuts in the kitchen, was startled by the crackling of burning timber. The upper floor already was ablaze. She helped her invalid husband to safety, but was unable to reach his widowed sister, who was living in the Heath home. When the last flames were extinguished, the house was a pile of ashes. Minnie Todd was dead, and the Heaths and their daughter, Dorothy Jaenicke, her husband and two young sons--were homeless.

While the Heaths and Jaenickes re-established their homes and lives in Branson, Ethel Paramore and Caroline Ballentine kept the library in operation. The Study Club held its customary anniversary dinner that April at Ye English Inn, but the celebration was muted by the tragedy.

The uncertainties of personal life were soon to be compounded by world affairs. In 1939, when events across the Atlantic and Pacific oceans were brewing a storm which would engulf the citizens of Branson and Hollister, the women in the Study Club included current events on almost every program. Some current subjects had a lighter tone, of course, like "Place Names in the Ozarks," "Personal Appearance," and "The 1939 World's Fair in New York City."

Local events, too, were demanding much of

Bringing Books to the Ozarks

the clubwomen's attention. Spring and summer headlines reported with growing excitement the progress of Branson's semi-professional baseball team, which won the regional championship. The bubble burst when the Branson Sluggers lost the first round of the national playoffs.

That May, another tragedy occurred, one which overwhelmed the graduating class at Hollister High School and grieved the members of the Study Club.

Fanny and Frank Dawes' son, Frank, Jr., was valedictorian of his senior class and scheduled to give the commencement address in lieu of a guest speaker. The popular twenty-year-old had starred in debate, participated in the band, glee club and quartets, been a reporter for the recently formed 4-H club, and served as secretary-treasurer of his class.

The Wednesday before graduation, he and his classmates went on a "senior sneak trip" to Jefferson City. Young Frank returned very tired. On the eve of the baccalaureate service, despite heroic efforts at a Springfield hospital, the hemophilia that had marred the young man's childhood claimed his life.

The planned baccalaureate service was altered to include a eulogy for young Frank Dawes. Two memorial book shelves were established in his name, one in the Hollister High library, the other in the Taney County Public Library. Friends who wished to send flowers were urged by the family to contribute a book to one of those shelves instead.

Battling the Powdery Scourge

Another "bell" was tolling across the hills of western Taney County. The Study Club's memorial shelf became a new tradition through which members honored departed loved ones and friends.

The year of 1939-40 was the last time that Fanny Dawes paid dues in the Study Club. Her husband already was involved in developing the area's Rural Electrification program. Several years later he was called to Washington, D.C., to work in the national REA headquarters. Until 1956, Frank and Fanny continued to own, and from time to time occupy, the "rocked-up" house south of Hollister. Fanny never lost her interest in the Study Club and library. However, after the death of her son, through all the years until her own life ended in Springfield in 1974, that concern was expressed only to close friends. Her donations reached the club treasury anonymously.

The events of 1939 held yet another sorrow for the families involved in the Study Club. On November 10th, Ella McHaffie, who only the week before had traveled to Springfield with her friends to enjoy the club luncheon at Heer's, was walking home from the Owen Theater after the evening movie, in company with two young neighbor boys. As they crossed the highway a speeding car bore down on them. The older boy's leg was broken, but he managed to push his younger brother to safety. Ella McHaffie was killed instantly.

Is there healing to be had in cooking for bake

Bringing Books to the Ozarks

sales, or in buying prizes for winners at Chinese checkers, pinochle, rummy or bridge? There were many grieving relatives and friends in Branson and Hollister that year who, if asked, would have answered "Yes."

In the summer and fall of 1939, keeping the library bills paid was the stated goal of the planning and work which went into serving two silver teas, preparing for a cakewalk and bake sale, selling tickets for a special movie, and carrying out two game parties and a jitney dinner. After the jitney dinner, ways and means chair Ellie Mitchell, noting that the highly popular five-cent meat portions were an economic disaster, vowed a change in pricing before the next such meal was served.

All things considered, lifting sorrowing spirits probably was a more tangible result from all that activity than was the seventy dollars raised. The club was given an added lift when the women were offered a set of the World Book Encyclopedia and a set of the New Standard Encyclopedia, thirty-seven books in all, for twenty-six dollars and thirty cents.

As Christmas approached, the women also busied themselves in other local activities calculated to brighten spirits through the holiday season.

Clubs and churches joined hands, as they had all through the Depression years, to insure that food, Christmas toys and needed clothing reached the area's less fortunate citizens. A gala holiday dance was sponsored by the Junior

Battling the Powdery Scourge

Chamber of Commerce at the Edgewater Pavilion on Lake Taneycomo.

Branson merchants delighted the town's youngest generation by organizing a "dollies and pets" parade in which curly-topped little girls, hugging their favorite dolls, trooped up and down Main Street in company with proud owners of cats, dogs, farm animals and tamed forest creatures. The lively, noisy march ended at the Owen Theater where Santa Claus made some agonizing decisions, passed out prizes, and pacified the losers with a lot of candy.

For many Study Club members the highlight of that last Christmas season of the 1930s occurred on December 20, when hundreds of Branson friends crowded Sammy's Lookout on Dewey Bald on a bright winter afternoon to witness the wedding of Pearl "Sparky" Spurlock to Lee Spurlock, the brother of her late husband. Rev. J. E. Chase, Sr., of the Branson Christian Church, tied the knot. Reva Ford and her husband Dwight served as matron of honor and best man.

The bride and groom were well known to vacationers and tourists. Lee Spurlock ran a gift shop next to the White River Hotel. Sparky's tour chats had, in 1936, been published in *Over the Ozark Trails*, a fact and fun-filled guidebook to Shepherd of the Hills country. When their unusual wedding was reported in the nation's press, congratulations arrived from all over the country. By far the most exciting letter, for the newlyweds and for their adventure-loving friends

Bringing Books to the Ozarks

in the Study Club, came from California, where Sparky's brother, who had been lost to her for many years, recognized his sister in her wedding story, reprinted in his hometown newspaper.

As the Taneyhills Study Club neared its seventh birthday celebration, there were forty-one names on the membership list. Eighteen of those women had attended the organizational meeting back in February, 1933. An additional dozen had been members since 1935 or before. Bill Ellen Hall, Josephine Madry and Ellie Mitchell were the only sponsoring Maids and Matrons still on the rolls.

Fourteen new members were added in 1940, among them several who expected to be in Branson only one year. In early January, the U. S. Corps of Engineers announced that twenty-five of its employees soon would arrive in the area to prepare for the building of Bull Shoals Dam, on the White River below Lake Taneycomo. Nine of those employees were married men who had been assigned apartments in downtown Branson. The engineers' wives found in the Study Club a route to active local involvement and friendship during their stay in the area. For others who joined that year, supporting Branson's library became a lifelong commitment.

Juanita Cunningham, a friendly, fun-loving young secretary, had joined her parents after they moved to Branson in the mid-1930s. In late 1939, she married her widowed employer, "Ike" Thompson. When the new Mrs. I. M. Thompson first paid dues, a few months after her wedding

Battling the Powdery Scourge

day, she little guessed that she would serve as an officer in the Study Club for much of the next half century.

The voice of actress Jill Edwards was familiar to some Study Club members before she became their neighbor. During the mid-1930s, radio listeners all over the nation tuned to the popular "First Nighter" drama series originating in Chicago, and heard the accompanying "Personality Pointers" offered by "the Campana Lady," who was introduced as Mary Morgan but actually was Jill Edwards.

In 1937, Jill married Don Gardner, a professional golfer, and the couple began looking for a way out of the highly pressurized life each had built in Chicago. Two years later they purchased the Judge McClary farm south of Branson and started building a new world for themselves and Jill's three teenagers. By early 1940, their rolling upland acreage was just beginning to take on the lines of the "Golf Ranch," and Jill's voice was heard in discussions at the Taneyhills Study Club.

Several newcomers were welcomed during the March meeting, held at the home of Ethel Paramore and Jessie Parks. Members noted sadly the death of Vitae Kite, whose colorful butterfly collection soon would be placed on display in the museum at The School of the Ozarks.

The day's program was a "progressive book review," in which the women shared their reactions to sixteen bestsellers recently donated to the library's rental shelf by Caroline Ballentine.

Bringing Books to the Ozarks

Dorothy Jaenicke reported that library patrons were enjoying the sunny atmosphere in the upstairs room and were very pleased that all the books which had been stored in boxes were now available for reading.

Before the meeting adjourned, Bill Ellen Hall was elected the new president of the Study Club.

Don and Jill Gardner and Their Family.
(left to right) Jean Edwards (Moore), Jill Edwards Gardner, Don Gardner, Clark Edwards, Lyn Edwards (Asselin).

CHAPTER X

"THE SHEPHERD" TO THE RESCUE
(March 1940 - December 1941)

New members may have been confused by Dorothy Jaenicke's discussion of library operations at the March, 1940 meeting. Women joining the Study Club sometimes failed to realize that they were volunteering to help support, maintain, and operate the Taney County Public Library. Those who were seeking cultural and social activities were sometimes surprised when asked to help raise funds and refurbish books.

That April seventy members, husbands and guests gathered at the Branson High School to enjoy a dinner prepared and served by Odelle Moore's home economics class and hear reports of the 1939 World's Fair in New York City.

Bill Ellen Hall remembers that Jim Owen was present to join in recognizing Ethel Paramore and Caroline Ballentine who were being awarded Honorary Memberships.

To confer that honor on Study Club members would have required a constitutional amendment, but no records confirm passage of such an

Bringing Books to the Ozarks

amendment. The earliest secretary's book available begins with April, 1941. In the constitution pasted in that book the phrase limiting such awards to those "not already members of the club" is lined out. The deletion is not dated.

Some reasons for such recognition were well known: the many hours both women had spent working in and for the library; Caroline Ballentine's repeated donations to the rental shelves. The Library Acquisitions ledger provides another part of the story. Thanks to Ethel Paramore, in the past three years, several hundred volumes of classical literature, general reference works and children's books had been added to the library shelves. In Chicago, her co-workers at the Quaker Oats Company, along with several friends who were school teachers, formed an "Ozarks Book Club," and regularly collected and shipped books to Branson's library. Other donations credited to Ethel had arrived from similar groups in Kansas City and Birmingham, Alabama.

There was one further dimension to the contributions which caused the clubwomen to remove that restrictive phrase from their constitution. Even as the awards were being made, Ethel Paramore was staving off a minus balance in the club's bank account.

Through the year just ending, bills for the club had totaled over fifty dollars. In support of the library, almost a hundred and fifty dollars had been spent, a sum which, for the first time, included the cost of a thousand dollars worth of

"The Shepherd" to the Rescue

insurance on the books and furnishings. Annual dues, plus the hundred dollars raised by the ways and means committee, fell short of covering the year's expenses. In early 1940, the treasury balance was so close to red ink that Ethel Paramore settled the bill for the March luncheon from her own pocket and delayed cashing the reimbursing check so other club bills could be paid on time.

Ethel and Caroline, though pleased with the honors being conferred, were not willing to give up voting rights or rest on past laurels. They paid their dues that spring and every year they continued in active membership. When Bill Ellen Hall announced her committee leaders at the April meeting, Ethel was continuing as the unpaid assistant librarian and Caroline would be responsible for fund-raising.

As chair of ways and means, Caroline planned a year filled with money-raising schemes. She also joined Dorothy Jaenicke in a search for some project offering a stable income for the library.

The shortage which Ethel Paramore had covered in March was reimbursed after the guest night dinner and the annual collection of dues. The treasury was swelled also by the seventeen dollar proceeds of a new project, the Gypsy Basket. The basket, filled with a variety of small household items, was passed from home to home. Each member took out what she could use, contributed what she thought was a reasonable price, and added new items in replace-

Bringing Books to the Ozarks

ment.

By early summer, Caroline also had enlisted many members in the production of "jellies and jams." Gift shops and resorts which had sold Ozark Lyrics offered a ready marketplace. Batch after batch of jellies, preserves and pickles, made with produce from members' gardens and berries collected along nearby country lanes, was poured into spare jars and glasses that summer. When the women ran short of containers and thought to stop, some of the profits were quickly reinvested in more jelly glasses.

Maude Horine and Stella Owen each paused in her canning chores long enough to host a summer breakfast meeting. September and October found the women preparing two successful jitney dinners. By the time Caroline's year of chairing the ways and means committee ended, club cookery had raised over a hundred and seventy dollars--a sum which, with members' dues, barely equaled the year's expenses.

Through 1940, the treasury balance was seldom less than forty dollars. That small backlog was all but wiped out at the end of the year, however, when the library was offered a hundred and twenty modern books for less than thirty dollars. The librarian at Galesburg, Illinois, was clearing his shelves of books which no longer were of interest to his patrons. He offered them to the Taney County Public Library if the club would pay the shipping costs.

At the same time, an extension librarian from the Missouri State Library Commission came to

"The Shepherd" to the Rescue

Branson to supervise the rearrangement of the library's fiction section in alphabetical order by authors and the recataloging of the nonfiction books using the Dewey Decimal System.

By January, 1941, the library's one thousand cardholders were enjoying four thousand books, almost double the number which had been cleaned and moved upstairs two years before. A news report noted that "The Branson library [has] graduated. . .from the class of small community libraries to a city bracket." The treasury supporting this sophisticated operation held a bit more than nineteen dollars, a sum which dropped to less than seven dollars the following month.

The Study Club's roster had grown to fifty-five, but members were finding it hard to concentrate on the Study Club programs or the needs of the library.

Since 1939, when Germany invaded Poland, the rumble of guns had echoed in the thoughts of these women half a world away. While many midwesterners were trying to ignore Hitler's conquest of western Europe, the bombing of Britain and the increasing belligerence of the Japanese, the club women in Branson were listening to lectures about such strategic outposts as Greenland, Iceland and northern Canada. Discussions of current events enlivened every meeting.

The war was intruding on life in Taney County in many uncomfortable ways. In the fall of 1940, the mobilization of the Missouri Na-

Bringing Books to the Ozarks

tional Guard awakened residents to the possibility of a military draft. When compulsory military service became a reality that winter, so many young Taney Countians already had joined the armed forces that no local men were summoned in the first of the national military lotteries.

With their world in turmoil, the Study Club members were too preoccupied to spend long hours in raising funds. Before the club year ended, the president, Bill Ellen Hall, and the treasurer, Minnie Whelchel, once again were planning their payment of bills so that the bank account would not be completely drained before members paid the next year's dues.

Meantime, Dorothy Jaenicke and Caroline Ballentine were pursuing an inspired plan for rescuing the library's finances.

Hollywood, with much national fanfare, was preparing to release a movie based on Harold Bell Wright's *The Shepherd of the Hills*. Dorothy reasoned that, with vacationers already poking about the area surrounding Dewey Bald, the movie surely would bring a renewed demand for the old novel--a demand which no one could meet since the book had been out of print for more than a year.

The librarian wrote to New York publishers Grosset and Dunlap, Inc., in January, 1941, pointing out the novel's renewed sales potential and urging that a new printing be considered. By return mail came the announcement that a new edition, illustrated with photographs from the movie, would be available by the time the film

"The Shepherd" to the Rescue

Harold Bell Wright, Author of *The Shepherd of the Hills,*
during the years he was a minister
in southwest Missouri and southeast Kansas.
(Swearingen Photo, Mt. Vernon, Missouri)

Bringing Books to the Ozarks

was released on April 11th.

The first report of the Study Club's new book project appeared in the *White River Leader* on February 14, 1941. Dorothy Jaenicke already had completed arrangements for the library to be the area distributor of that movie edition of *The Shepherd of the Hills*. The enthusiastic librarian also had made a hurried trip to the state capital at Jefferson City to complete legal arrangements. When the first books arrived from the Kingsport Press of Kingsport, Tennessee, the library committee would be able to distribute them to nearby resorts and stores without becoming entangled with the law or the tax collector.

As with Mrs. Mahnkey's *Ozark Lyrics*, the problems of financing *The Shepherd of the Hills* project were not made public. The books, to be retailed for fifty cents a copy, would cost the library thirty cents plus shipping charges, payable when each shipment arrived. When the first three hundred books were received at the end of March, the treasury contained less than eleven dollars and the librarian's eight dollar monthly paycheck was due.

The complicated way in which those financial obligations were met is documented in the files at the Taneyhills Community Library. The bottom line was that Ethel Paramore and Caroline Ballentine loaned the money to pay for the initial supply of *The Shepherd of the Hills* books.

Most resort owners who had been selling *Ozark Lyrics* and the Study Club's jellies agreed to participate in the new project. Ethel spent

"The Shepherd" to the Rescue

longer hours in the library so that Dorothy Jaenicke could help Caroline distribute the books and find more resorts willing to sell them. Dorothy also began setting up ledgers to keep track of all the books and buyers, bills and receipts.

When the Study Club members gathered in March, 1941 to elect Margaret Bell their new president, they shared reports of the growing library, enjoyed a lecture on the spring wildflowers which soon would decorate the Ozark hills, and discussed the new book project and prospects of relief from budgetary problems.

The first shipment of *The Shepherd of the Hills* books arrived several days before the release of the much anticipated movie. Copies were available at Ye English Inn on April 5th, when the club held its annual guest night dinner. Bill Ellen Hall presided, welcoming the many guests, including the wife of Missouri's ex-governor, Mrs. Henry S. Caulfield, who was staying at the hotel.

No installation service was conducted that evening. Many of the new officers were at the side of Margaret Bell, mourning the death of her daughter. A frivolous program had been planned and Effie Fechner's minutes (the first such report available for any Study Club meeting) assure that, despite the tragedy, the guests had an enjoyable time:

> Most of the ladies came bedecked in Easter Bonnets both old and chick with very few egg-scuses from those without hats . . . .

Bringing Books to the Ozarks

> Mrs. Mitchell . . . took Charge of a very entertaining program as follows.
> Ladies hat contest with a prise [sic] for the oldest best Looking hat going to Ann Thompson and Chickest hat to Mrs. Horine.
> Quiz Contest which although stiff revealed the egg-stream brilliancy of our members & friends.
> Men's Hat trimming contest honored Dean [John] Bennett with the prize for the best trimming.

The warmhearted atmosphere at the April dinner carried over into May, when each member arrived at the White River Hotel bearing a picture of her mother or of herself as a child. A time of shared memories brought the women to the luncheon table in a happy mood.

When Vice President Dorothy Garner rose to conduct the meeting, she first read Margaret Bell's resignation as president. Then, in accents which betrayed her English birth and in a clever manner that brought smiles to every face, Dorothy told the club members what she, as their new president, would expect of them in the coming year.

Dorothy Jaenicke explained cheerfully that two of Ethel Paramore's friends in Chicago, school teachers Irene Cushing and Marjory Williams, had sent a hundred and twenty-five more books to be enjoyed by the children of Branson. The day's program honored mothers in music and pictures, concluding with a simple and moving candlelighting service.

"The Shepherd" to the Rescue

Electing Reva Ford to the vacant vice presidency was left for a called meeting held several days later. The twelve members who attended that extra session also introduced two constitutional amendments which were ratified at the regular meeting in June. The rule allowing those joining late in the club year to pay fifty cents for a partial year was eliminated, the first real change in dues since they were instituted in 1933. The second amendment removed from the honorary membership rules the restrictive phrase "except the right to hold office," so that women whose service to the club and community had been so honored could participate fully in the Study Club without payment of dues.

With three of the group's most diligent and supportive women now honorary members, that decision probably seemed both prudent and essential. As war clouds darkened, the possibility of maintaining a stable working membership diminished alarmingly. Through the next four years, as wives followed husbands to military training camps, then returned home to wait out combat tours, absent members' names were kept on the rolls for varying lengths of time with no payment of dues. Many families moved to "war plant towns," nearby or half a continent away. Club records reveal that some who were considered to be temporarily absent settled elsewhere when the conflict ended.

The women watched husbands, sweethearts, sons and brothers being inducted into the armed forces in 1941-42 and planned Study Club pro-

Bringing Books to the Ozarks

grams emphasizing patriotism and things American. Speakers encouraged Red Cross work and volunteer labor in the Branson box factory, then operating in the old tobacco barn by the railroad tracks. It was, the women were told, amazing how many war materials were packaged in boxes.

In July, the thirty-two women who gathered at the White River Hotel chuckled through Lyta Davis Good's assessment of "Trends in American Humor," then listened gravely as fellow member Jean Huntley described the plight of infants in wartorn China.

Jean and her husband, Dr. G. A. Huntley, had served in China as medical missionaries for many years. Now retired, they were living in a cottage near their daughter, Jill Gardner. The Study Club members, heartsick following Jean's report, undertook in spare moments to make many tiny sweaters for babies they would never see.

Before the July meeting ended, Dorothy Jaenicke announced that she now was delivering *The Shepherd of the Hills* books to twenty-three resorts and shops, and that sales seemed very brisk. The delighted women, realizing that Dorothy was burning a lot of gasoline in the making those book deliveries, immediately voted to reimburse her "for expenses, 2c for each book sold after the first 500."

Two months later, Dorothy brought the astounding news that "more books would have to be purchased before Hillbilly Day," the upcoming

"The Shepherd" to the Rescue

fall street carnival in downtown Branson. Of the seventeen hundred books received from the publisher in April, a thousand already had been sold. The book profits, at ten cents per copy minus shipping and distributing expenses, were months away from actually adding to the treasury. Nonetheless, that September concerned supporters of the Taney County Public Library breathed a sigh of relief.

For many it was a very tired sigh. Following a successful bake sale in May, the women again had produced jar after jar of pickles and preserves, and glass after glass of jams and jellies for distribution along with *The Shepherd of the Hills* books.

Caroline Ballentine, intrigued with Ozark sunbonnets, made several from gingham scraps. When tourists eagerly bought the first few, she began sewing up old-fashioned bonnets in great numbers and encouraged the other women to make them also.

Apparently the sewing and cooking projects created a temporary aversion to library and household chores. The suggestion was made that someone be hired "to clean the library," and only one special breakfast was held that summer.

When the cooler days of autumn arrived, however, members returned to the kitchen with vigor to support several money-making projects, including an "oyster supper" and the raffling of Irene Couchman's handmade rug.

As the end of 1941 approached, the club treasury, which eight months before had been juggled to avoid red ink, was carrying a balance of two hundred dollars or more.

That November, the Taney County Public Library passed another milestone when Study Club members responded to their healthy bank balance by voting to give Dorothy Jaenicke fifty dollars "to purchase new books."

The librarian did not have a supporting committee to share in this new duty. Since 1938, she and Ethel Paramore had run the library, calling for help as it was needed. Now Dorothy Garner and Caroline Ballentine were asked to help with the book selections. When the next year's chairmen were announced, the library had the support of its own committee.

Meantime, in the euphoria of having a solvent treasury, the head of the ways and means committee introduced an idea which caused a ripple of excitement among the members and some dubious glances among the club officers.

Caroline Ballentine "brought to the club the urgent need of a library building," pointing out that the shelves again were crowded and there was little space for more bookcases. Ellie Mitchell, Dorothy Jaenicke, and Edna Evans were appointed to a committee chaired by Minnie Whelchel, to "inquire about suitable lots and report the cost of same."

It was an idea whose time had not yet come. Events of December, 1941, forced the plan from the club's list of priorities. Many years would pass before it was brought up again.

CHAPTER XI

SISTERS IN ADVERSITY
(Late 1941 - Early 1944)

The members of the Taneyhills Study Club gathered at Ye English Inn on Saturday, December 6, 1941, for a meeting filled with the beauty of Yuletide. Lydia Ellison, as chairman of the day, introduced Margaret Bell, who spoke on "The Advancement of American Music." Then Edith Hayes led her girls' chorus from The School of the Ozarks in a program of Christmas songs.

The following afternoon, a quiet, balmy Sunday, Helen Alexander and several friends planned to stroll across Lake Taneycomo by way of the Highway 65 bridge, down the road beneath the eastern bluffs and back across the Main Street bridge. As they approached Marie Tiffany's house to ask her to join them, she rushed out.

"Hurry, hurry, there's terrible news on the radio! The Japanese are bombing Pearl Harbor!"

Through the months that followed, with their world torn by crisis, it was a blessing for the women that community events continued in

Bringing Books to the Ozarks

their familiar monthly progression.

In January, twenty-seven members and seven guests attended the club's covered dish luncheon and book review held in the Civic League rooms. Among those present were Lyn and Jean Edwards, the daughters of Jill Gardner, attending as guests of their grandmother, Jean Huntley. Also visiting was charter member Hazel Vaughn Johnston, then living in Maracaibo, Venezuela.

By February, wartime conservation had become a byword. The women shared a "Thrift Luncheon" at the White River Hotel, and Ellie Mitchell gave a whimsical dissertation on American cookery, covering the kitchen arts from soup to nuts and, in Ozark fashion, from soap to cake. Then the women voted a five dollar donation to the Red Cross.

There was an omen in that donation. At the March meeting, when Reva Ford was elected club president, the day's speaker, Dr. Florence Boehmer, who was elected recording secretary, provided an enlightening view of Branson's city government.

Dr. Boehmer had been a member of the Study Club for more than a year. In the late 1930s the Drury College professor had suffered a broken back while vacationing near Branson. Through months of recuperation, she remained in the Lake Taneycomo area and, in 1940, joined the Study Club. When she returned to teaching, she did not go back to Springfield. Her classrooms were at The School of the Ozarks and in

Sisters in Adversity

Branson. Installed as club secretary in April, 1942, she relinquished that post a month or so later. Both before and after the war, the club enjoyed her strong support. Meantime, she developed wartime Red Cross services and brought assistance to many troubled Taney County homes.

Minnie Whelchel, who took over as secretary, was herself scarcely a lady of leisure. A licensed embalmer, she operated the Whelchel Funeral Home and prepared several young men and women, including Juanita Thompson, to qualify for their embalming licenses.

Also, at the March meeting, the women congratulated newlywed Mrs. Norman Whelchel, who the month before had been known as Delsie Edwards. They voted another fifty dollars for new library books, and drew the winning ticket for "the rug" purchased the previous summer. Twice the ticket sales had been extended, in an effort to at least cover the club's outlay of a hundred dollars. That goal finally had been reached. Now, as Virginia Boehm reached into the box, each woman hoped to be the lucky owner of the beautiful rug.

The winner's name was greeted by a collective sigh. The rug was going to Bernice Jaffee of Dallas, Texas. When Miss Jaffee received her prize, she was so pleased she sent a five dollar donation, bringing to fourteen dollars the profits on the project.

After twelve months of hard work and imaginative planning, Caroline Ballentine and her

Bringing Books to the Ozarks

ways and means committee had netted only a bit over a hundred dollars. Two hundred and sixty dollars was spent on books, library insurance, utilities, and a large fan to stir the air in the library on hot summer days.

Club costs had exceeded the amount collected in dues. The number of members had fallen to forty that spring when fifteen names were dropped from the rolls for longtime non-payment of dues.

Any "red ink" would have been hard to find in the treasury records, however. During the first year of handling *The Shepherd of the Hills*, costs and profits on eighteen hundred and twenty books were mingled with donations, dues and operating expenses. More than a thousand dollars credited to the club's "income" would soon be needed for new supplies of the books to be wholesaled to resorts and tourist attractions around Branson and the old farm.

Bill Ellen Hall, as head of the ways and means committee, quickly realized that the illusion of a well filled treasury, the many calls to support war-related activities, and the clubwomen's growing need for supportive social events, could make getting those books distributed and carrying out other money-raising efforts very difficult.

That Bill Ellen accepted the fund-raising post in 1942 was probably a surprise to her friends. Through most of the previous year she had been "indisposed," and a substitute had taught her classes. Her son, Jerry, was born in October, 1941.

In later years she enjoyed recounting the

Sisters in Adversity

A Teenager Was Hired by the Library Board
to work part time as library assistant in 1942.

many trips she, Dorothy Jaenicke and tiny Jerry made through the Ozark hills, delivering books, bonnets, honey and preserves to tourist shops.

Actually there was little other than the books to distribute. With nationwide shortages of both sugar and jars, Study Club members were confining their canning endeavors to filling their own larders, and Caroline Ballentine had little time for creating sunbonnets. Increasingly, the responsibility of the library fell on her shoulders, as Ethel Paramore and Jessie Parks took care of their terminally ill mother, and Dorothy Jaenicke pursued book sales.

In June, 1942, the club hired teenager Joan Campbell to work eight hours a month as library

Bringing Books to the Ozarks

assistant. She was paid twenty-five cents an hour. Through the next eighteen months her part-time help was a boon to the librarian, but added to the drain on funds.

When the women met in July, the treasury had not yet received any money from the summer's sales of *The Shepherd of the Hills*. The balance had sagged to a little over a hundred dollars. Dr. Boehmer's audit of the club books, delivered following treasurer Stella Owen's monthly report, revealed that the women were still far short of recouping the borrowed funds which had financed *The Shepherd of the Hills* project. The money the clubwomen had so happily spent on library books the previous year had contributed to a sizable deficit.

Despite the reported shortage, when Bill Ellen Hall tried to generate enthusiasm for her money-raising ideas that day, she got little response. With a hint of exasperation, she asked, "What would you like to do?"

Stella Owen offered to serve a mid-month breakfast and guide a stroll through her gardens. That event plus a second breakfast, and a "white elephant" book sale cleared twenty-nine dollars. In November, Bill Ellen Hall enlisted the whole club in preparing a benefit dinner. She also planned a talent show. The dinner netted nineteen dollars. There are no records to indicate that the talent show ever took place.

The following January, having raised only fifty-one dollars, Bill Ellen again pleaded for suggestions. Ellie Mitchell, Ethel Paramore and

Sisters in Adversity

Jessie Parks volunteered to organize "cook and pay anyway" luncheons for the next two meetings. Those efforts pushed the ways and means committee's total for the year over the eighty dollar mark.

Through World War II, the burden of supporting and operating the library was carried by a handful of the club's members. It was suggested several times during those tension-filled years that too many of the women viewed the club as a social outlet and overlooked its serious intent of study and of providing reading materials for the community.

If self-improvement and fund raising were sometimes neglected in 1942, the Study Club members' need for support in a time of much insecurity was not.

During the spring and summer, Sybil James planned monthly programs that took the women on adventures real and imaginary. Lunch, a lecture and shopping at Heer's in Springfield; a retrospective view of Caroline Ballentine's "journey" to the Philippines; Mrs. F.L. Moore's exciting book review about the world everyone would enjoy "after the war," and an August boat cruise to Rockaway Beach, soothed many personal anxieties.

In the fall and through the holidays, they "went" to India with Margaret Bell, to the Orient with Reverend Yates, and to the East Indies with Dorothy Garner. And at the December meeting, Jean Huntley recited the Lord's Prayer in Chinese and told about China's holiday tradi-

Bringing Books to the Ozarks

tions.

The year's programs prompted an increase in reading. Branson's volunteer library loaned a record number books in August, and in late summer became a certified member of the American Library Association. In celebration, the club voted to use some of their funds to replace a few worn-out books. That, along with many gifts, brought the year's expenditures on new books to two hundred and eighty-four dollars. In January, 1943, Dorothy Jaenicke reported some four thousand three-hundred volumes available for check-out. Even as she spoke, new memorials were being received for the late Kate Scudder, a charter member.

When the year's financial dealings were reviewed that March, Bill Ellen Hall realized with much relief that the two hundred and sixty-four dollars it cost to operate the library was not being balanced solely against the eighty dollars her committee had managed to raise.

The figures in Stella Owen's treasury report probably left the club members more confused than enlightened. She had handled, over the past twelve months, more than eight hundred dollars, including expenses of the library and club, and the costs of and receipts from well over a thousand *Shepherd of the Hills* books. The treasury, marginally solvent with a balance of a hundred and two dollars, again presented a monetary tangle which everyone was happy to leave to the annual auditing committee to verify.

Those treasury records were about to become

Sisters in Adversity

even more complicated. In February, 1943, with interest in other fund-raising projects lagging, a letter was received from the publisher of *The Shepherd of the Hills* asking if the club would like to handle sales of *Take to the Hills*.

Some of the women were familiar with the offered book, an Ozarks autobiography on sale since 1941. The author, Marguerite Kemp Lyon, and her husband Robert, in 1935 left behind the business and publishing world of Chicago to take up farming in the sparsely populated mountains of south central Missouri. With the Depression making city life difficult at best and miserable at worst, many struggling couples found the "back to the soil" movement very appealing. That movement was reversed by the war, but Marge Lyon's picturesque and sometimes zany adventures with her new Ozark neighbors attracted many readers.

In May, the first sales of *Take to the Hills* were entered in the Study Club treasury records.

By then the club had a new president. Daisy Cook, installed at the April dinner at Ye English Inn, had joined the group in 1941. A lively and talented teacher, and mother of five school-age children, she also was a self-taught artist whose paintings were receiving wide recognition.

On the first Saturday in May, when the women met at the White River Hotel, the new president introduced a request that the club take on sponsorship of the Hollister book collection.

The library in the resort community across Lake Taneycomo was popular among local read-

Bringing Books to the Ozarks

ers and vacationers, and had operated from time to time even before the church women took up sponsorship in 1936. However, most of those women had soon transferred their interest to the Taneyhills Study Club.

In 1943, the Hollister Library was housed in the City Hall, a building previously used by the Madry Lumber Company. The city clerk kept an eye on the books. However the effort required to save them that spring, when the waters of the flooding White River filled the first floors of all the buildings in downtown Hollister, made it clear that those one thousand volumes needed care and support as well as supervision. The Study Club members voted to discuss the request with Townsend Godsey, Hollister's mayor, but if such a conversation occurred there is no record of it and nothing was done.

When he was not being Hollister's mayor, Godsey, a journalist, photographer, and educator, was engaged in capturing on film the life of Ozark villagers and isolated farm families, before the old ways and the older generation disappeared entirely.

Godsey's wife, Helen, was one of the Study Club's newest members. Her time usually was occupied with raising her children and teaching piano students. In the Study Club, she joined in encouraging musical entertainment at the meetings. The club members, after enjoying several musical performances and sessions of group singing, voted to have a few minutes of music in each monthly program.

Sisters in Adversity

The head of the ways and means committee, Jessie Parks, keeping in mind the women's lack of enthusiasm for time consuming projects, was postponing her money-raising plans until the fall and winter so members could enjoy the summer as a social time.

Interest in fund-raising was drained away more by the anxieties of the times than by the summer heat. Each month more names of local men were added to the Servicemen's Honor Roll on the wall of the Branson Post Office. The women agreed, as they shared a July breakfast, to pay the cost of inscribing twenty additional names. It was a donation with personal meaning to each member. Those who had no relatives involved in the fighting shared the concerns of friends such as Jill Gardner, Bill Ellen Hall and Ingrid Almon Russell, who anxiously waited at home when they were not traveling to distant military stations to be near their husbands.

At the July meeting, Townsend Godsey told of the fascinating arts and crafts he was discovering in his travels through the hills. Helen Godsey read an article on folk music, and Dorothy Jaenicke reported the cataloging of a large number of books donated by Florence Smith.

The relaxed summer meetings concluded with a cruise down Lake Taneycomo past forested shores, towering craggy bluffs, and tiny meadows where cattle browsed on lush green grass at the water's edge. At Rockaway Beach, the women had dessert in the big resort hotel and reviewed the club's finances.

Bringing Books to the Ozarks

In the fall of 1943, the war was coming much closer to home. Every weekend the streets of downtown Branson and Hollister were filled with men and women in uniform. Most were either patients or on the staff at O'Reilly military hospital in Springfield.

Wartime problems were the center of attention at the October meeting, when Dr. Boehmer spoke on the organization and purposes of the American Red Cross, and Mrs. E.K. Boles told of the help which that organization's home service office was providing the families of servicemen. Both women were adept at encouraging the natural neighborliness of their Ozarks friends to help meet the problems created by tension-filled family separations.

Bill Ellen Hall was not present to benefit from the information provided. "I didn't get to any meetings that year," she later recalled. "Ingrid Russell and I worked out our own self-help plan. She took care of my Jerry so I could teach school, and I kept her daughter, Karen, while she went to club meetings."

In December, Study Club members celebrated the tenth anniversary of the Taney County Public Library. The luncheon was held at Ye English Inn, hosted by Virginia Boehm and her sister, Juanita Weaver, who were operating the hotel and restaurant while their husbands were away at war.

Maude Horine brought a gaily decorated birthday cake; Ethel Paramore's five years of volunteer service were applauded with a standing

Sisters in Adversity

ovation; and Caroline Ballentine presented Dorothy Jaenicke with a dozen roses as a token of the club's appreciation for her selfless dedication to the library through all the years since its beginning.

The librarian was reminded again of that appreciation, in January, 1944, when her salary was increased from eight to ten dollars a month. This time she did not refuse the larger amount.

Ingrid Russell and Helen Godsey led the January program on "Music and the Emotions." A few days later, Ingrid and her daughter joined Ray Russell at his duty station and were away until the war ended.

In hindsight, many people think of World War II as "almost over" by January, 1944. In reality there was no end yet in sight for those doing the fighting. The struggle to reclaim the continent of Europe from the Nazis and free the island chains of the Pacific and much of the continent of Asia from the Japanese had barely begun. Many problems complicated the lives of the worried women at home, who struggled to maintain a house, care for children, and often also keep the family business alive. The tourist trade, a part of Branson's "industry" since the town was born, had diminished to a trickle. Vacationers who did appear brought with them an ever present need for scarce items--soap, butter, and sugar, china dishes and kitchenware. Each fall local merchants found it more difficult to restock their increasingly empty shelves.

The women pushed their frustrations to the

Bringing Books to the Ozarks

background by sharing hours in the Red Cross craft center, weaving material for mufflers and socks, or rolling bandages. Study Club programs reflected dreams of improved housing and normal home life.

In February and March, 1944, Jessie Parks dispelled the midwinter doldrums with a games party and a mood-brightening project called "Pennies from Heaven." The object of the latter event was to celebrate days of sunshine, add cheer to cloudy ones, and collect a few pennies for the club. No one remembers how it all worked out, but those two projects brought the year's fund-raising total to a hundred and twenty-three dollars.

After Ethel Paramore was elected Study Club president at the March meeting, Dorothy Jaenicke reported twelve new books on the rental shelf, and sixteen much traveled favorites had been repaired. Sales of eight hundred and sixteen *Shepherd of the Hills* and *Take to the Hills* books had netted a hundred and twenty dollars for the library.

In their third year of distributing books for sale to tourists, members listening to the annual financial report waited for the bottom line. It had cost two hundred and fifty dollars to operate the library, leaving a hundred and seventy-nine dollars in the treasury.

The women were reminded that no action had been taken on the year-old appeal for help from the Hollister librarian. For those who remembered earlier efforts to organize libraries

Sisters in Adversity

throughout the county, it was hard to turn aside from such a request. The book collection at Rockaway Beach had long since been absorbed into the local school. If the Hollister library could not be put on a self-sustaining basis, only Branson and Forsyth would have "public" library services available.

However, funding and overseeing the Branson library weighed heavily on the executive committee. Sponsoring a second library would require more donated hours, and volunteers were not rushing to meet the club's present responsibilities. The Hollister library recently had sold several dozen copies of *Take to the Hills*. Following the March meeting, corresponding secretary Sara Heath sent the Hollister librarian, Mrs. Peyton, a check for ten dollars, explaining that it represented the profits from those book sales, and suggesting that perhaps a similar project might be found to support their library.

Mrs. Peyton answered with her thanks, but the Hollister library ceased operation a short time later. Townsend Godsey remembered that the books were offered to the Branson library. However, the majority were duplicates which had come from across the lake originally. Most of Hollister's books went to the library in Forsyth.

CHAPTER XII

THE NAME'S THE GAME
(April 1944 - Early 1946)

Ethel Paramore was installed as library club president on April 1, 1944, at Ye English Inn, the site of guest night dinners for eight of the past nine years. The evening's festivities included several hilarious games led by Ellie Mitchell, and Eve Griffith singing, accompanied on the piano by Helen Godsey.

Helen would soon be leaving Branson. Her delightful way of presenting programs would be missed, as would her kind personality. Through the next twenty years, while her husband taught photojournalism at the University of Oklahoma, and at Stephens College in Columbia, Missouri, the family would come and go in the Branson area. Her membership was broken by long absences until the family became permanent Taney Countians in the mid-1960s.

Ethel Paramore's presidency began with the acceptance of two donations. Sara Heath offered to pay for a supply of cards imprinted with the Collect used at the opening of each club meeting, and Caroline Ballentine paid to have the Study

The Name's the Game

Club constitution included in the 1944-45 yearbooks.

The constitution had not been rewritten for ten years. The 1944 printing, prepared from the 1934 document pasted in the secretary's book, raised quite a stir. Included were the three amendments for which there were records of club approval after the required two readings at regular meetings, the deletion of part-year dues, allowing the nomination of only one candidate for each office, and permitting honorary members to vote and hold office without payment of dues.

However, the phrase limiting honorary memberships to "persons not already members of the club" was left intact, there being no minutes or other records verifying its deletion.

Thus, women already members of the club could not be named to honorary membership, but new honorees could hold office in the club without paying dues. The resultant "stir" was understandable. Dorothy Jaenicke's honorary membership, conferred before she became a regular member, was not affected. The 1940 awards to Ethel Paramore and Caroline Ballentine raised so much controversy that, though new candidates were suggested for the honor from time to time, twenty-five years would pass before any further honorary memberships were awarded.

Caroline Ballentine had her name removed from the honorary members list in the 1947 yearbook. It did not reappear until sixteen years later, when she no longer could be active in the

Bringing Books to the Ozarks

club. By 1947, Ethel Paramore's health had failed. Her name was never missing from that special list.

Also omitted from that printing of the constitution was an amendment, penciled in and dated February 6, 1943, stating that "the President shall serve only one term and not succeed herself." It had been introduced and voted on without a second reading. Whatever the story was behind its improper approval, several more years passed before any president ran for a second consecutive term.

When the club gathered in May for a picnic at Dorothy Garner's country home, members mourned the passing of Honorary Member Rose O'Neill. Bonniebrook, Rose O'Neill's secluded home, stood unused for three years, then burned to the ground. Her fetching little Kewpies and other characters continued to stir memories among visitors to the Ozarks and brought collectors from around the world. In the 1980s, Bonniebrook was named to the National Register of Historic Places and, in the 1990s, the rebuilt O'Neill house again welcomes visitors to the lovely wooded setting of yesteryear, along with an elegant restaurant, gift shop and museum.

In the spring and summer of 1944, memories of Rose O'Neill were shared by library club members as they "cleaned and culled the books." For Marion Brown and her fellow library committee members, Caroline Ballentine and Dorothy Garner, that task seemed endless. Carton after carton of donated books arrived, by car and by

The Name's the Game

freight, from Galesburg, Illinois. Not until the end of July were the eleven hundred and thirty-three usable volumes identified, logged in, cleaned, and shelved. The discards, sold at five cents each, brought over a hundred dollars. Those cartons from Galesburg had contained over thirty-three hundred books!

Youthful readers were enjoying an additional thirty-nine "juveniles" donated by Mrs. Davis; and Etta Mann and Ellie Mitchell went to an auction and bought twenty-two recent Book-of-the-Month Club selections for the rental shelves.

Sales of *The Shepherd of the Hills* and *Take to the Hills* did so well that summer that Ethel Paramore and Caroline Ballentine were finally repaid the money they had advanced in 1941 to get the project started.

At the August meeting, held at The School of the Ozarks, club finances were looking healthy. When Lyta Good concluded her speech on conservation by announcing there would be no charge for the luncheon the women had just enjoyed, the twenty-five dollars already collected also went into the club treasury.

With so many things going well, why were the Study Club members so upset that day?

Because Dorothy Jaenicke had taken a job at the Webb Novelty factory and was resigning as librarian.

For eleven years the Study Club had accepted Dorothy's services as a reliable blessing. The library was always well run and open on schedule, and she unfailingly kept the club abreast of

Bringing Books to the Ozarks

its needs and operation.

Hiring a clerk would not bridge the gap between library and club. The August minutes addressed that problem:

> Mrs. Garner brought up for discussion changing the name of the club to the Taneyhills Library Club.
> Mrs. E.J. Beimdick made a motion that it be left to the executive committee for consideration and that they bring the matter before the club at the next meeting. Motion failed to carry.
> Mrs. Mitchell suggested that it be settled then. She made a motion that we change the name of the club to Taneyhills Library Club and the library to Tanehills [sic] Library. Motion was seconded and carried.

A constitutional amendment changing the club's name was approved in October. Changing the name of the library proved more difficult. The club's governing document still contained no mention of the library or any responsibility for it, and the women were not ready to make major revisions in their constitution. They still were assessing the resignation of Dorothy Jaenicke and whether they could keep the library open without her.

Meantime the library committee took on supervising the library, and a clerk was hired at ten dollars per month.

More space was needed for the ever expanding book collection and in the final weeks of 1944 the reading room again became noisy and very

The Name's the Game

dusty, as Albert M. Worthing built new partitions and additional shelves. When order and quiet returned early in 1945, the library had a new entrance to fit its enlarged interior and a fresh sign again proclaimed its identity as "The Taney County Public Library."

The twenty-seven members of the library club who gathered at the White River Hotel on January 6th were too delighted with the library improvements and encouraged by the news from the world's battlefronts to see any ill omen in the day's events. They had expected to meet in the home of Ruby Worthing, but she was ill. They anticipated hearing a talk by Winnie Blain. Instead, Sybil James and Daisy Cook led discussions on postwar problems and juvenile delinquency.

Rev. Waller and Winnie Blain had moved on to a different church in another town right after Christmas. Before the end of January Rev. George and Margaret Bell also moved away.

For several weeks Evelyn Runyon was the only "complimentary" member on the club rolls. In late January, however, the Gardners' cottage at the Golf Ranch, empty since Jean Huntley's death in August, became the home of Rev. Guy Howard, the "Walking Preacher of the Ozarks," and his family. By March his wife, Mary Louise, was a "free-dues" member of the library club.

A light-hearted group of clubwomen met at the home of Sybil James in February for a "Kid Party." Daisy Cook, dressed in hobo garb with her covered dish tied in a kerchief and dangling

Bringing Books to the Ozarks

from a pole, took home the prize for best costume. Mrs. William A. Sailor's humorous poem also won a prize.

The following month, Ruby Worthing hosted the luncheon she had planned for January. Year-end reports revealed a drastic change in the club's finances. Florence Blanchard, by capitalizing on every social occasion and making each money-raising event fun as well as work, had cleared almost four hundred and twenty dollars. Over the preceding twelve months the club's income had totaled fourteen hundred and seventy dollars. With all the bills for enlarging the library paid, four hundred and eighty-nine dollars remained in the treasury.

That April, the guest night dinner, with installation of the new president, Berniece Coday, and other officers, was held in the student cafeteria of The School of the Ozarks. In the midst of the evening's games and entertainment, conversation often turned to Branson's colorful taxi driver, Pearl Spurlock. The women in the library club were well aware that Sparky's activities had contributed much to the success of their book sales. Her death the previous month had prompted the Missouri House of Representatives to pass a resolution recognizing her achievements in encouraging improved roads in the area around Lake Taneycomo and all over the state.

No local meetings of any kind were held the following weekend, when record-breaking rains turned the White River into a rampaging monster which submerged much of downtown Branson

The Name's the Game

Branson's Main Street Bridge, Built in 1913,
Was swept away in the flood of 1945 and not rebuilt.
(Photo taken from Mt. Branson in 1920's)

and Hollister. For the second time in three years the lobby of Ye English Inn was filled almost to its high ceiling. The iron bridge across Turkey Creek was pushed from its supporting pillars, and had to be reset. The bridge at the foot of Main Street in Branson was swept away forever.

Branson's volunteer library was well above the floodwater and any danger from gushing springs, but the officers of the sponsoring library club suddenly found their responsibilities, always complicated, taking a bizarre turn.

In early March, a newcomer to Branson requested membership in the library club. A few days later, the woman and her husband brought to the library a number of books and pamphlets which they wanted put on the shelves. The mate-

Bringing Books to the Ozarks

rial was blatantly communistic.

Almost simultaneously, a letter arrived at the library warning that people who had brought similar material to a library in an eastern town were now living in the Branson area.

The clubwomen who heard about that letter, the offered material and the request for membership were, after three-and-a-half years of war, very conscious of propaganda and alien ideologies. In the spring of 1945, as the Allies won control of central Europe, club discussions centered on unsettling reports of the territorial tug-of-war with the Soviet Union then taking shape.

In later years, the librarian, when asked what she would do in similar circumstances, felt she had ample tools to deal with the problem. Asked what she would have done in 1945, given the prevailing attitudes, the organization of the club and the lack of clearly defined responsibility for the library, she had no ready answer. Neither did the women then faced with the situation.

The club women managed to weather the storm, but several changes in library procedures and operations were made. The letter of warning, which had been seen by many people, created an uproar in Branson. When the new officers met with their predecessors on March 17th to transfer responsibilities, a post office box was rented. In the future, the library supervisor would be the first to review all incoming mail.

The retiring president, Ethel Paramore, agreed to become the supervising librarian, relieving concerns about decision-making in the

The Name's the Game

library, but when the new executive committee met the first of May, strong views were expressed about current member admission policies. A constitutional amendment was suggested, but no action was taken.

When the club met two days later, Forrest Runyon, the editor of the *White River Leader,* introduced an army intelligence officer, Major Ottic, who spoke on "China, Japan, and their aims in this war." The Major's comments did little to allay the women's fears. In the business meeting which followed, they approved a motion "That the membership be closed at the present number for the year."

The strangers who precipitated the furor in the club and library left the area within a few months, but the questions remained.

Many changes occurred in the world, the nation, and the communities along Lake Taneycomo during the year in which the Taneyhills Library Club accepted no new members. In May, the fighting ended in Europe and servicemen began coming home. In August, Japan surrendered and anticipated postwar developments became current events.

By the spring of 1945, many Taney County's sons already were coming home. Families from other places, uprooted by the war, decided to relocate in or near Branson. But it became obvious also that many pre-war neighbors were settling elsewhere and other longtime residents also moved away. Among the latter were Dean and Mrs. John Bennett who, after ten years of "work-

Bringing Books to the Ozarks

ing" retirement," moved back to their native Nebraska.

Early that summer, Irene Couchman was hired as librarian, and immediately started logging in and shelving forty children's books which arrived from Kansas City, a collection of boys' books donated by Mrs. Benton of St. Louis, another large shipment from Galesburg, and twenty dollars worth of new books paid for by the club. The library committee looked at the many new children's books and decided that using them to establish a junior rental shelf would speed the development of a better young people's section.

With all the additions to the book collection, finding wanted books on the crowded shelves sometimes involved much searching. Caroline Ballentine and Dorothy Garner offered to cross-file the entire collection by subject, title and author, if the club would buy more cabinets to hold the new file cards. With that project underway, the library committee, exasperated at the club's failure to fully acknowledge responsibility for the library, ordered a new sign for the outside door of the library. Instead of "Taney County Public Library," this one read "Taneyhills Public Library."

In July, with the conflict still raging in the Pacific, the club gathered at The School of the Ozarks, to hear Lyta Good discuss compulsory military training and Capt. Harold Horine recount his experiences in wartorn Europe. Before the war, young Horine had developed a

The Name's the Game

process for making pottery and garden ornaments from cement. Now he was again working with his mother, Maude Horine, at Como Craft, a sprawling combination of home, factory, and store where those ornaments were made and sold.

The club women listened attentively to both speakers. However, that meeting had in store yet another trauma for the library supporters. When Daisy Cook rose to give her ways and means committee report, she announced that the supply of Shepherd of the Hills books had been cut off. She did not know why, nor when or if they might be available again.

For the time being, at least, *Take to the Hills* would still be available, but losing Wright's long-time bestseller, even for a short time, brought visions of red ink to everyone's mind.

In discussing the problems the loss would create, the clubwomen assessed again Dorothy Jaenicke's continuing management of the book sales, and voted to give her a fifty dollar war bond to show their appreciation.

Daisy Cook, forewarned that the book supply was ending, discussed plans for a thrift shop to replace the lost revenue. A ripple of laughter and applause greeted her announcement that the first donation already had been received--one very lively nanny goat.

The thrift shop opened a few days later, in the "weaving room just east of the Community Building." Club members and friends of the library were invited to donate anything that

Bringing Books to the Ozarks

might be sold--fancywork, baked goods and novelties, as well as used clothing and furniture. The shop netted a hundred and fifty-eight dollars over the next six months, but was closed in December. Each member, having been asked to bring in one item a month, ransacked her closets, kitchen and basement until she had little left to spare.

From the thrift shop, catering the high school's junior-senior banquet in May, a bazaar in November, a games party, and proceeds from two luncheons, the ways and means committee raised two hundred and sixty-four dollars that year. However, with the bazaar behind her and faced with the closing of the thrift shop, Daisy Cook temporarily ran out of witticisms. In early 1946, the executive committee hosted a scheduled games party so she could relax awhile at her painting easel.

As the year's financial reports were prepared, it was hard to assess, in the club's six hundred and eighty-five dollar balance, the problems ahead once all *The Shepherd of the Hills* books were sold. By the spring of 1946, however, every member of the club was aware that the publishing house had been sold and the new owners were not planning any more reprints of Wright's most famous book.

CHAPTER XIII

DECISIONS, DECISIONS
(1946 - 1947)

In the summer of 1945, as the war ended, youth groups in and around Branson launched a drive for funds to build a War Memorial on a hill overlooking Lake Taneycomo, a tower whose carillon would be heard for miles. The library club appointed a representative to the Memorial Tower Council, as did most other local organizations.

Through the war years, Taney Countians had helped each other and their fighting men by supporting Red Cross activities and repeated war bond drives. The Servicemen's Honor Roll Plaque had received continuing contributions from individuals, businesses and clubs. By early 1946, however, personal and community priorities were changing.

All over Taney County, homes, jobs and schools for returning veterans and their families were a primary concern. Down river from Lake Taneycomo, construction was underway on Bull Shoals Dam, and before it was completed the citizens of Forsyth must move their county seat

Bringing Books to the Ozarks

town from the bottom land at the mouth of Swan Creek to higher ground to avoid recurrent flooding. Between Forsyth and the Arkansas state line, several river front villages and much rich farmland would be covered by the new lake. Many families would be forced to move and find other work.

Civic leaders in Branson encouraged development of new local industries and worked to revive and expand the tourist trade. Recovering four "lost years" seemed more important than building reminders of war. Support for the memorial tower soon faded.

Long dreamed of postwar improvements were slow in arriving. Library club programs focused on better housing and anticipated visits to distant places, but grocery bags contained little sugar or margarine. Not even the most basic home appliances were on sale in area stores and it would be three or four years before new cars were available again.

Improvement of telephone service in Taney County was agonizingly slow. Each town still was served by its own small switchboard. In Branson and Hollister, residents requesting a telephone faced a long wait. Not until well into the 1950s did company consolidations and expansions begin bringing telephones to rural homes.

The women planning library club luncheons bought quantities of two-penny postcards to remind members of meetings, and often avoided the expense of unclaimed reservations by planning covered dish luncheons in the Civic League

Decisions, Decisions

rooms or private homes.

By early 1946, the consequences of the decision to accept no new members for a year were distressingly apparent. Despite the return of several members who had been "away" for months or years during the war, the number of women actively participating again dropped below fifty. That January, as thirty-eight members climbed the hill to the Paramore-Parks home for their monthly luncheon, they knew they would be saying farewell to Sara Heath, since she and her husband Willard were moving back to St. Louis. She had served the club through twenty-one terms of office since 1934!

Tearfully, the women gave their former president and longtime corresponding secretary a basket overflowing with small gifts and mementos. Until new officers were installed in April, Juanita Thompson would handle club correspondence as well as keeping the minutes.

The day's reports set off a lively discussion of club finances. Librarian Ethel Paramore noted that, for the second consecutive year, four hundred dollars had been spent in providing books for local readers. Income from rentals and fines, dues, and fund-raising projects had not covered library and club expenses. Though the treasury still contained a healthy six hundred and seventy-five dollars, much of that was money which would be needed to buy more supplies of *The Shepherd of the Hills*, if the books became available again.

A suggestion of developing more money-raising projects to cover annual expenses met with little enthusiasm, however. With returning husbands, changes of jobs, and large investments of time and resources in refurbishing long-neglected businesses or resorts, almost all the women were coping with re-ordering of their own lives.

Evelyn Runyon proposed that the dues for both active and associate members be raised to five dollars a year. Evelyn (a dues-paying member since the recent sale of the *White River Leader* to William and Minnie Freeland, the owners of the *Taney County Republican*) pointed out that such a plan might overcome the club's money problems. Immediately, enthusiastic supporters drafted and read the required constitutional change. In February that amendment received a second reading and when the vote was called for, the response was a firm "Yes."

Voices of dissent began to be heard as soon as the vote was cast.

The many complaints could not be ignored. By March, Evelyn's amendment had been revised, resetting the annual dues at three dollars. At the same time, two additional amendments were proposed: that "all amendments to the constitution and bylaws be voted by written ballot" and that "the club shall not use moneys for any purpose other than the benefit of the Taneyhills Library or the Taneyhills Library Club."

In that third amendment, the library received its first mention in the sponsoring club's constitution! All three amendments were ratified, by

Decisions, Decisions

written ballot, amid the festivities of the guest night dinner the following month.

Ye English Inn rang with song and laughter that April evening in 1946. Dorothy Garner led members and their husbands through hilarious games and Mrs. Ronald Portman gave her "impressions of England." Eve Griffith, who had been an officer in the club for two of the four years since she joined, was being installed as president. As Berniece Coday handed Eve the gavel and "retired" to the ways and means committee chair, both women were aware that there were several controversies still to be resolved.

When the moratorium on new members expired in May, the women had reached no agreement concerning membership requirements. However, many neighbors and friends were anxious to join, and the library and club needed more support. No new rules were passed, but with the understanding that, to apply, a woman must have lived in the area for a year, and that each applicant would be considered carefully by the membership committee, the club roster began to grow.

Within a month, more than a dozen new members were accepted. Eve Griffith planned a welcoming tea for early June, to acquaint the newcomers with the club and its library. That event would have been a "first," but it, and also the picnic which was to be the monthly meeting, were called off when the president became ill.

Despite those cancellations, there was plenty of participation available for all who would vol-

Bringing Books to the Ozarks

unteer. The library clerk, Irene Couchman, was unable to work that summer. In June, while Ethel Paramore and her new assistant, Flora Beimdick, loaned over five hundred adult and two hundred and forty-six children's books, Caroline Ballentine and Dorothy Garner continued the seemingly endless job of cross-filing all the books. At the same time, the library committee, realizing that charging a fee to check out the most popular juvenile books had discouraged youthful readers, cancelled the juvenile rental program and began installing new "shelf tables" so the children's books could be grouped according to grade level.

Activity in the library room reached the point of hysteria when all the shelves were shifted first one direction and then another to enable painting the floor.

On the first Saturday in July, the busy library volunteers took a well-earned break to attend the luncheon at The School of the Ozarks, enjoy Lyta Good's enlightening tales of "The School of the Ozarks Then and Now," and renew acquaintance with honorary member Mary Elizabeth Mahnkey. More volunteer workers for the library were recruited from among the eighteen new members present, and the many teachers attending that day as guests were urged to join the club.

Sybil James, her program plans completed for the coming year, reported that the *White River Leader* had offered to print the yearbooks "for free if we would wait until September." The cost would be twenty-eight dollars if the club needed

Decisions, Decisions

them sooner.

With so many new names on the club's roster, no one wanted the yearbooks to be a month late. However, there were strong objections to paying that price.

In the club archives, the outsized 1946-47 yearbook (which includes the constitution) is easily recognizable. Typed, mimeographed, and assembled by Betty Chase at a cost of ten dollars, that yearbook is a lasting symbol of protest against the onset of forty years of inflation. Its cost was barely covered by proceeds of a midsummer rummage sale.

Before the yearbooks were distributed, Edith Hayes, listed as corresponding secretary, resigned her post. Dorothy Jaenicke, now divorced and working as manager of the Branson Hotel, agreed to accept the office which her mother had held for so many years.

In planning the year's programs, Sybil James had enlisted the talents of several friends who had been away during the war. In October, Steve Miller demonstrated silkscreen printing, assisted by Jill Gardner's husband, Don. Nadine Miller had joined the library club in 1942, shortly after she and her husband first moved to the area. During the war, Steve Miller designed aircraft in Kansas City, and he, Nadine and young Ron had only recently returned to the Ozarks. Now the artist was developing a market for his advertising illustrations among local merchants and tourist attractions.

December's program featured music per-

Bringing Books to the Ozarks

Elizabeth "Lizzie" McDaniel

Decisions, Decisions

formed by returning member Ingrid Russell and readings by new member Lyn Asselin, long known to the women as Jill Gardner's daughter, Lyn Edwards.

Through the fall, monthly reports from the library told of a growing readership. With Irene Couchman still unable to work regular hours, patrons were assisted by volunteers. The library committee received another shipment of Marge Lyon's *Take to the Hills*, all distributed and sold by the end of the 1946 tourist season. There were no more *Shepherd of the Hills* books. The last copy had sold at the inflated price of one dollar.

The women struggling to meet library expenses often thought longingly of Wright's bestseller. The market for those books had never seemed better. In the winter of 1945, after Lizzie McDaniel died, the Branson Civic League again had borrowed funds, this time to finance a winning bid on the Shepherd of the Hills farm out on Dewey Bald Road. The following year, with title to the one hundred and eighty-four-acre parcel in the League's name, Branson's intrepid "city mothers" sold all except the state-leased park on Inspiration Point and the refurbished "Old Matt's cabin and barn" to Dr. Bruce and Mary Trimble, who then leased both buildings for inclusion in their planned tourist attraction.

Library club members recall that, through the late 1940s, in an effort to meet visitors' continuing requests for the book which the farm represented, Mary Trimble sought out and bought every copy of the old Wright novel she could find,

Bringing Books to the Ozarks

Old Matt's Cabin: Elizabeth McDaniel Bought & Restored the log house at the Shepherd of the Hills farm in the 1920's.

both locally and on trips all over the country.

In 1946, ways and means committee chair Berniece Coday was determined to prove that the library and club could survive without the support of *The Shepherd of the Hills*. Through September and October, she encouraged and cajoled the women to handcraft items for a bazaar and luncheon. That November event cleared over eighty dollars. A much enjoyed "games night" raised an additional thirty-three dollars.

Ways and means receipts totaled a hundred and twenty-seven dollars which, along with a hundred and eighty-eight dollars from library fines and rental fees, fifty dollars in profits from *Take to the Hills*, and a hundred and forty dollars

Decisions, Decisions

in club dues, more than covered the three hundred and eighty dollars spent on the club and library. The year, which had begun with worries over decreasing membership and loss of income from book sales, ended with twenty-seven new members on the rolls and a record nine hundred and thirty five dollars in the treasury!

Meanwhile, the club constitution was being overhauled. Evelyn Runyon, Ingrid Russell and Berniece Coday wrote and argued and rewrote-- defining the duties of each committee and each elective and appointive officer. They set up new membership rules to satisfy current club perceptions, and gave recognition to responsibility for the library by building into the document a separate library board.

In February, after listening to the lengthy document for a second time, the women voted. Twenty-five affirmative votes were needed for passage. Only twenty ballots read "Yes."

A copy of the rejected document is still in the club files. The constitutional committee had restated the organization's identity to be "a community institution primarily for the purpose of providing library service" and secondarily "to further cultural interests and social life among the members." The framers of that lengthy document offered what they thought would be an acceptable resolution to virtually every difference of opinion which had accumulated through the past decade. Obviously too many of those differences were not yet resolved.

Rejection of the constitutional revision left the

Bringing Books to the Ozarks

library and the club with many problems, concerns which loomed large in the early months of 1947, following the January announcement that both librarian Ethel Paramore and assistant librarian Flora Beimdick were "retiring."

For nine years, Ethel had walked down the steep Pacific Street hill to work in the library. She no longer could manage the six-block-long climb to her home at the end of each working day. Flora, too, was struggling with ill health. Juanita Thompson recorded the resignations in her minutes, adding, "The loss of the Librarian and asst librarian is a very severe blow to the club."

Through several months Florence Hamilton and Martha Chase were hired as interim library clerks, until Irene Couchman returned as full time librarian in May.

Juanita Thompson, who moved from recording secretary to president that spring, inherited continuing arguments over the club's relationship to the Taneyhills Public Library. There were no rules delegating authority over its operation, or even mandating its existence. The library committee, which coordinated the club's supportive efforts and provided volunteers to run the library, also was not mentioned in the club constitution.

The new library chairman was Ruth Wiley, then teaching in the Branson area, whose interest in the Taneyhills Library had brought her into the club the previous year. Ruth's husband, Ralph, a retired army officer popularly known as

Decisions, Decisions

"Cap," was a native of Crane, Missouri, who had taught in Branson for a year or two before he entered the service and subsequently married St. Louis schoolteacher Ruth Snyder. After "Cap" Wiley's retirement in the late years of World War II, the couple chose the Branson area as their permanent home.

Ruth was taking on a fast-growing responsibility. In May, 1947, the Galesburg librarian, Mr. Wynn, delivered to the library some very nice books and said he would send a thousand more if the club would pay the freight costs. Initially that offer was declined. Volunteers still were trying to sort and find room for the volumes they already had. A few weeks later, with the backlog of newly acquired books processed and the library cross-filed, the women changed their minds and decided to accept the latest donations from Galesburg.

By August, patrons of Branson's library had five thousand books readily available for reading. Also available were several periodicals. For ten years Stella Owen's son, Dr. Lyle Owen, had renewed his mother's gift of the *Reader's Digest* and added other magazines. His generosity inspired others to follow suit. The newest subscription, from Caroline Ballentine, was *The Book List*, a catalog of the latest offerings of the nation's publishers. That gift contributed to many daydreams and much frustration among the women running the library.

The ways and means committee, led by Mary Roberts, was trying hard, in the summer and fall

Bringing Books to the Ozarks

of 1947, to back up those daydreams with hard cash. On a hot August afternoon, the clubwomen entertained their neighbors and friends with a benefit garden party and ice cream social. Two months later, members collected and sold a mountain of rummage, including in the sale any of the books from Galesburg which could not be used in the Branson library or one of the other public book collections in the area. And all fall the gypsy basket traveled from home to home, speeded by the admonition, "Don't keep it for more than three days, please."

At the September luncheon, one of the differences of opinion which had divided the vote on the proposed new constitution the previous winter came sharply into focus. The speaker was Edna Boothe, from the Missouri State Library. She had been invited to explain how a public library system might be established in Taney County.

The idea of developing a tax-supported, county-wide library network had been suggested before, usually by new members who had come from towns where such institutions were supported by city or county taxes. Miss Boothe's plan caught the interest of several longtime members, women who had invested years of volunteer effort to keep books available in Branson and now were much concerned about rising costs and the future of their library.

However, when club leaders talked to local realtors and merchants about the possibility of a tax supported library in Branson, they were told

Decisions, Decisions

that the required tax increase would be resisted strongly by area property owners and lobbied against by Branson's Chamber of Commerce, then trying to attract more small factories to the area. It was suggested, too, that revenue from a county-wide tax almost certainly would be used first to develop the library at Forsyth, the county seat. If such a tax were approved, western Taney County might have a long wait for a genuine public library.

Little further was said, in the late 1940s, about a tax-supported library in Branson. There was, however, much conversation about the role of the club in running the increasingly popular Taneyhills Public Library.

CHAPTER XIV

SOME CLEAR DEFINITIONS
(1947-1950)

In the early summer of 1947, Dorothy Jaenicke married Marshall Todd and moved to Oregon. Through the first decade and more of the library's existence she had been given virtual autonomy in its operation. Ethel Paramore had continued the library policies with which she was familiar. Since her resignation, no one had offered to take on such total responsibility, though with many new members joining the club because of their interest in its library, there was no shortage of willing hands to help with the work.

There were many different opinions as to how that work was to be done. During Juanita Thompson's year as president, reconciliation of those ideas was a major task. Frequently she looked to Minnie Whelchel for advice, counsel which often was accompanied by a gentle reminder that each of the women had the best interests of the library at heart. In the 1990s, Juanita remembers that at year's end she was

Some Clear Definitions

Library Club Officers 1947-48
(left to right) Agnes Parnell, Laura Eiserman,
Rose Eiserman Fechner (later Merritt), Flora Beimdick,
Josephine Madry, Juanita Thompson (president), Eve Griffith,
and Stella Owen.

grateful that the library and club were still in existence.

Again there was talk of enlarging the library rooms, and complaints of crowded conditions. Through the year, the enthusiastic library supporters spent four hundred and fifty dollars on furnishings, salaries, insurance and books.

Financially, it was just as well that the space needed for expansion did not become available that year. By the time Evelyn Runyon took over as president in April, 1948, annual operating expenses had exceeded receipts by a hundred and seventy dollars and the treasury held only seven hundred and sixty-three dollars, considerably less than the previous year's record balance.

Bringing Books to the Ozarks

The new president was not intimidated by the task she was taking on. Most of the members, perhaps inspired by a March peak of a thousand and ninety-two library loans, accepted the club's responsibility for the library. Evelyn selected her committee leaders carefully, keeping in mind the many problems she had been unable to get solved through the rewriting of the constitution.

Apparently music and entertainment had been the focus of their meetings long enough. In response to the frequently heard complaint, "I thought we were a study group," program chair Nadine Miller planned a series of events which would foster a better understanding of the members' home state. An interest in Missouri's role in frontier history had been awakened in February, 1947, when John Neihardt read to the club from his epic poetry of the opening of the West.

The group's early mentor, after spending the war years in St. Louis and Chicago, returned briefly to his house west of Branson but, before 1947 ended, the Neihardt family had moved permanently to Columbia, Missouri.

The 1948-49 yearbook, designed by Steve Miller, lists the year's study activities. Lois Holman's historical overview was followed by reports on the northwest, central and southeast regions of the state, prepared by members Edna Evans, Mary Field, and Ingrid Russell. For a new view of their own region, the club called on Southwest Missouri State College history professor Harry Suttle. In other months, Hollister school superintendent R.S. Thurmond told

Some Clear Definitions

about the northeast region of the state. Caroline Ballentine reviewed a book by a Missouri author; Mildred Dawson spoke on native wildflowers; Lyn Asselin read from the works of Missouri poets, and Dee McClure presented a timely program on "Christmas in the Ozarks."

At each meeting, in preparation for the program, members sang "The Missouri Waltz." The nostalgic words sometimes brought tear-filled eyes and a catch in many voices. During that year of broadened acquaintance with Missouri, the women mourned the death of Gwen Binkley and shared Juanita Thompson's grief over the loss of a longed-for child.

In June, when Ethel Paramore died, members recalled again her long years of service to the library, the many books her friends had sent from faraway places, and the anxious days when she rescued the club from financial disaster. Unanimously the women approved a resolution memorializing Miss Paramore's unselfish contributions to their common cause.

Two months later, on August 13, 1948, Mary Elizabeth Mahnkey passed away. Taney County's talented country correspondent had continued writing from her hospital bed and in her last days at home. The final entry in her journal was dated July 24th.

Through the months that followed, Mary Elizabeth's poems were read repeatedly at club meetings. Dorothy Garner's brother, Frank Wise of Montreal, Canada, handcrafted a scrapbook filled with many of those poems to place on the

Bringing Books to the Ozarks

Branson's Community Building.
Until the 1970's the Taneyhills Library Club did not own any land but it really did own all those books at the top of the stairs in Branson's Community Building!

library's memorial shelf.

Donations of memorial books honoring these special friends provided much enjoyable reading for library patrons that year. Also received in late 1948 and early 1949 were several cartons of books given by "the Dr. Smith family." A much needed librarian's desk was provided by Caroline Ballentine. And from the Union Pacific Railroad came a highly prized map of the "Old Oregon Trail," which was soon framed and on display in the library.

In the summer of 1948, so many book borrowers were climbing the outside staircase to the Taneyhills Public Library that, when Irene Couchman resigned in July and Gertrude Miller took her place as librarian, Dorothy Dickerson

Some Clear Definitions

was hired to help with checking out and reshelving books each Saturday.

President Evelyn Runyon became increasingly certain that she must try again to get written into the club's constitution responsibility for the library. This time she had the able assistance of Mary Sansom, then leader of the library committee.

Mary had been a member for less than a year. Ten years earlier, she had received her first invitation to join the Taneyhills Study Club while she and her sons were camping on a bend of the White River in the distant eastern part of the county. In the early 1930s, the Sansoms, then living in Chicago, bought land at "Bright Elbow" as a vacation retreat, but by 1936 they were aware that what they had planned as the site of their future home would become "lake bottom" if Bull Shoals Dam was built.

In search of a more secure retirement location, Mary drove to Hollister and, with the help of a real estate agent (possibly Sara Heath), looked at property in the nearby hills. When an invitation to join the Study Club arrived in the mail a few days later, the surprised vacationer wrote her husband about it. Her letter was written by lantern light as she sat cross-legged beside an Ozark campfire.

In January, 1947, having settled with her husband, William, on a hilltop east of Hollister, Mary accepted a renewed invitation to join the club. The following fall she was appointed to the library committee.

Bringing Books to the Ozarks

The constitutional amendment which Mary Sansom presented to the club in December, 1948, was approved in January with only one dissenting vote. The library became an official, semi-autonomous entity run by a six-member board drawn from and elected by the Taneyhills Library Club membership.

The approved amendment gave the library club final say on all major decisions and placed responsibility for the operation of the library--book selection, hiring of the librarian, and dealing with maintenance problems--firmly in the hands of the six-member board.

Mary Sansom's constitutional committee did its work well. Though the number of library board members has, over the years, been doubled, and firm requirements for regular board meetings added, the duties and authority of the library board have remained the same through several extensive revisions of the club's governing rules.

At last the club's relationship with the library was clearly defined. Still to be resolved were many questions concerning the club itself.

In late 1948 and early 1949, membership matters were a tangle which almost defied unraveling. The women firmly believed that attendance at the monthly meetings was vital to the club and library. Through the 1940s, officers spoke of a "rule" that to be an "active member" one must attend at least eight meetings each year. Such a requirement had been included in the rejected constitution of 1946. Yet in the past

Some Clear Definitions

two years, with membership nearing eighty, fewer than twenty women had achieved that attendance record.

Indeed, there still were few meeting places around Branson able to handle even groups of forty for lunch. Reservations had become a must, and though a growing number of members had telephones, cards continued to be mailed to those who did not. Luncheon planners were now asking members to make "permanent reservations." Members whose lives were too complicated to allow such a commitment saw their attendance possibilities lessened with each new name added to the roll.

Club finances formed the final dimension to the problem. The year's receipts were nearing five hundred dollars, almost half of which had come from members' dues. The latest season of fund-raising, though filled with enjoyable social occasions, had netted only a hundred dollars.

In October, the executive committee recommended that "because of our large membership of eighty members and due to limited accommodations the members be requested not to submit any more names for membership until after the first of the year." Women desiring membership would be put on a waiting list.

The following March, after months of debate, a constitutional amendment was proposed limiting the membership to eighty and affirming that a candidate must be proposed by a member and considered and accepted by the membership committee. The women refused to approve it.

Bringing Books to the Ozarks

Rewritten, and read again in June and July, it still did not carry. Through the next several years the number of members remained at approximately eighty, but not because any new rules had been passed.

Meanwhile, at a catered dinner held in April, 1949, in the Civic League rooms, Evelyn Runyon relinquished to Ruth Wiley the president's gavel, responsibility for some fifty-six hundred books and an eight hundred and seventy-two dollar treasury balance.

The speaker that evening was Rev. Hanna Almon, Ingrid Russell's mother, who traced the development of literature, beginning with the oldest versions of the Bible. Hanna Almon, an ordained Presbyterian minister, spoke several times to the library club during the 1940s. Following her husband's death in that spring of 1949, she served as pastor of the Hollister church for two years, then left to work in the foreign mission field.

The Taneyhills Library Club programs provided many enjoyable afternoons during the last club year of the 1940s. In May, writer Lucile Morris Upton completed the Missouri study, telling in fascinating detail of interviews with some of the state's most outstanding personalities. The following month, after "a delicious dinner" in The School of the Ozarks dining hall, the clubwomen adjourned to the school's new music hall to enjoy songs in four-part harmony sung by members of the faculty.

"Women's Status in the World Today" was Dr.

Some Clear Definitions

Florence Boehmer's subject at the July luncheon. Her listeners, almost all women who had worked for part or all of their adult lives, followed with intense interest her comments on "the importance of the woman worker to the nation, the importance to the national economy of equal pay for the woman worker & her right to equality of opportunity and reward without discrimination."

That August, sixty-four members and guests crowded the Civic League rooms to hear Rev. Guy Howard review his novel about the Ozarks, *Give Of Thy Vineyard.* The book, though not yet released for sale, already had been awarded a seventy-five hundred dollar prize in the International Christian Fiction contest. Also a guest that day was Steve Miller, who had illustrated Reverend Howard's book.

Steve Miller's talents were on the way to becoming legendary in southwest Missouri. In the fall of 1949 he designed and helped construct huge wooden figures for an "Adoration Scene" which was erected atop the bluff across Lake Taneycomo from downtown Branson. Each evening through the weeks before Christmas--as darkness enveloped the little town--the Babe in the manger, Mary and Joseph, shepherds and wise men, camels and sheep, were illuminated against the black hill and sky, a continuing reminder of the meaning of the season.

In the months leading up to that Christmas, library club members, inspired by ways and means chairman Mayme Boren, worked indus-

Bringing Books to the Ozarks

triously to support Branson's books. Mayme had joined the club in 1946, shortly after she and her husband, Charles, purchased the Stonewall Motor Inn in Branson. In August and September's simmering heat she encouraged many willing hands to assemble piles of sandwiches which netted a bit over seventeen dollars when sold by club members at baseball games in the lakeside park. A "white elephant" sale provided extra merriment at the August meeting and put another seventeen dollars in the treasury.

In October, everyone again raided closets, attics and basements, collected surplus plants from gardening enthusiasts and spruced up books being discarded from the library. The resulting rummage sale raised over sixty-five dollars.

New Year's Day was celebrated with a progressive silver tea, for which several members held open house. Through the winter and well into spring the women entertained with a series of card parties and teas. The many activities brought the year's ways and means total to a hundred and seventy-six dollars and cemented many new friendships among the clubwomen.

All in all, 1949-50 was a very successful year for the library club. Unfortunately Ruth Wiley, who had embarked on her presidency with high hopes and many plans, became ill in late July and could not take part in Mayme Boren's season of festivities. Vice president Esther Wing presided at the August meeting. When teaching duties at The School of the Ozarks kept her from

Some Clear Definitions

the September meeting, Sybil James, the vice president from the preceding year, was asked to preside and receive the monthly reports.

With the glories of autumn foliage in mind, a picnic was planned in October, but on the meeting day a chill wind gusted through the hills. No business was discussed by the seventeen members who "enjoyed" what turned out to be a very short outing.

The following month Ruth Wiley, still too ill to conduct the club's business, asked to be replaced. Esther Wing declined the office and Ellie Mitchell was elected by acclamation to fill out the term as president.

Fifty-two members and guests enjoyed the Christmas luncheon, held at The School of the Ozarks. The reading of the Club Collect was led by Elizabeth Clark, who had joined the Taneyhills Library Club shortly after her husband, Dr. M. Graham Clark, became a member of the administrative staff of The School of the Ozarks in 1947. The festivities, with Ellie Mitchell presiding, included special recognition for Stella Owen, who was celebrating her Golden Wedding Anniversary, and a beautiful Christmas program performed by members of the music club, most of whom also were members of the library club.

The women met in January, 1950 at Miller's Family Style Restaurant, on the southeast corner of Main and Commercial streets. Daisy Belle Wright, chairman of the day, had planned a program based on the musical comedy *South Pacific*,

Bringing Books to the Ozarks

but Branson's newest restaurateurs were unable to borrow a piano in time for the occasion. The performers were unwilling to attempt the nation's latest hit songs without accompaniment; so, with tremendous aplomb, Ingrid Russell narrated a script synopsis interwoven with recordings from the Broadway show.

When March arrived, Ellie Mitchell found herself presiding, as she had in 1938, at her own re-election as president. Both Ruth Wiley, her health returned, and Josephine Madry, whose participation for the past few years had been in donating books for Branson readers, were elected to the library board, filling two of the several vacancies which occurred as the women worked through the establishment of library responsibilities.

By the spring of 1950, though there still were many adjustments ahead, members of the Taneyhills Library Club were trying diligently to meet their redefined responsibilities. And with the women's staunch refusal to place any constitutional restriction on membership, the way already was opening to broader participation in the club and stronger support for the library.

CHAPTER XV

LEARNING TOGETHER
(1950 - 1952)

When, at the end of 1948, the library club formally admitted that it "owned" the Taneyhills Library, few members gave thought to the fact that their collection of books was far from a well-rounded selection of reading materials.

Now, however, with a card file cataloging the more than fifty-five hundred volumes by subject, title, and author, library volunteers could see that they had nothing at all to offer by many authors and on numerous subjects, yet had to keep selling or giving away books which never were read.

Always, of course, there were waiting lists for bestsellers on the rental shelves. For the library as a whole, the enthusiastic book borrowing which marked its early years had settled into a predictable pattern in which annual checkout totals were one and a half to two times the number of books available. Loans to adults usually outstripped those to children and young teenagers by two, three, sometimes even four to

Bringing Books to the Ozarks

one.

Actually, there was no shortage of youthful readers. There just weren't enough books for them. Additional children's books were purchased as often as possible, and donated ones were welcomed. Few had sturdy library bindings. Volunteers repaired and rebound their precious "juveniles" over and over again. Even so, the shelf-life of the most popular ones was comparatively short. Reference materials and particularly sets of encyclopedia were outdated from the start, having been received as gifts from individuals, or from libraries which were updating their own collections.

All in all, young people intent on study or research were finding the Taneyhills Public Library of limited help, particularly since it was open only four hours on Wednesday and Saturday afternoons.

In the late 1940s, when rural students began riding busses to schools in town, funds were found to provide or improve reference libraries in Branson and Hollister grade and high schools.

Members of the first Taneyhills Library board: Dorothy Garner, Mary Sansom, Evelyn Runyon, Lyn Asselin, Rose Fechner and Josephine Gray, began the long struggle to turn their club's collection of books into a wide-ranging modern public library. In the 1950s, the board welcomed the continuing assistance and advice of Janet Lamb, the librarian at The School of the Ozarks.

That neighboring institution, which had been a high school for more than forty years, in the

Learning Together

1950s and 1960s responded to the educational needs of the region with a gradual changeover to a full four-year college. By the early 1950s, courses designed to bring entering students up to high school entry level already had been eliminated.

Through 1955, as Mrs. Lamb removed books for young teenagers from The School of the Ozarks library to make room for more advanced materials, many of those discards were donated to the Taneyhills Library.

The world along Missouri's White River also was changing. In 1950, eighty-seven miles down river, the half-finished dam at the foot of Bull Mountain promised further expansion of the network of electric power lines which had already transformed life in the towns and hamlets adjacent to Lake Taneycomo. Progress reports on Bull Shoals Dam were now accompanied by plans for an even higher dam soon to be built a dozen miles upstream from Branson and Hollister, near the spectacular bluff known as Table Rock.

As townsfolk and farmers realized the size of that planned impoundment, they were torn between the prospect of an end to disastrous flooding and the fact that most of the surrounding scenic White River bottom lands soon would be permanently under water.

Land speculators and retirees rushed to buy Table Rock "lake front" homesites before prices rose too much--trying to guess where high water lines would be on a lake which would not exist

Bringing Books to the Ozarks

for another eight or ten years. Along Lake Taneycomo, property previously considered too flood-prone for development now became the target of reappraisal.

In January, 1950, in anticipation of residential growth and increased tourism, a modern, twenty-five bed hospital began operation on the U.S. 65 hill north of Branson's Roark Creek. It was a cooperative community venture. Local doctors managed the hospital which was built with money donated by M.B. and Estella Skaggs. Businessmen and doctors on the board of directors had agreed to underwrite any operating deficits which might arise in the first few years. Furnishing and equipping the Skaggs Community Hospital became a top priority for local citizens.

Meeting that commitment demanded many volunteer hours. Library club membership dropped from more than eighty to seventy-four in 1951 and to sixty the following year. In the spring and summer of 1950, president Ellie Mitchell, whose husband, Guy Mitchell, had been a doctor in Branson for forty years, was uncomfortably aware that the hospital's fund-raising efforts and continuing need for volunteer services were drawing away from the library potential donations, volunteer fund-raisers and library workers.

Late that spring, the club leaders welcomed Irene Couchman back as librarian and began a quiet search for more members to support the library. Within a few months, Etta Mann, Jessie

Learning Together

Gansz, and Maude Horine, whose declining health made full participation impossible, were welcomed as associate members with dues at two dollars a year; Dr. Florence Boehmer returned to the active roll, and several new members were welcomed.

Meantime, in May, members gathered at Stella Owen's home for a covered dish luncheon. After Stella "took the group for a stroll through her flower gardens," Dr. Alice Nightingale introduced the women to her nephew's internationally famous peony industry at nearby Sarcoxie, Missouri. Many of her listeners were avid gardeners who listened in fascination as the highly educated botanist described her personal experiences in trying to develop a double yellow peony. At the end of the afternoon, secretary Lois Holman noted in her minutes that, "Few of us will ever attempt to develop a new flower."

Two months later, when the group met in Mary Sansom's pleasant rural home, Alice Nightingale recounted her terrifying experiences as a resident of Hawaii in the first days of World War II. By August she had become a part of the club, and entertained thirty-five fellow members and guests on her porch overlooking Lake Taneycomo.

Other summer programs brought reports on the lives and accomplishments of famous Missourians: artists Caleb Bingham and Thomas Hart Benton; several authors, past and present; singers Marion Talley and Vera Courtney Thomas, and the careers of operatic favorites

Bringing Books to the Ozarks

Helen Traubel of St. Louis and Gladys Swarthout of Davenport, Missouri.

The developing world of Ozarks arts and crafts received much attention at the September meeting, held at Ye English Inn. Sam Weaver described the pottery-making processes in use at Branson's Walker Novelty Shop with which he was connected, and Ann Shreve talked about "early handcrafts and heirloom patterns and designs." Then Virginia Jenkins told of the weaving that Mabel Bishop was teaching at The School of the Ozarks, dried apple dolls made by Mrs. Bates of Branson, and manufacturing processes used in producing Ozarks-originated Blair China.

The season of fund-raising that fall and winter might best be described as one long canasta game. With Mayme Boren's enthusiastic encouragement, party after party was planned, featuring the card-playing craze which was sweeping the nation. If bridge also was played, there was no mention of it. Of course, the proceeds from all those sessions of canasta--just short of a hundred dollars--went to the library.

Also, in the fall of 1950, the women of the Taneyhills Library Club were organized to sell Christmas cards, designed by Steve Miller and featuring a photograph of the "Adoration Scene," then being readied for its second Christmas on Mount Branson. Unfortunately, the cards did not arrive until early December. By then potential buyers already had bought their holiday cards elsewhere. After Christmas, having sold barely

Learning Together

enough cards to cover their costs, the clubwomen voted to store the remainder for sale the following fall.

Ways and means committee efforts cleared only a hundred and twenty-eight dollars that year, a sum slightly less than the rental fees and fines collected by the library. What wasn't received in monies, however, was made up for in donated books. The only purchases were two or three dozen rental books, but five hundred gift volumes were added to the shelves. At year's end, the treasurer reported that the club's seven hundred and twenty-one dollar balance was a hundred dollars above that of the year before.

The emphasis on game parties again reflected growing personal concerns among the club members. For the women who so recently had welcomed husbands, sons and fathers returning from the battlefronts of World War II, the United Nations "police action" in Korea, initiated in the summer of 1950, brought much consternation. Locally many reservists and young men subject to the draft were called to active military duty.

Early in 1951, Dr. Gertrude Law, a university psychology professor and writer who recently returned to the Ozarks to retire, addressed those fears when she spoke to the club on "Woman, her work, and war." From Dr. Law the women also learned that the thought-provoking Collect which had been used to open their meetings since the club began, and which was used by clubs all over the nation, was written by one of her acquaintances, Mary Stewart, though most

Bringing Books to the Ozarks

often it was signed "Author unknown."

Another month, Caroline Ballentine told the club about the background and achievements of Dr. Ralph Bunche, recently chosen by the United Nations to arbitrate disputes between the Arab countries and the two-year-old nation of Israel.

The Korean conflict affected the women's lives for several years. Concern about the Arab-Israeli "disputes" continues a half-century later.

The March election meeting was held in a new restaurant south of The School of the Ozarks, Mount Como Inn. To many of the women, the setting was very familiar. The sprawling white building had long been Como Craft, the Horines' home, shop and factory. Recently the younger Horines, Harold and Mary Elizabeth, had moved to Colorado, seeking a more healthful climate, and Maude Horine now lived in Branson, only a block or two from the library.

The club returned to Mount Como at least once each year through 1955, and twice held their annual installation dinners there. In those years, luncheon planners constantly searched for adequate space, good food and affordable prices.

Ye English Inn, which had hosted so many gala activities through the past two decades, disappeared from the library club programs when that charming old hotel closed its doors in January, 1951. It would not reopen for sixteen years. On the other hand, between 1950 and 1954 the "new Miller's Cafeteria," now moved across Main street to the lower floor of the Whelchel Building, hosted the club fifteen times,

Learning Together

including three guest nights.

When the Millers later moved their restaurant to Hollister and could no longer handle large luncheon groups, the women transferred that loyalty to the Sportsman's Inn, on Highway 65 in Branson, and held many meetings there in the late 1950s.

For covered dish luncheons and money-raising dinners they continued to rely on the Civic League rooms, on the lower floor of the Community Building.

In 1953, another dimension was added to possible meeting places. The women's groups of the Christian Church in Branson and the Episcopal congregation then located in Hollister saw in such club meetings a chance to fund church projects. Enthusiasm for that way of raising church monies peaked in 1955, when seven meetings and a part of an eighth were held in some local church.

Through those years there were occasional jaunts to more distant locations, a boat ride to Rockaway Beach, a drive to Shadow Rock Park Hotel at Forsyth, a trip to Springfield to tour the Public Library there and have lunch at Heers Department Store. One or two meetings each year were held at The School of the Ozarks. Summer meetings were most often picnic luncheons at some member's country home.

When the club held its guest night dinner at Miller's in April, 1951, Aletha Kennedy, supervisor of the guest house at The School of the Ozarks, was accepting the president's gavel. She

Bringing Books to the Ozarks

immediately announced that the executive board would convene on the Tuesday before each meeting day. The second of those monthly sessions, on May 31st, turned into a celebration.

The Shepherd of the Hills was back!

Earlier in the spring, the library board had sent the latest of many anxious queries to Grosset and Dunlap. Couldn't they please provide some copies of Harold Bell Wright's most famous book for the Taneyhills Library to sell?

The club has no copy of the reply received from Grosset and Dunlap's vice president in May, 1951, but the minutes of that month's executive meeting contain Ruth Wiley's library board report that, at that moment, *The Shepherd of the Hills* was being reprinted:

> The Board...finding they could obtain a franchise of Taney County for this purpose--and realizing the value of time They decided to and did order 500 copies of the new edition to place at various points for sale during the [tourist] season. She [Ruth] further reported that these books were purchased at a discount of 40% and are to be sold [retailed] for $1.50 per copy. She then asked the Executive Board to approve their action and lend funds from the treasury to cover purchase price and freight.

The executive committee's discussion of these actions was not recorded, but Reva Ford's approved motion tells the result-- "That the said Library Club lend the Library Board the...total

Learning Together

sum of $460.67 (the purchase price of the books plus freight charges) to be repaid as the books are sold."

The check issued on June 4, 1951, to get the library supporters back into wholesaling *The Shepherd of the Hills* reduced club funds to two hundred and fifteen dollars. Once the money loaned was back in the treasury, profits could be used to order more books. The project would bring no support to the library for a long time, but book sales during the 1951 tourist season brought the club's bank balance above five hundred dollars.

Again the library board had the responsibility for distributing those books to motels, shops and tourist attractions and reestablishing bookkeeping procedures. Board members Caroline Ballentine, Juanita Thompson and Ellie Mitchell were familiar with the sales procedures in the early 1940s. Virginia Jenkins, Josephine Madry and Ruth Wiley, soon realized that *The Shepherd* would be creating much extra work for the library board.

Long before the summer ended, the clubwomen learned that their "franchise of Taney County" was a monopoly which stopped at the county line. The proprietors of the Shepherd of the Hills Farm, whose property straddled the Taney-Stone County line, also had been pleading for a new printing. They considered the book too vital a part of their undertakings to be handled through a third party, and ordered their supplies directly from the publishers.

Bringing Books to the Ozarks

In June, 1951, amid much excitement over the renewed book sales, the women were treated to a display of Opal Parnell's "homemaking treasures" from her family's pre-1912 Taney County household, and Mr. Holman gave an enlightening eyewitness account of those days so powerfully depicted in Harold Bell Wright's novel.

Hot days of July and August brought two picnics. One was hosted by the eight or nine library club members associated with the faculty and staff of The School of the Ozarks. That afternoon Lyta Good told of the developments and changes she had witnessed since the 1915 days when she helped re-establish The School of the Ozarks at Point Lookout after the original school at Forsyth burned.

The other picnic was shared on the porch of Mr. and Mrs. Ned Mann's Hollywood Hills Hotel overlooking Lake Taneycomo north of Branson. Ned Mann, introduced by his sister, Edna Evans, entertained the women with some lively revelations about the movie industry and tales of his recent experiences in Italy while producing special effects for the prizewinning movie *Miracle of Milan*. During that day's business meeting, the club noted sadly the death of the club's early president, Sara Heath, and the passing of Forrest Runyon, the longtime editor of the *White River Leader*.

Earlier in 1951, the clubwomen's interest in photography had been piqued by a detailed history provided by Townsend Godsey, who was in the area temporarily. A few months later, further

Learning Together

inspired by Ned Mann's exotic world of movie making, they invited Godsey back to explain "how to get good pictures with color slides," which were becoming very popular.

Although Helen Godsey did not renew her membership during that brief sojourn in the area, she too spoke to the club, on Ozark folk music. In response to local interest in the region's folk music, a four-volume set of books on the subject had recently been purchased for the library.

To pay for those new books and other library purchases, that fall the clubwomen brought their "Adoration Scene" Christmas cards out of storage, inserted updated explanatory notes, and soon had them all sold. A cookie sale and a financially rewarding card party added further to the library club's funds.

For the Christmas tea at The School of the Ozarks, Josephine Madry concocted a "Modern Attempt to Revive the Christmas Spirit," in which "nine veiled ladies" shared some interesting ideas for helping others, inspiring "silver offerings" of forty dollars and much laughter.

The following February, with a hundred and sixty-nine dollars to their credit, Reva Ford and her ways and means committee vowed to boost their receipts over the two hundred dollar mark, a goal which was more than met with an Irish Stew Dinner and Card Party held at the Branson High School in early April.

For the library supporters it had been a very satisfactory year. Almost all of *The Shepherd of*

Bringing Books to the Ozarks

the Hills loan was back in the treasury. Progress in updating the library, and the happy social times during the winter, brought increased participation in all the club's activities.

One problem did arise that winter, as Aletha Kennedy's term neared its end. The president became ill at the January meeting and was not able to preside. Vice president Lois Holman was in the hospital. Of the elected board members, only the treasurer, Elsie Stephens, and the secretary, Ann Shreve, were present. Quietly, the two women asked Sybil James to conduct the business meeting.

With exuberant humor, Sybil accepted the yearly library summary and the monthly committee reports. In the absence of the corresponding secretary, she instructed the secretary to send a get-well card to Lois Holman and a thank-you letter to Lyle Owen for his renewal of the library's subscription to *Consumers Reports*. Then she adjourned the meeting and went home smiling.

When the executive board met the following month it was noted, a bit sharply, that a temporary president should have been elected to run the meeting. Suggestion was made that a parliamentarian could have recommended the proper procedure. The club had been without a parliamentarian for fifteen years.

No one was nominated or appointed to that office for 1952-53, but the board did purchase a new copy of Robert's *Rules of Order*.

CHAPTER XVI

BOOKS FOR A DEVELOPING TOWN
(April 1952 - June 1959)

Mayme Boren was actively involved in the management of Stonewall Court on Highway 65 in Branson when she accepted the office of the library club president in April, 1952. That same year she served as the first president of the Estella Skaggs Hospital Auxiliary. One of her goals as president of both organizations was increasing cooperation between the hospital and library volunteers.

That cooperative attitude was much needed. In the early 1950s, with the population growing and new enterprises multiplying in the Branson area, many local chapters of fraternal, service, and veterans organizations were formed. For the library club's ways and means committee, setting dates for a dozen or more small parties and several club teas in 1952-53 was often hampered by conflicting meetings. Juanita Thompson remembers rising at one luncheon to observe that Branson needed a community-wide calendar just to keep meetings and special events from interfering with each other.

Bringing Books to the Ozarks

In addition to the many new social groups, club members and other potential library supporters also were operating local businesses or busy developing some craft or hobby, as evidenced by many of the club's programs.

At one memorable meeting, business partners Wilma Pulliam and Dora Erbes presented "A Day in the Eubank Doll House," a skit using several of Wilma's character dolls to tell how she had originated their manufacture and how the business grew. Ann Shreve displayed her large button collection, exploring the origins and history of her most prized specimens and pointing out the many variations which fascinate collectors. And Etelka Galbraith, who traveled for a batting company, used her talents as a quilting artist to demonstrate the development of quilting in the making of clothes and bedding.

Similar programs were enjoyed throughout the 1950s. At the June, 1952 meeting, Marguerite Lyon reviewed for the members her 1930s book, *Take to the Hills*, introducing the club's newer members to the humorous adventures and misadventures in hardscrabble farming she and her husband Robert had shared in the Ozarks during the depression years of the 1930s.

In 1952 the Lyons were living in Eureka Springs, Arkansas, but the following year, after her husband's death, Marge moved to The School of the Ozarks campus to serve as Director of Public Relations and in 1954 she joined the Taneyhills Library Club. She assisted in many

Books for a Developing Town

fund-raising projects and was generous in sharing her experiences as a Chicago newspaper reporter and as a novice Ozarker. Until her death in 1965, Marge provided a strong voice in support of the Taneyhills Library.

Each new business or professional woman who joined the club, each retiree who climbed the library stairs to borrow a book and became involved in the club's volunteer efforts, helped bring the library a bit closer to standard operating practices. Records remind that in 1950, when the library board was notified that the state bookmobile was to visit Hollister, the leaders of the Taneyhills Library, with some eight thousand books to offer readers, decided that the services offered by the Missouri State Library were not needed. However, the annual library report brought to the club two years later showed that in the past twelve months sixty-five books had been borrowed from the state library service. Obviously, opinions had been revised.

The popularity of having access to the Missouri State Library's extensive book collection became a matter of record the following year. When cutbacks in the program were threatened, Juanita Thompson urged club members to back State Library appropriations so the Taneyhills Library would have the continued service of the state Bookmobile.

Irene Couchman resigned her job as librarian for the last time, in the summer of 1952. She was replaced by Georgia Owen, a trained librarian. Miss Owen, paid by the hour, received about

Bringing Books to the Ozarks

twenty dollars a month. The library she was to supervise was cramped beyond belief.

Once again the room so recently labeled spacious and light filled was crowded with bookshelves. Browsers could find little space to sit and read, and every nook and cranny was stacked with boxes of *The Shepherd of the Hills* books awaiting distribution to local retailers.

Members of the Branson Civic League, having repeatedly contributed funds for new library books, took stock of conditions in the crowded library, reviewed their own finances, and gave Juanita Thompson a message to take to the October meeting of the library club:

> ...Mrs. Thompson announced that the Civic League was planning to build a library building on a corner of the Community Building block...providing the Library Club would furnish a heating system for the new building.

Delighted, the women quickly approved Ellie Mitchell's motion that the offer be accepted. A committee would work out the details.

Plans for a library building at the southeast corner of Pacific and Highway 65 were short-lived. It seemed important to keep the books in a downtown location, but the land involved had been donated to the city back in 1936. Even if the town council agreed to the proposal, the location right next to busy Highway 65 posed parking and safety problems.

Through the remainder of Mayme's term of

Books for a Developing Town

office and the full tenure of her successor, the women struggled to build up their treasury and searched for a larger site on which to develop a library.

Opal Parnell volunteered to give the club her mother's double log cabin, and to pay to have it moved to Branson from the old home place in eastern Taney County, if the women could find a suitable lot which might later accommodate a modern library. However, no one really wanted to move the books very far from their present central location, and available downtown properties were very small. A few years later, Opal's log cabin was relocated in the Herschends' Silver Dollar City theme park, where it stands today, a permanent reminder of nineteenth century living.

Minnie Whelchel offered to donate her downtown residence for conversion into a library. An architectural engineer, asked to assess the expense of restressing the house to support the tremendous weight of the books and bookcases, reported that such an undertaking would cost more than a new building.

Each new proposal raised hopes and brought frustrations for the women in charge of the club and library. Efforts to accumulate a building fund were discouraging. By April, 1953, after months filled with fund-raising events, less than a hundred dollars had been added to the monies available for such a project.

The annual cost of running the library was nearing five hundred dollars. Through the fol-

Bringing Books to the Ozarks

lowing decade, the club treasurer (an office Juanita Thompson filled from 1954 to 1959) faced the challenge of figuring out when and how much social security to withhold from the current librarian's salary every time the latter worked in the library three months in a row.

All but one of the librarians who served through the remainder of the 1950s were members of the library club. Between September, 1952, and the end of 1959 six women served as paid librarian. Non-member Georgia Owen served from September, 1952, through January, 1954. The other five were Gladys Buntin, February to October, 1954, and March, 1955 to April, 1956; Myrna Escher, November, 1954, to February, 1955, and May, 1956 to July, 1958; Marion Stark, September, 1958, to May, 1959; and Thelma Hester, September to December, 1959.

The 1953 nominating committee called on the retiring president and vice president, Mayme Boren and Virginia Jenkins, to add strength to the library board. Perhaps, with their wise assistance, Ellie Mitchell, head of the library committee, could find more space for the books, good leadership for *The Shepherd of the Hills* book project which was finally showing a little profit, and dependable supervision for the library.

Nelle Combs assumed the club presidency in 1953. She had been a member for only a year, but her energy and her dedication to the library already were apparent. She was to guide the club through twelve remarkable months.

Books for a Developing Town

Nelle's list of appointive officers included Caroline Ballentine as parliamentarian. The challenge to that long-empty post was obvious. Since 1934, the constitution had been amended several times, but not successfully rewritten. Through all those years, the library's treasury books had been closed for audit on December 31, and reports delivered at the January club meeting. The club's year ended on March 31, new officers were installed in April, and programs were planned for June through May.

Caroline Ballentine, Helen Cole, and Juanita Thompson were instructed to research the club records, incorporate all legally approved amendments, and make "such additions as seem advisable."

The resulting "conformed constitution" of 1953 incorporated most of the goals which Evelyn Runyon's committee had envisioned in 1946, but without the strict and confining rules for each office and committee. Evelyn was not present to participate in the updating. After her husband's death she had moved away, and her membership expired in the spring of 1953.

That August the women assembled in the Civic League rooms, on the ground floor of the Community Building, where County Extension Clubwomen were serving a "Hillbilly Luncheon" for the benefit of Skaggs Hospital. After lunch the library club members walked around the corner to the new Christian Church, where Mary Margaret Turnbeaugh, a teacher of speech, drama and remedial reading at The School of the

Bringing Books to the Ozarks

Ozarks, opened what was billed as a dramatic presentation--

...with the startling announcement that she would talk of the only two important things in any woman's life, namely "Men & Dieting." Following this hilarious interpretation...Mrs. Turnbeaugh [better known as "Tub"] gave us a one act play "At the Sign of the Cleft Heart," another sketch "Pinky Panky Breakfast Food;" also a section of the Book "Shepherd of the Hills;" a poem "French Clock" and closed with "The Land of Beginning Again."

Though the secretary recorded little business that day, Mildred Dawson and her ways and means committee already were hard at work on a new money-raising idea.

For several years, thanks to Caroline Ballentine, birthdays had been remembered with greeting cards. In 1952, Mayme Boren inaugurated a birthday box, and at each meeting celebrants were serenaded as they contributed a penny for each of their years. That practice became a continuing luncheon custom, though through the years members learned to avoid announcing their age by donating a dollar.

Now Mildred proposed linking the need for a social calendar and the club members' shared interest in birthdays with a popular new plan for a "community birthday calendar." The work involved proved to be enormous. The financial results were astounding.

Through the summer, Helen Rubesam,

Books for a Developing Town

Harriet Rinehart, Elizabeth McDougal, Mable Binney, Edna Evans, Mayme Boren and Mrs. Fred Stephens managed to convince over a hundred area merchants that four dollars for 365 days of advertising was a real bargain. The entire membership was called on to sell birthday and anniversary listings at twenty-five cents each, so the calendars would have added value to the purchasers.

At the beginning of November, 1953, Mildred Dawson still was exhorting each club member to "get at least 20 more names by November 16." Sales of listings were to end when the first date box was filled to capacity, but that cut-off point came much too soon for the women of the library club, who were trying to obtain every possible quarter for the library. "Editors" stood by the composing table in Neal Dean's print shop in Hollister and fitted excess listings into empty spaces at the beginning and end of each calendar page.

In January, thirty-four jubilant library club members gathered at Mount Como Inn to receive Mildred's carefully audited report of the "1954 Calendar" project. After all the bills were paid, the club received a four hundred and fifty-five dollar profit!

With that amount, plus "silver offerings" from the Christmas Tea, and a luncheon and program about antiques, held at the home of Harriet Rinehart, ways and means funds that year exceeded five hundred dollars.

Many thanks were extended at that meeting,

Bringing Books to the Ozarks

to the calendar committee and to Ruth Wiley, Mary Sansom, Alice Nightingale and Mary Anna Fain, who had worked on the library's float for the "Nativity Parade" which, in 1953, was added to Branson's Adoration Scene Ceremonies.

The January business meeting came to an abrupt end "due to the freezing conditions outside making travel hazardous," but not before it was announced that the library club would sponsor a "Gay Nineties Review" at the Branson School on February 20.

There were many people in Branson who treasured memories of the last years of the 1800s, and many more with an interest in that era fostered by books and motion pictures. That wintry night, old time tunes urged feet into half-forgotten dance steps. Party clothes which had been the height of fashion sixty years before were judged for authenticity by Nelle Combs, Elizabeth McDougal, Wilma Pulliam and Hazel Lowe.

The Gay Nineties Review cleared eighty dollars, bringing the ways and means total to five hundred ninety-five dollars and contributing to a treasury balance of eleven hundred and eighty-three dollars at year's end. For almost two years, as the women searched for a way to provide a permanent home for their library, they had struggled to increase their annual revenues. The 1953-54 treasury balance lifted many hopes.

Enthusiastically, the women embarked on further projects without waiting for the installation of new officers. At the March 6th meeting,

Books for a Developing Town

Library Club Officers 1954-55. (left to right) Harriet Rinehart, president, Josephine Madry, Ann Smith, Mayme Boren, Marge Lyon, Nell Shaw, Bernice Mottesheard, Helen Skinner, and Mildred Dawson at the 1954 Silver Tea.

Ila Swinney was called on to organize several card parties in the next two months, and the club members agreed to provide books from the library along with a wheeled book cart to set up a library on wheels for patients at Skaggs Hospital.

When the newly elected officers met in May at the home of the new president, Harriet Rinehart, at the top of the Board's planning list was the possibility of a new library building and the need to "raise funds during this year" to help pay for it.

Library building fever was abroad in Branson. Helen Cole, the new leader of fund-raising, challenged each member to host a coffee or a simple

Bringing Books to the Ozarks

breakfast sometime between the June and July meetings. Each hostess was to invite the three women whose names appeared just before and immediately following her own in the yearbook, and collect twenty-five cents from each guest.

That initial plan was overly ambitious for such a brief time period. However, by September twenty of the women, singly or in a cooperative effort, had held such a party. At year's end that number had reached thirty-eight. Well over half those actively involved in the club hosted such events that year, and there were several fundraising luncheons and card parties. Each member also embroidered her own name on a block for a "friendship quilt" which was raffled off. It was a very busy summer and fall.

Through 1954, volunteer efforts of library club members were spurred on by the donation of hundreds of fine books, and by programs recounting unusual achievements of several remarkable women, now neighbors to the Taneyhills Library. Marian Cox, of The School of the Ozarks, told of her years in military service on the island of Okinawa. A few months later Mrs. R. R. Abarbanell, also an employee at The School of the Ozarks, described the life of wives of American businessmen in Manila before Pearl Harbor, and recounted her own survival experiences through two wartime years in a Japanese concentration camp.

Library club member Helen Skinner, a music teacher, related how she had learned to fly after her fiftieth birthday, and became known as "the

Books for a Developing Town

Flying Grandma" at airports all across the United States. Listeners sat enthralled as Helen recounted her adventures on a solo flight from her former home in Galesburg, Illinois, to Fairbanks, Alaska, following the Alcan Highway.

Local readers, children and grownups, also were enjoying many adventure-filled tales and mind-broadening ideas, as the librarian at The School of the Ozarks continued passing along books for young readers, many memorials were contributed, and Edna Evans donated the book collection of her late husband, Dr. Harry Evans. In addition, the library board began making regular purchases from the Literary Guild, the Junior Literary Guild, and the Doubleday Mystery Book Club. As Christmas neared, Caroline Ballentine suggested a book shower for the library.

Privately purchased books gradually became a part of many people's home life. Beginning in the early 1950s, club members were allowed to order books through the library at cost, a move which seemed to increase use of the library as well as participation in club activities. Such purchases brought no profit to the library, but many of the books later appeared in the library as donations. Those book sales ceased after a few years however, because they created too many problems.

All the extra activity added to the strain on the library, described in the early fall of 1954 as a "twelve by sixteen foot room jammed with 10,000 books."

Bringing Books to the Ozarks

That October, word was received that the Civic League would pay fourteen hundred dollars to the American Legion so that the library would have a twenty-five year lease (the unexpired term of the American Legion's contract with the city) on the present library room plus a small adjoining room and part of an entry hall then being used by the Legion.

Planning the building alterations began immediately. The library was closed after the first week in December and did not reopen until the middle of January. The cost to the club for remodeling materials and labor, plus new equipment, and 1,440 square feet of linoleum blocks was seventeen hundred and forty-one dollars. On the hard-working building committee were Mildred Dawson, Juanita Thompson, Caroline Ballentine and Virginia Jenkins.

When Elsie Stephens took office as president in April, 1955, only three hundred and seventy-one dollars was left in the club's bank account, and five hundred *Shepherd of the Hills* books must be ordered before the tourist season began. In June the club members voted to raise their annual dues to five dollars, retroactive to April 1, 1955. Still, to have the four hundred and thirty-eight dollars available to pay for those books when they arrived, two hundred dollars was borrowed from Caroline Ballentine. That loan was repaid before the end of the year. However, the women on the club and library boards, faced with treasury records which included the costs of wholesale book orders as well as resale

Books for a Developing Town

receipts, were finding it virtually impossible to parse out what funds were available for operating the library and club.

It was just as well that the idea of constructing a new library building was set aside, in the mid-1950s, in favor of enlarging and renovating its current home.

The first of a trio of fall money-raisers was held on October 25, when Professor Merrill Gage, head of the sculpting department of the University of Southern California, presented a demonstration lecture under the auspices of the library club.

Before a captivated crowd of children and adults, the professor recounted the life of Abraham Lincoln while his talented fingers fashioned the craggy face of the young lawyer from a large egg-shaped mass of clay. As Lincoln's life story evolved, the likeness changed and aged, at the end taking on a startling similarity to the well-known photograph taken just four days before President Lincoln's assassination.

The lecture was a resounding hit with the audience. The receipts were ten dollars short of covering the lecturer's fifty dollar fee.

The second venture was much more successful.

Newspaper ads asked, "Are you a Cake Eater?"

The General Mills Company was introducing its new Betty Crocker cake mixes. The library club was offered a commission of five cents on every package sold in Branson and Hollister gro-

Bringing Books to the Ozarks

cery stores during the third week of November, if the clubwomen would be on hand to help sell the cake mixes on that Friday and Saturday. Sixty women each worked for two hours or more, garnering seventy-nine dollars for the treasury. The wage, someone figured out, was sixty cents an hour.

Of course, after the success of the 1954 birthday calendar, selling advertisements for a 1955 calendar was much easier. The printing was to be done this time by the *White River Leader*.

The calendars were tremendously popular in the community. They netted nine hundred and fifty-five dollars for the library in that second year, and the project was repeated many times during the next decade.

In the spring and summer of 1955, when Elsie Stephens became leader of the library club, membership reached a record ninety-four. However, the new president almost immediately faced the pressure of losing ten members, as The School of the Ozarks began its shift from high school to junior college level courses.

Alice Nightingale, with a doctorate in science, had for five years been teaching in local grammar and high schools. In 1955 she joined the fledgling college staff, and was too busy helping organize a science department and assisting in setting up the college level administration and curricula to participate in local volunteer work.

On the other hand, the school's secondary teachers were seeking employment elsewhere as high school graduates began filling the campus

Books for a Developing Town

classrooms and dormitories. On the library club's 1955-56 membership rolls only Elizabeth Clark, Bernice (Bunny) Mottesheard, and Marge Lyon represented The School of the Ozarks.

Despite the drop in membership, late 1955 was filled with fun and fund-raising events: a hillbilly dinner, a covered-dish luncheon at Harriet Rinehart's, entertainment by the Shepherd of the Hills Garden Club, and a lively Christmas Tea.

When March winds blew in 1956, the members shared a "Let's Get acquainted with Lilly Dache" party, again taking part in a mirthful hat exchange. Hazel Harris's sister, Myrna Escher, described some of the hats from out of her past and told about Lilly Dache and her famous hats. In the midst of the frivolity, Hazel was elected the club president for the coming year. Then everyone went home with a "new" chapeau, and cakes, pies or cookies which also were auctioned to raise funds for the library.

That summer, with the raise in dues comfortably settled, the library club board presented and the membership unanimously approved bylaws changes mandating regular board meetings, better defining officers' duties, allowing a club president to succeed herself for one term, and eliminating the July and August meetings!

Before the 1956-57 year ended, the women voted to join the Missouri State Library Association. They also approved changing their club year. When Dr. Margaret Jones took office in April, 1957, she knew that she and her board

Bringing Books to the Ozarks

were embarking on a fourteen month term. The next year's election would be held in May and 1958-59 officers, installed in June, would have the summer months to get organized before officiating at their first meeting in September.

Meanwhile, in 1957, Dr. Margaret was installed in the midst of a library club sponsored banquet held in the student dining hall at The School of the Ozarks. Dr. Robert M. Good was the guest of honor that evening, though he did not know it ahead of time. The theme for the occasion, borrowed from a then popular television show, was "This is Your Life," and Dr. M. Graham Clark was master of ceremonies. Local newspapers reported that--

> Everyone is still marvelling at the way he [Dr. Clark] acquired pictures and facts of Dr. Good's early life. His hardest job was getting Dr. Good to attend the party. Until the final hour, the "victim" was still protesting he could see no reason why he should go to a woman's club party.

Dr. Clark presented a photo-biography of Dr. Good's life, from his babyhood in Mississippi through his thirty-seven years as administrator of The School of the Ozarks. Then long time friends O.K. Armstrong, a magazine writer of Springfield; May Kennedy McCord, one of Springfield's nationally known radio stars; and Fred Jenkins, the chairman of the Board of The School of the Ozarks who lived in Kansas City, alternately teased Dr. Good and "praised his life-

Books for a Developing Town

long efforts" in behalf of the region's young people and The School of the Ozarks.

Over the next decade, as the high school was phased out and the four-year college became a reality, the two school administrators were to serve in tandem, Dr. Clark as president of the college and Dr. Good, officially president emeritus, as director of the high school.

Dr. Margaret Jones and her husband, Dr. J. Leland Jones, who had been residents of Branson for only two years, were said to have thoroughly enjoyed that evening's proceedings. Both were osteopathic physicians who for thirty-seven years had practiced medicine together in Kansas City and taught at the Kansas City College of Osteopathy and Surgery. Since their retirement in 1955, this friendly couple, known for their lively sense of humor, had lived in a stone house atop the bluff across Lake Taneycomo from downtown Branson, and were now an integral part of the community.

The nostalgia of that evening set the tone for the months which followed. That summer Evelyn Runyon, presently instructing at Warrensburg State Teacher's College, came back to Branson bringing her theater arts students to perform *The Shepherd of the Hills* at a theater on the Lake Taneycomo waterfront.

When the library club resumed its monthly meetings in September, 1957, members were celebrating their library's twenty-five years of providing books for their community. Jessie May Hackett set the atmosphere for the evening, per-

Bringing Books to the Ozarks

forming on the vibraharp and the piano. A third generation library club member, Jessie May was the daughter of Cora May and Rolland B. Kite, Jr. and granddaughter of the butterfly artist, Vitae Kite. Present to share their memories of earlier years were charter members Josephine Madry, Gay Miser, Minnie Whelchel, Edna Evans, Reva Ford, Sybil James, and Ellie Mitchell. The last named four plus Etta Mann, Dorothy Garner, Eve Griffith, Juanita Thompson, Ruth Wiley, Aletha Kennedy, Mayme Boren, Harriet Rinehart, and Elsie Stephens, all past presidents of the club, were asked to recall the highlights of their time of leadership. Of the twenty-two women who had served as president, only Sara Heath and Ethel Paramore were no longer alive, though five others had moved away.

October's speaker was lawyer Tiera Farrow, the first woman to be admitted to the bar in Missouri. After fifty years of law practice, she had retired the previous January. The focus of her speech was her recently published book, *Lawyer in Petticoats*.

The club members learned that day that thanks to the Civic League, which had offered to pay for the librarian's extra salary, the library would be open from 7 to 9 p.m. each Wednesday evening in addition to its regular hours from I to 5 p.m. on Wednesdays and Fridays.

The following April the Taneyhills Community Library held an open house, joining in celebration of the first National Library Week. Publicity about that occasion brought the Taneyhills

Books for a Developing Town

Library many donations of books for young people. Afterwards the women on the library board, Nelle Combs, Mildred Dawson, Ellie Mitchell, Mable Binney, Helen Cole, and Ruth Wiley, looked over the library's collection of second hand encyclopedias and decided a new set of *Encyclopaedia Britannica* was needed.

When the club board assigned Harriet Rinehart the task of raising the needed funds, reported to be a hundred and fifty-five dollars, she had already done her arithmetic, and immediately stated that five dollars each from thirty donors would be needed. She had eight pledges in hand before that board meeting was adjourned.

The thirty pledges were received by the end of April, but Harriet searched for ten more donors in May, when it was learned that the price actually was two hundred dollars. The club board paid the five dollar shipping charge.

The following month, when Dr. Margaret Jones was installed again as president, the Taneyhills Library's first new set of the *Encyclopaedia Britannica* was on its way to Branson.

Through the ensuing summer and fall, library patrons again enjoyed many new books: thirty-five review copies donated by the *Springfield News-Leader*; a long list of bestsellers, and the latest in juvenile fiction, made possible in part by a gift of a hundred dollars from the Rotary Club.

Enthusiasm was high in September, 1958, when the club met at the Christian Church for a

Bringing Books to the Ozarks

luncheon served by the women of the congregation. Being honored were some fifty members who had joined the club in the previous twelve months! Strangely, the roll call that day included only about eighty members, a dozen less than the previous year. Branson's world was changing fast. Many people who had lived in the area while the dam was being built were moving elsewhere since that project was now almost completed. Growing tourism brought new businesses, and women who wanted to work usually found jobs, if only for half the year. During the 1950s, while the group's membership numbers "failed to grow," a hundred new members actually joined the library club!

"The New Look" was on center stage at the October meeting, and seventy members and guests discovered that many of the season's hats, shoes and dresses strongly resembled the fashions of the 1920s which older members had dug out of their closets and cedar chests. New fall fashions were supplied by local dress shops: Peterson's, the Band Box, Dillon's, and Parnell's, with jewelry provided by Davidson's.

Several months later, Jack Herschend of "Marvel Cave" spoke to the women about cave exploration. Since the late 1940s the Herschend family, Hugo, Mary and their two sons, Peter and Jack, with a long-term lease on the land around the mouth of Marvel Cave, had been conducting thousands of visitors into the cavern's depths each summer. To make it easier for vacationers to see the cave, Hugo had envisioned them

Books for a Developing Town

descending a spiraling staircase from the entrance to the floor two hundred feet below, and being led through the picturesque depths on cement walkways, then returning to the surface on a steep railway.

When Hugo died in 1955, it fell to his sons to help fulfill their father's vision and their mother's desire to continue developing the cave and its surroundings as a tourist attraction. In 1957, with visions of ever-growing crowds of visitors now that the construction of Table Rock Dam was well underway, Jack explored and mapped the cave, planned the tour route and picked the best place to drill his railway tunnel to the surface. On May 11, 1958, with the railway completed and ready for operation, Casey Jones, Jr. was enlisted to operate the train on its maiden trip up the steep incline.

Jack Herschend had many stories to tell at that February, 1959, luncheon. Records show that his mother was able to take time off to hear him. Mary Herschend joined the library club in 1955. She played an active role through that decade, and remained a strong supporter even after the family's burgeoning tourist business demanded most of her time and attention.

In June of 1959, Bess Kelso assumed the presidency of the library club. She had become parliamentarian in 1958 during her first year as a member, and after her term as president she served as membership chairman for three years. Such was the enthusiasm of the women who joined in supporting Branson's library during the

Bringing Books to the Ozarks

decade which saw the creation of Table Rock Hydroelectric Dam and the huge recreational lake it impounds.

CHAPTER XVII

HOME FOLKS AND THRIVING TOURISM (1960 - 1969)

When the calendar turned to 1960, a new era was dawning. The nation was embarked on a series of space experiments that Jules Verne would have applauded as great science fiction. In and near Branson, fledgling enterprises were begun which gave promise of turning the region into a popular tourist area.

Already the newly impounded expanses of Table Rock Lake were attracting crowds of visitors. Many took time to cross the swinging bridge to the Herschends' "1800s mining village" Silver Dollar City, developing around the mouth of Marvel Cave.

A few miles east toward Branson, on the highway now known as West 76, the Trimbles set up several hundred folding chairs on the north side of a high ridge looking across miles and miles of Ozarks hills, and welcomed play-goers to a dramatic version of Harold Bell Wright's *The Shepherd of the Hills*. Audiences gathered on warm summer evenings to experience the excit-

Bringing Books to the Ozarks

ing, heart-rending old story as it unfolded in historic detail and vivid action. During daytime hours visitors wandered about the ridgetop homestead, walked up Inspiration Point to survey the far-flung hills and valleys, then visited the rustic log cabin and barn, and hiked the old road where the author of the bestselling novels of the first quarter of the twentieth century met the people and tales which would form his most famous book.

In that year of 1960, Nelle Combs, the latest Taneyhills librarian, was serving an ever increasing number of patrons, many of whom were retirees now living in new houses along the shores of Taneycomo and Table Rock Lakes. Since her presidency in 1953-54, Nelle had served the club continuously in one office or another, and also frequently filled in as volunteer librarian in the paneled library upstairs in the Community Building.

The bestsellers she was renting to library patrons included *Hawaii* by James Mitchener, *Dear and Glorious Physician* by Taylor Caldwell, Pearl Buck's *Command the Morning*, Dr. Thomas Dooley's *The Edge of Tomorrow*, *Teen Age Football Stories* by Frank Owen, and a popular autobiography *Groucho Marx and Me*.

The supporting library club entered 1960 with seventy-four active members. Club planners were relying primarily on local churches to provide meeting space, and on the women of the host church to prepare and serve their luncheon. The March meeting was held at the Branson

Home Folks & Thriving Tourism

Christian Church and author Edith McCall told about her book, *The Land Where Rivers Meet*. A writer of school textbooks and children's fiction, and a resident of Hollister, Edith was the daughter of Mary Sansom, and a member of the library club in the 1950s and 1960s. In future years, her friends and neighbors would enjoy many historical books and articles, non-fiction self help books, and juvenile fiction based on midwestern history written by this adopted daughter of the Ozarks. In 1969 she published *English Village of the Ozarks*, an in-depth history of Hollister. All of her books published both before and since, have appeared on the Taneyhills Library shelves, gifts from the author to the library's readers.

On the June day when Eleanor Coleman was installed as library club president for 1960-61, the members shared a covered dish luncheon and enjoyed the eagle's eye view of Lake Taneycomo from Harriet Rinehart's blufftop home.

The new president, a friendly and outgoing person, worked long hours in support of both the library and Skaggs Hospital. Eleanor and her husband, Edward, had moved to Branson after his retirement in the early 1950s, and she joined the library club in 1954. During her first year as president, the club's seventy-four active members were organized into ten groups, each pledged to raise a hundred dollars toward support of the library. Among their projects were a cakewalk, and a hat exchange in which, once again, the women bought one another's cast-off

Bringing Books to the Ozarks

headgear.

During Eleanor's second year as president, the club membership rose again to eighty-five. Most of the women were getting accustomed to the constantly changing membership roll. Fewer than a dozen of the charter members were still active in the group; those who had joined as young brides in the 1930s were now middle-aged. New members added to the roll from year to year lent their vigor and enthusiasm, ideas and experience to each fund-raising project. And of course new members frequently possessed talents and expertise that added to the group's prospects for leadership and lively, interesting programs.

In the fall of 1961, Molly McGee gave a fascinating account of life in Ecuador. She and her husband, Edward, affectionately referred to as "Fibber McGee and Molly" after the long-lived, popular radio program of that name, had spent some time in South America, and were always happy to tell others about their experiences, insights, and artifacts. A few months later, Molly and Marge Lyon were co-hostesses of the club's traditional elegant Christmas party, a highlight of the women's holiday season.

Joyce Wilhelm, a retired school teacher with a dynamic personality, was installed as club president in June, 1962. The following September, with vacations over, she opened the club's yearly activities with a speech on "Wisdom From Books." There was little question why books were uppermost in her mind.

Home Folks & Thriving Tourism

Nelle Combs had resigned as librarian that summer, and Marion Stark was hired to take her place. Since Marion and her husband, Walter, a retired baker, arrived in Branson in 1951, she had been librarian at the Branson High School and also occasionally helped out in the Taneyhills Library. Delighting in her new responsibilities, she kept the shelves in order, assisted patrons, and did all the cleaning chores except washing the windows. She enjoyed every minute of her job.

Often children would stay in the library on Saturday while their parents were shopping. Marion sometimes read to them and when they begged to be allowed to help in the library, she taught them to straighten the books on the shelves while they waited for their parents return.

From mid-1962 until the end of 1974, the library operated under the watchful, efficient supervision of Marion Stark, with coordination and assistance from the library board.

There was no restroom available to the library, nor was there a telephone anywhere upstairs in the community building. The librarian used the telephone in the police department then located downstairs, and visited the beauty shop across the street when she needed a restroom.

In May of 1963, a silver tea was held at Michel's Restaurant out on East Highway 86 (now 76). Harriet Rinehart presented a program on her favorite subject, antiques, and members

Bringing Books to the Ozarks

of the club bade a reluctant farewell to Caroline Ballentine, who had served the library and club faithfully for thirty years and whose timely loans had repeatedly averted financial disaster. Now she was moving to California. When the yearbook was published the following fall, her name was returned to the honorary members list.

The women attending that silver tea wore their "Plumb Nelly Days" costumes--sunbonnets and long, calico dresses. An oft repeated celebration first held in Branson in 1960, Plumb Nelly Days (the phrase translates to "pretty near anything can be bought here") brings crowds to town to shop at booths which line the downtown streets or, in more recent years, are sheltered under tents on a downtown parking lot. Then and now folks gather around the fiddlers to do some fancy square dancing. Sometimes the celebration honors some local citizen, as fishing and movie entrepreneur Jim Owen was one year, with a procession of horses trotting down the main thoroughfare. The men dressed in overalls, the women rode side saddle or daringly astride wearing split skirts.

Most of the library club members were wearing slacks, however, the following month when Joyce Wilhelm was installed for her second term as president. The installation took place aboard an excursion boat plying the waters of Lake Taneycomo.

That summer the local newspaper, then referred to as the *Branson Beacon and Leader*, began publishing a "recommended reading list,"

Home Folks & Thriving Tourism

a practice which continued for several years. The local library was acquiring many memorial books from patrons and well-wishers, and regularly the librarian or the library board ordered bestsellers, and other popular novels. Regular purchases also were arriving from the Dollar Mystery Guild, the Junior Library Guild, and the Double Day Book Club. The Encyclopaedia was modernized by the purchase of fact-filled yearbooks. Marion Stark, whose salary as librarian now ranged from eighty to ninety dollars a month, also was donating books from time to time.

Though it was the continued money-raising activities of the club which kept the library doors open, benefactors in the community and modest donations from citizens of all ages contributed a significant amount to its continued operation.

Native-born Ozarker Elmo Ingenthron shared his knowledge of Taney County history with the library club in September, 1963. Through the past thirty years, Ingenthron had been a teacher, principal, and county superintendent of schools in Taney and Stone Counties. For the club-women he also related some of his own experiences in educating local youths, and told of his active participation in forest management studies, his continuing research into regional history, and the books he hoped to write after he retired.

Over the next quarter of a century, Ingenthron completed and published three of his four planned volumes on Ozarks history: *Indians of the Ozark Plateau*, *The Land of Taney* (a county history), *Borderland Rebellion*, about the Civil

Bringing Books to the Ozarks

War in Missouri and Arkansas. His fourth book, *Bald Knobbers, Vigilantes on the Ozarks Frontier*, was researched by Ingenthron before he became terminally ill. He chose another local author, Mary Hartman, to write this detailed study of the baldknobber phenomenon of the 1880s, a dark aftermath of the Civil War which lasted for little more than a decade, but colored regional history well into the twentieth century.

It was current history that the women on the ways and means committee had in mind in the fall as they once again sold birthday calendars throughout the area. From those sales they turned seven hundred and forty-seven dollars in profits over to the club. The calendar cover featured *The Legend of the Dogwood*, and a "Happy New Year 1964." Inside were hundreds of birthday entries, church and organization information, and planned community events.

In December the library acquired modern editions of McGuffey's *Third, Fourth, Fifth and Sixth Eclectic Readers*, concerning which the local newspaper reported, "Best pieces of the old books are retained and to these have been added a long list of selections from the best English and American literature...." Thus a long ago favorite, updated with material in tune with today's world, became useful again, much as the Taneyhills Library has over the decades, ever growing and improving to meet its original purpose in a changing society.

Josephine Madry, who had recently taken time out for some world travels, provided several

Home Folks & Thriving Tourism

light-hearted moments at the February, 1964, meeting with a humorous account of her three-month journey to Scandinavia, France, Greece, Egypt, and the Holy Land.

It was down to business in March, when representatives of the Missouri Library Association met with interested patrons of the library to discuss the library's specific needs, such as a new library building. Once again the library board members and officials from various civic groups were advised on the problems and hazards involved in pushing for municipal or county tax support for their library, and the particular problems facing a municipality of under five thousand population.

So thoughts of a library building were set aside. Yet, in the back of many minds the library club members knew that something must be done about a building.

In April, right after National Library Week, Marion Stark spoke to the Branson-Hollister Lions Club, whose theme that year was "Reading is the key to new worlds of opportunity and understanding." She reviewed for them the history of Branson's library and the scope of its present collection of books, emphasizing the important role their organization had played through the years in the continued growth of the library.

That June, 1964, Bill Ellen Hall was installed as president of the library club. She would be leading some one hundred and ten members in support of the community's books. It had been twenty-four years since her first term as presi-

Bringing Books to the Ozarks

dent. Her son, Jerry, was a grown man, and she and Ted were now operating a general store near The School of the Ozarks. At the same time, she also was librarian at the Branson High School, and soon to become teacher and principal at the Hollister Grade School.

Immediately after Bill Ellen took office, she traveled to Jefferson City to participate in the Governor's Conference on Library Development, a meeting designed to improve library services throughout Missouri. She was among two thousand librarians, library trustees and civic leaders invited to the conference.

Back home in Branson, volunteers were determined to improve their local library. Working particularly hard toward that goal, in 1964, was Catherine "Cathy" Hunt, then serving as corresponding secretary and also chairing of the ways and means committee. On a recent visit to Atlanta, Georgia, Cathy had enjoyed the taste of fresh southern pecans and realized that her friends in the Ozarks might like them for their holiday baking.

Back home, she proposed selling packages of shelled Georgia pecans as a money-making project, and twenty-five cases were ordered. When the pecans arrived, Cathy and Eleanor Coleman drove all over the countryside, selling them at homes and motels.

Mayme Boren also sold the pecans at Stonewall Court and Bill Ellen Hall offered the packages to vacationers and everyone else she met. The initial shipment was soon gone and ten

Home Folks & Thriving Tourism

more cases were ordered. Before the November meeting, the ways and means committee had reaped four hundred and eighty-one dollars in profits from the sale of pecans!

Each succeeding fall, to the present time, the library club has sold fresh Georgia pecans. For the rest of her life, Eleanor Coleman ran the project. Still today, friends often speak of her as "our Pecan Queen."

After the holidays, members of the Taneyhills Library Club had an opportunity to meet Douglas Mahnkey and enjoy his "Anecdotes of Taney County History." A lawyer, writer, and local historian, Mahnkey was the oldest son of columnist and poet Mary Elizabeth Mahnkey and certainly inherited his mother's talent for storytelling.

Later in the spring of 1965, Dr. O. Myking Mehus reviewed for the club two new books from his ancestral land, *Norway Today* and *The Folk Arts of Norway*. He also displayed examples of Norwegian embroidery, weaving, rosemalling, metal crafts, silver and enameled jewelry, woodcarvings, china, glass and pewterware, and told of life in Norway and how it compared to life in the Ozarks.

Dr. Mehus and his wife, Jewell Ross Mehus, a new member of the library club, had retired to the Ozarks from the Kansas City area and were operating the Old Shepherd's Book Shop on the highway between Shepherd of the Hills Farm and Silver Dollar City. Jewell was a member of the library club for many years. Through the remain-

Bringing Books to the Ozarks

der of her life she endeared herself to area readers through her weekly column, "The Old Shepherd's Book Shop," published in Southwest Missouri newspapers.

Election time in 1965 brought Cathy Hunt to the club presidency. Cathy worked in Canote's Drug Store, where her husband, Eugene, was a pharmacist. She also was active in the hospital auxiliary and the Eastern Star. An accomplished pianist, she accompanied the clubwomen in many a "sing along."

During Cathy's presidency, the board in charge of the library began keeping its own permanent records. Separate records of the *Shepherd of the Hills* books also were instituted, those purchases and sales having become increasingly complicated over the years.

By 1966, Branson enjoyed a thriving, constantly increasing tourist business. Improvements to existing attractions, new housing developments around Table Rock Lake, and the growing crowds of fishermen enjoying fall and winter trout fishing on Lake Taneycomo each year lengthened the tourist season and broadened the appeal of the area to vacationers.

Lyn Asselin and her husband Vi, having acquired the Sammy Lane Boat Line from Charles and Lenore Fain in 1964, began entertaining vacationing families with a "Pirate Cruise and Water Pageant" on Lake Taneycomo. Folks ashore could follow the progress of each trip by the firing of a cannon and the excited screams of the children as a pirate came aboard to abscond

Home Folks & Thriving Tourism

with the "gold" just picked up at an old mine at the base of a towering lakeside bluff.

"Ellie's Guided Tours," became a new feature for the tourists in 1965. Ellie Jennings had been hired by the Don Gardners' Golf Ranch on East Highway 76 during the late 1940s, to drive the station wagon which picked up "golf widows" and their children at various motels each morning. While husbands and fathers played golf, Ellie gave their families a grand tour of Shepherd of the Hills country, returning them to the golf ranch for lunch.

Ellie had grown up admiring Pearl "Sparky" Spurlock, the colorful granny character whose exciting taxi tours entertained many a visitor to the area during the 1920s and 30s. As a child, Ellie rode with "Sparky" whenever she could, enthralled with the old tales repeated so dramatically by the pipe-smoking lady in old-fashioned dress and sunbonnet. Always she dreamed of one day being behind that wheel and telling stories "like Sparky did."

After several years spent away from Branson, in 1966 Ellie Jennings returned to live out her dream. Her first nine-passenger Volkswagen bus had a big sign on top announcing "Ellie's Guided Tours." Her investment was in her vehicles, which grew to a fleet of two Volkswagon buses, two fifteen-passenger Dodge buses, and a school bus, offering many tourists the opportunity to learn much about the Ozarks in one fascinating ride.

By the mid-1960s tourist accommodations

Bringing Books to the Ozarks

included a growing number of motels and resorts. Along the main streets of Branson were the Paramount, Southern Air, Newhaven, Lamplighter, Travelers, and Roark Motels. Between the Taneycomo Bridge and Roark Creek were the Taney, Rains and Crescent Motels, the Branson Hotel, Stonewall Court, Branson Court, and Anchor Village.

On East Main Street, near the lake, was the White River Hotel, and along the lake were Sammy Lane and other resorts, all of which had been serving vacationers for several decades. Beyond the top of the Main Street hill on today's West 76, and along the then winding U.S. 65 north of Branson and south beyond Hollister's resort area there were only a few scattered tourist cabins.

From time to time vacationers visited the library in the Community Building, but only if they were actually living in summer homes in the area could they check out books.

Cathy Hunt accepted a second term as president. In 1966-67, she presided over the rewriting of the constitution and bylaws, some library remodeling, and a club vote which initiated a voluntary fund for a future library building.

A year later Eve Griffith was installed as president for a second time. The library and club had changed vastly since her 1940s presidency. The membership had doubled and the annual budget had multiplied. This time she served through the spring of 1969.

The Griffiths now owned and operated the

Home Folks & Thriving Tourism

local freezer locker plant. Jack was secretary of the White River Booster Club and Eve's beautiful voice was being enjoyed in local churches and many musical performances. She was the organizing director of a Christmas chorale which sang for the annual Adoration Festivities on the first Sunday in each December.

Library patronage steadily increased, with 13,689 books checked out in 1969, and two hundred and seventy-one new patron cards issued. In the late 1960s the club and members were enjoying interesting and educational programs each month, happy to have cheerful, knowledgeable Marion Stark as librarian.

Club members were soon to find, however, that steady growth was not enough. A new generation of young people was growing up in the Ozarks. More and more reading material would be required to get them started reading books at an early age, and a broader base of reference material would be needed to help advance their education.

Meanwhile, an after-school stop at the Taneyhills Library in the now aging Community Building revealed shelves packed floor to ceiling with books. Once again there was little open space, and wheeled carts were loaded with books, and no shelf space left on which to put them.

CHAPTER XVIII

GROWING PAINS AND BUILDING FEVER
(1969 - 1975)

On July 20, 1969, in the midst of the turbulence, confusion and protest of the Vietnam War years, three American astronauts made a successful landing on the moon, then returned to earth to brag about it. Our country had carried out mankind's most daring and challenging technical and scientific project to date.

But would the 1970s bring to fulfillment the Taneyhills Library supporters decades long dream of a permanent home for all their books?

In January, 1970, the library board met to consider adding to that book collection. Through the mother of a teenager, the librarian had learned of a new book, *The Stork is Dead*, by Charles Shedd. After careful consideration, it was ordered for the library. As Marion Stark, Josephine Madry, Jane Davis and Sue Morlan made that and other selections, they again were faced with boxing up books so the new ones could be shelved.

Growing Pains & Building Fever

Three months later, library club president Mildred Dawson and the library board were making plans for a public tea to be held during National Library Week in April, amidst all those books and boxes. They decided that their librarian, Marion Stark, who was to speak at the next local Parent-Teachers Association meeting, should issue a special invitation to those parents of school-age children. Invitations also were sent to local service organizations. The community turn-out was very gratifying.

At the installation meeting in June, for the first time in three decades, an honorary membership was awarded. The recipient was Dorothy Garner who, in the years since she joined the club in 1937, had served in every club office except secretary.

After Betty Stewart and all the club officers who would serve with her were properly installed and every committee head except the ways and means chairman was pledged to service, Mildred Dawson turned the president's gavel over to Betty Stewart and moved immediately into the role of head of the library board.

Betty, who was moving up from a year as vice president and head of the program committee, had two sons, eleven and fifteen years of age. Her husband Birl owned and operated Chick's Barber Shop in downtown Branson. Betty's family roots went back to the nineteenth century pioneer settlers in the great loop on the White River where Branson had its beginnings.

The crucial ways and means committee was

Bringing Books to the Ozarks

still leaderless because Betty hoped to enlist faithful Mayme Boren for the job, but hesitated to ask because her husband, Charles, had died just the week before. After the meeting, in conversation with Mayme and her daughter, Mary Helen Benson, Betty asked the question anyway.

Mayme hesitated, but behind her Mary Helen, knowing that being busy would help her mother through her grief, was nodding. Mayme did accept the challenge, and led the club's fundraising efforts through both years that Betty Stewart was president.

Betty's presidency had barely begun when the library board approved a list of recommendations compiled by retiring board members Josephine Madry, Ruth McCullom, and Jane Davis, and continuing board member Helen Fletcher. In the interest of offering better service to the community, the library would be kept open more days of the week, a training program was to be set up for students interested in library work, and club members were to be encouraged to become library volunteers. A standard catalogue system was to be set up. It was recommended that Bob Anderson at The School of the Ozarks be contacted to learn more about such a project.

By summer's end, the library's thousands of books were being reclassified, recatalogued, and rearranged on the shelves by a team of industrious volunteers. The library was now open all day Wednesday and Friday, and from 9 a.m. to noon on Saturday.

Growing Pains & Building Fever

Other volunteers were tracking down long overdue books and culling those on the shelves, replacing or retiring worn out books and mending those in need of repair. When one well known resort owner kept eight books over long, volunteers made a visit to "repossess" them, returning with all but two.

That fall someone suggested that the American Legion might donate more space for the library. On December 2, 1970, Martin G. Gallon, commander of Pemberton-Jennings Post #220, confirmed the granting of approximately eleven more feet across the south side of the library room, adjacent to the Legionnaires' Hall.

There had been no remodeling done for more than fifteen years. Mabel Sarber, who had set up a card file for the library and was compiling a staff manual, immediately drew up plans for the alterations. Josephine Madry and Helen Radcliff began seeking bids on installing floor covering, rewiring, moving the wall, and rearranging the shelves and books.

Three thousand dollars was set aside for the enlargement project. The library was closed from mid-December through January, 1971. While the work was being accomplished, Marion Stark enjoyed a holiday tour of the Holy Land.

With noisy saws and flying dust, the construction work was soon completed. After the carpeting was laid, the books were all dusted, and reorganized on the shelves. The new addition was actually twelve feet deep, rather than eleven.

Bringing Books to the Ozarks

Thanks to sizable gifts from the Lions and Rotary Clubs, the library desk was refurbished, other needed equipment had been purchased, and on February 1, 1971, there was almost two hundred dollars left in the building fund to begin rebuilding the club finances. The first Saturday that the library was reopened, a hundred and ninety-eight books were checked out!

Marion returned from her long holiday on February 20th, eager to share her experiences with friends in the library club and at church. But when the Taneyhills Library held open house during Library Week in April, all the librarian could talk about was the enlarged and modernized library.

While the library board saw to the remodeling project, other club volunteers were busy raising money. To the balance from the fall's card parties, pecan sales, and a very successful birthday calendar assembled under Lou Chilton's leadership, there was added the proceeds from the sale of six thousand, one hundred and seventy-four Shepherd of the Hills books. And, with a hundred and sixth-six members on the library club roll, even the passing of the birthday box was proving a good fund-raiser. On May 28, the club's income for the year was just forty-five dollars short of three thousand dollars.

Thanks to many long hours of work by Donna Canote, on the June day when Betty Stewart was installed for a second term, club members all wore permanent name tags. Among the other elected officers being installed was Josephine

Growing Pains & Building Fever

Madry, the new club historian. Always before, that job had been filled by an appointee. Through the next two years Josephine industriously compiled a collection of notes, clippings and pictures, creating a valuable, lasting record of current club activities. She also reconstructed lists of the women who had shared in the beginnings of the club and library, resources much appreciated in more recent years.

Two faithful, hardworking friends were made honorary members of the library club in June, 1971. Minnie Whelchel, who had worked behind the scenes even before she joined the club in 1934, was failing fast. Her warm-hearted support and gentle wisdom would be long remembered. Stella Owen's generous gifts of books and magazine subscriptions had been offering new dimensions to the pleasures of reading for patrons since the earliest years of the library, long before she joined the club in 1940. Her generosity was destined to continue even beyond her death in 1981, at 104. Her son, Dr. Lyle Owen, who had long shared in providing magazines for the library's readers, continues in the late 1990s the donations his mother began all those years ago.

The newly enlarged library welcomed many new patrons, but often during the summer months those who had to drive found Branson's downtown streets highly congested and parking non-existent. Traffic through the intersection of Highways 65 and Branson's Main Street was so heavy that often cars were backed up in all direc-

Bringing Books to the Ozarks

tions. New businesses being built on West 76 (Main Street) added to the tie-up.

In late 1971 help was on the way, though things would get worse before they got better. The highway department was buying homes along Main Street and nearby thoroughfares, to make way for the construction of a Highway 65 by-pass. One of the original Maids and Matrons, Florence Campbell Hamilton, would remember that, on November 19, that year, she gave up her home on the Main Street hill, along with the house next door where she had lived as a child. It was with mixed emotions that she, along with twelve neighboring families, left their houses vacant awaiting demolition. The hill where for so many years sledders' happy shouts greeted winter snows, would never again be safe for such activities.

Florence did enjoy her smaller, modern house several blocks away, however, and the sound of distant blasting through the months and years that followed soon consigned the past to memories.

Mary Herschend brought the positive side of Branson's growth to those attending the March, 1972, meeting. Attendance was increasing rapidly at Silver Dollar City, and the demand for Harold Bell Wright's famous book was such that they were ordering another two thousand copies from the library club; welcome news, of course, for the committee handling book sales.

The dedicated club members were quick to cheer such continuing generosity from Branson's

Growing Pains & Building Fever

business community, though many among the almost two hundred library club members were not fully aware of the group's responsibilities.

Since November, 1971, the library had been open five days a week, Tuesday through Friday from 1 to 5 p.m., and Saturday from 9 a.m. to 5 p.m. The librarian's salary now averaged a hundred and twenty dollars a month. New books cost an average of six to nine dollars each, and much time and thought went into selecting them, and raising the money to buy them.

The club and library boards, in an effort to encourage more participation in fund-raising and volunteer assistance, placed reminders of the library before the members at monthly meetings. Book covers became table decorations, and colorful children's books formed centerpieces.

During Plumb Nelly Days in 1972, old library books being discarded were sold at the Veterans of Foreign Wars' booth. Helen Fletcher and Rosabelle Durr netted almost fifteen dollars selling the library's cast-offs and Johnnie Quistgard's crocheted "bookworms."

When Delores German was elected president in June, 1972, the club was entering its fortieth year. In the mid-1960s, Delores and her husband, Ralph, had moved from Illinois to the Branson area to enjoy their retirement years. In 1968, she joined the library club and almost immediately became involved in supporting the library and club, and encouraging others in their volunteer efforts.

Her presidency began inauspiciously. In early

Bringing Books to the Ozarks

September she and the board reviewed the club's financial situation and shared the news that donations from the Rotary and Lions Clubs, which had totaled eleven hundred dollars in the past year, would be given this year to Skaggs Hospital and to other more pressing community needs. Furthermore, sales of *Shepherd of the Hills* books had slumped to less than three thousand. The challenge was very apparent to the club, and particularly to Fran Applehans and the twenty-three members of her ways and means committee.

Through the winter, while blasting nearby on the new highway by-pass continued to rattle windows and shift books on the library shelves, the club members concentrated on money-raising schemes even as they enjoyed their monthly programs and made plans for that big anniversary celebration in the spring. For the latter they called on club member Pearl Hodges to bring to life for them the earliest days of the Study Club, when Rose O'Neill, originator of the world-famous Kewpie doll, was a familiar figure in their midst. Pearl, who cherished her own teen-aged association with the artist and writer, reviewed Rose's life and works for her fellow members, many of whom knew little about this early honorary member of the club.

Pearl, herself a well-known artist, was prominent in the establishment of the Ta-Co-Mo Art Club (now the Steve Miller Art Association), the National Rose O'Neill Club, the International Rose O'Neill Club and the Forsyth Art Guild. This

Growing Pains & Building Fever

descendant of Branson and Kirbyville pioneers enjoyed a successful career in fashion illustration for a Kansas City department store. In 1961, she returned to Branson with her husband, Frank, settled in the house her Grandfather MacFarland built on Mount Branson and joined the library club. However, her knowledge and interest in Rose O'Neill soon led her to employment at the Shepherd of the Hills Farm, where she shared with tourists the famous artist's story.

Pearl's interest in Rose O'Neill helped bring about the annual Kewpiesta which each April draws throngs of Rose O'Neill fans to Branson from all over the world to share in Kewpiemania.

In the midst of preparations for the 1973 Kewpiesta, eighty-nine library club members had lunch in the White Frog Restaurant at the Branson Inn and shared memories of the club's founding and forty years of keeping books available to the public in Branson. Three weeks later they and many of their neighbors celebrated together in a marathon day of card parties, from 9:30 a.m. to 12:30, 2 p.m. to 5, and 7:30 to 10:30 p.m!

The organizers of those card parties, Merle Brooks, Rosabelle Durr, Virginia Powell, Mildred Dawson, Irene Nalle and Mabel Sarber, added their names to a long and growing list of women whose efforts had kept the doors of the library open through four decades. At the end of the day, exhausted, Fran Applehans totaled her ways and means receipts and found that her

Bringing Books to the Ozarks

frazzled committee members had raised nine hundred and fifty dollars. That, along with pecan sales, several private donations, and an unexpected gift from the Rotary Club, helped the club finish the year with almost a thousand dollars in its treasury.

There was talk of using some of that money for a new set of *Encyclopaedia Britannica,* or installing an air conditioning unit in the library to increase the comfort of readers and the librarian. That quandary was solved shortly after the June, 1973 meeting, when the Lions Club donated the four hundred dollars needed for the air conditioner.

The president installed that June was Jane Arend, an attractive woman with considerable organizational training, a vast reservoir of energy, and a strong discontent with conditions in the Taneyhills Library. Her husband was Jim Arend, nephew of Josephine Madry, and president of the Security Bank in Branson.

Jane's work notes reveal a deep interest in every facet of the library and its sponsoring club. She was concerned that "Merle Brooks (the library board chairman) is spending an enormous amount of time on the library and we are going to need much organization to carry on when she goes off the board."

Early in 1974, Merle told the club women that, "It is very rewarding to work in the library. You hear so many comments of gratitude."

On the other hand, Jane brought to the library board's attention the continuing unpleas-

Growing Pains & Building Fever

antness of not having restroom facilities available in the community building.

As winter's doldrums gave way to a glorious Ozarks spring, the club members presented Marion Stark with a plaque in appreciation of her loyal service to the library. They also named Marion and the late Mildred Dawson honorary members of the Taneyhills Library Club.

During Girl Scout Week, a crew of industrious little girls helped the librarian clean the library, their personal contribution to the place which offered help with their studies and exciting stories to read.

That June, when Jane Arend was installed for a second term as president, the annual library report showed that 14,940 books had been issued in the past twelve months. There were three hundred and sixty-four new patrons, and sales of *Shepherd of the Hills* books were a very satisfactory six thousand, netting eighteen hundred dollars for the club treasury.

There were, however, many problems in the library. The recently added space had done little to relieve overcrowding. The librarian, nearing eighty years old, was having difficulty handling the five day a week schedule, the increasing number of patrons, and the lack of a telephone. Marion preferred to handle the library alone, yet more and more frequently library board members were filling in because she was ill.

Late that fall, announcement was made that Marion Stark would resign at the end of 1974. During December, arrangements were made for

Bringing Books to the Ozarks

Margaret Cram patiently Ran the Library amid the loaded shelves and boxes of books in the Community Building library, but found running the larger library, dealing with the much needed volunteers and the growing list of patrons intimidating.

Margaret Cram, a club member, to become the new librarian.

Already Margaret was studying the Taneyhills Library procedures, and was scheduled to attend library science classes at The School of the Ozarks through the spring semester. She began work in December at the current hourly rate of a dollar and seventy-five cents, which would be raised to two dollars an hour in January.

Marion Stark was honored by the library board at a coffee held in the library on the afternoon of December 13th, and she was extended a lifetime invitation to attend the club's luncheons without charge.

Growing Pains & Building Fever

The library patrons were still getting acquainted with Margaret Cram when People's Bank and Trust Company in Branson set in motion a remarkable adventure for all who supported and used the Taneyhills Library.

During January and February the bank made contributions to the library of one per cent of all new certificates of deposit, new savings accounts over twenty-five dollars, or additions to existing accounts. To get the plan off to a good start, the bank made an advance payment to the library of a thousand dollars, or one per cent of the next $100,000 of new deposits. President Jane Arend and the leader of the library board, Merle Brooks, accepted that check.

As head of the finance committee, Bill Ellen Hall remarked that day, "We're very happy to get the money. We sure know how to put it to good use." When asked how the money would be used, Bill Ellen replied that eventually they hoped to have a new library building.

The bank's president, Smith Brookhart, commented,

> The concept of the Peoples Bank promotion is to appeal to the residents of the area to become more involved in our community by bringing their money from other cities to Branson. Therefore the bank evolved the idea of giving to the Taneyhills Library in lieu of a premium for deposits.

Employees of Peoples Bank were gratified by the response to the promotion, which brought

Bringing Books to the Ozarks

over four thousand dollars to the Taneyhills Library.

Within days Jane Arend, in passing by the corner of Fourth and Pacific Streets in Branson, thought, "That would be such an ideal location for a library." The corner was a block south of West Highway 76 and only three blocks from Highway 65.

The First Presbyterian Church, the Tri-Lakes Adult center, and a senior citizens complex, Oak Manor Apartments, were less than a block away. It was only a short walk to Branson's elementary school. And across Fourth Street was a paved parking lot belonging to the Presbyterian Church.

Realizing that the two houses on the property were vacant and quite old, at the next club board meeting, Jane requested and received permission to contact the owners and find out how much it would cost the library club to purchase the property.

Inquiries led her to the Stewart family of Republic, Missouri, who agreed, in response to her telephone call, to sell the property for nine thousand dollars. Thrilled with the reasonable price, but wondering where the club could get the additional five thousand dollars, Jane set out that evening to find a woman, experienced in fund-raising, who might give her advice on how to raise that amount.

As darkness approached, Jane lost her way and stopped at the home of an acquaintance to get directions. She was told that her destination

Growing Pains & Building Fever

Three Librarians
(left to right) Norma Root who would direct the Taneyhills Library from 1983-1997, Marion Stark who after a career as school librarian, served eleven and a half years as Taneyhills librarian, and Bill Ellen Hall whose lifelong career as a teacher in Taney County schools was capped by several years as a school librarian and a lifetime as a "public library" volunteer.

was far across Table Rock Lake. Then the woman invited her in and asked the reason for her search.

When told of the club's need for a library building and the opportunity to purchase a fine lot if only five thousand dollars could be raised quickly, Jane's hostess offered to donate the entire amount, provided she could make the gift anonymously.

Bringing Books to the Ozarks

In March, 1975, the library club became owner of that fine building lot!

However there was much to be done before a campaign to raise building funds could go into full swing. In all its years of existence, the club had never owned land or buildings. It was just a private club acquiring, maintaining and lending books. Before the club could purchase real estate, or solicit donations to a building fund, it would need to be incorporated as a not-for-profit educational organization.

By the time the library club took title to the lot, articles of incorporation were adopted and the first board of directors was formed, its members to be Jane Arend, Jeannette Street, and Betty Yates. In April, 1975, the State of Missouri issued the new certificate recognizing the Taneyhills Library Club as a not-for-profit corporation!

Through the next eighteen months, at almost every club meeting, revisions to the bylaws were introduced, or passed, carrying out the organizational changes required to sustain that impressive new status.

CHAPTER XIX

THE FEVER MOUNTS
(1975 - 1977)

Meantime, in June, 1975, Jeannette Street, a retired school teacher and a very active member of the library club for the past five years, was installed as president. A special bank account was opened to receive donations for the new building, and an application was submitted to the Internal Revenue Service for tax exemption under the Federal Revenue Code.

The government ruled that the club and library already were considered "not for profit", exempt from the social security act, the unemployment act, excise tax, income tax, sales tax, and would be exempt from taxes on the building and its contents.

That summer the services of a public accountant were secured, assuring possible donors that their gifts would be properly applied to the building project. With the need to restructure not only the rules the club operated under but the organization itself, the elected leaders also enlisted

Bringing Books to the Ozarks

the professional advice of several Branson businessmen, forming a permanent library advisory committee. Those two moves, Jeannette later pointed out, provided a strong bulwark which served the library and its supporters well during the great challenges and adjustments of the decade which followed.

The most visible of those changes, implemented two years later, was the strengthening of the two major committees through the designation of their leaders as vice president of finance and vice president of library, and establishing them in that order as emergency successors to the president and the vice president of program. A vice president of membership was added in 1982.

In the summer of 1975, following Jeannette Street's installation as president, retiring president Jane Arend took on leadership of the building and planning committee. In early July she invited her three committee officers, treasurer Virginia Lucas, corresponding secretary Eleanor Coleman, and recording secretary Betty Yates, to a meeting at her home near downtown Branson.

At that meeting, fund-raising projects were assigned. Delores German's door-to-door solicitation drive was already underway. Merle Brooks, assisted by Ruth Hush, Mayme Boren, Johnny Quistgard, and Josephine Madry would develop the sure-to-be-successful community activities calendar. Ruth Hush was to organize a fashion show, as well as a house tour, and Virginia Lucas would plan and carry out a giant

The Fever Mounts

auction at Mang Field, on the lakefront.

Some neighbors in Branson, reading of the club's many money-raising schemes, were heard to remark that the whole thing was crazy, impossible. To which Jane Arend replied, "It's time we start a building. If it is the Lord's will, we'll get it done."

Through June and July, the door bell ringers canvassed their neighborhoods and sought out areas where no members lived. Some gave as much as a hundred dollars. If met with "Oh, I can't afford to give a donation," the library volunteer was to reply, "Can you give us a dollar?"

Every dime and dollar was appreciated.

As Bill Ellen Hall canvassed from door to door along Lake Shore Drive, she thought of their cause and the $100,000 needed to get it constructed, and said to herself, "We've just got to go out and do it."

The people answering Bill Ellen's knock often asked, "What are you collecting for this time?" for each year she canvassed for the Red Cross, Heart, Cancer and many other funds.

When she replied, "The library" one householder countered, "What are you going to do if you don't get enough money?"

"Why, of course we are going to get enough," she countered indignantly.

Still skeptical, the gentleman gave her ten dollars.

Ultimately Bill Ellen collected five hundred dollars, and the "door to door" campaign netted over five thousand dollars.

Bringing Books to the Ozarks

Construction was not to begin until the $50,000 needed to buy and erect the basic building was in hand. However, preparing the building site was underway by mid-summer. With the approval of the executive board, the two old houses were sold to the highest bidder. Shortly thereafter the land was cleared, and a sign was erected there which read, "Future Home of the Taneyhills Library."

In the public press, Jane Arend stressed the need for a children's library, as well as a reference library for junior and senior high students, the two estimated to cost $20,000 to $25,000. She envisioned a bookmobile, staffed by volunteers and stocked with adult and children's reading materials to share with readers in outlying areas.

Newspaper articles about the club's fund-raising projects were often accompanied by photographs taken in the current library, where every shot of the crowded stacks revealed boxes of books ranked ceiling high against the walls.

With advertisements, pictures and publicity bombarding the town, it was a virtual certainty that the library's auction, held at Mang Field in late September, in conjunction with Branson's Autumn Daze street fair, would add substantially to the building fund. Local auctioneers Bill Holt and Jewell Snowden and their assistants, Clifford Crouch, Brenda Persinger and Don Furman, donated their services for the auction sale.

Auction items were delivered to the site by

The Fever Mounts

the donating merchants, or picked up by the Jerry and Martha Hess U-Haul or other volunteers from among the families and friends of members. The sale raised over fifteen hundred dollars for the building fund. Several volunteers dressed in their Plumb Nelly outfits and manned booths to sell donated baked goods, flowers, and handcrafted and small antique items.

When the fair was over, the *Branson Beacon* announced that the building fund held $21,000 in donations and pledges. Throughout the campaign, advertisements about the fund drive were run without charge by Lee Beasley and the Tri-Lakes Press.

September, 1975, also brought Jane Arend's announcement that Carl Harris had agreed to donate his services as architect for the project.

The building was to be faced with brick, and soon full-page ads appeared in the Beacon inviting one and all to "Buy a brick or a book." The appeal went home with visiting tourists, and donations began arriving from all over the country.

Encouraged by library club member Pat Shue, who handled tour bookings, the *Kansas City Star* reported the campaign and more donations arrived in the mail. Pleased with that success, Pat appealed to various foundations, and one of them sent fifty dollars.

The *Beacon's* publisher received a check from the Rose O'Neill Association in California, given in memory of one of their founding members, Ellie Mitchell, who with her daughter Jane

Bringing Books to the Ozarks

Mitchell Pierce, and her sister, Ann Thompson had died in a terrible automobile accident just north of Branson in 1969.

Branson lawyer Clay Cantwell brought in a thousand dollar contribution from a Florida couple who had read of the library and thought it a fine project.

At the October, 1975, meeting of the library club, Jeannette Street shot off a toy cannon to herald the country's upcoming bicentennial, and announced that in keeping with the day's theme, library club members, in partnership with members of the Business and Professional Women's Club, would be selling attractive necklaces, which marked the nation's two hundredth birthday, for a dollar each. At the end of that month, Elaine Nelson, head of fund-raising, reported that a hundred necklaces had been sold, for a net profit to the building fund of a hundred dollars. The women also sold candles, which turned out to be a slow-moving venture.

It should be noted that, with little fanfare, the women tasked with funding the day to day operation of the library faithfully carried out their other, more mundane, duties.

As Christmas approached, Bill Jones donated the pay he received as Branson's Santa Claus; the Branson-Hollister Jaycee wives gave the money raised through their "Miss Merrie Christmas" campaign, and Bill Ellen Hall, with an eye to a future few could visualize, quietly arranged an option on the lot and house on Pacific, just east of the building site.

The Fever Mounts

On New Year's Eve, as library supporters sang "Auld Lang Syne," many thought of the recently dedicated Highway 65 by-pass and the building fund that was halfway to the $50,000 mark, and toasted 1976, which promised to be a momentous year for the community and the library.

At the executive board meeting in January, plans were made for ground-breaking ceremonies which would include filling a box to go into the cornerstone and also tie in with bicentennial celebrations.

Through the months which followed, the club women continued their fund-raising: planning cookie sales, card parties, and the annual spring fashion show. They dug out their favorite recipes for a cookbook Dorotha Douglas was putting together, a project which stretched to two books instead of one. Both cookbooks became local "bestsellers" and contributed to the support of the library for the next fifteen years.

The Security Bank gave their campaign a boost by setting up a table inside the bank's front door and inviting club members to sell those slow-moving candles there until all were gone.

Delores German and her thirty-three "door to door" canvassers reported in January that their collection had reached almost five thousand four hundred dollars and three areas were still to be canvassed.

The club officers, on the other hand, were swamped with corporate technicalities. Lawyer Gary Allman drew up the new articles of incor-

Bringing Books to the Ozarks

poration for the library club, and stipulated that a Board of Directors should be elected that June. After President Jeannette Street read the articles of incorporation aloud to the club, Lola Charleston, herself a lawyer, commented on the changes which would be needed in the club bylaws, and it was agreed that parliamentarian Delphine Sedwick should consult with Allman on those needed changes. Turning the forty-three-year-old library club into a corporation was indeed a complicated business.

Meanwhile, at the March club meeting, the women received word that the Taney County Court (now called the County Council) after much consultation, was giving the Taneyhills Library twelve hundred and fifty dollars to buy books. The announcement was greeted by a standing ovation.

The money arrived with explicit directions concerning its use. Elaine Nelson reported these were

> . . . monies received from the judges of the county from revenue sharing funds. This can only be used for the purpose of books as a supplement to our book budget. It must be spent this fiscal year and clarification will have to be made as to whether it is the court or our club year.
>
> Acknowledgement must be made in these books that they were obtained through revenue sharing funds provided by the county court. It was suggested that purchase should be made of reference books or children's books. The library board is to keep a list of books purchased from

The Fever Mounts

this fund and report their cost.

Library board representatives, Merle Brooks, Grace Eckert, Audrey Williams, Pearl Hodges and Jane Arend met with school librarians, Vena Anderson and Elizabeth Warder from Branson and Madge Schimpf and Connie Jones from Hollister, who helped select the suggested children's books and reference material.

As the library club members canvassed their neighbors and friends for donations for the new building, they thought about their own annual dues, which were still five dollars despite many years of inflation. The club, when the point was made, voted to change the dues to ten dollars a year. Despite fears that the raise might be a hardship for some members, the club roll continued to grow.

Meantime the women were busy selling tickets to a benefit performance promised by the Foggy River Boys. In 1974, this popular singing group had moved from Kimberling City, joining the Mabe Brothers' Baldknobbers Show and Presleys' Mountain Music Jubilee in entertaining visiting tourists out on Highway 76 west of Branson. None of those first three theaters were very large in the mid-1970s, and the fourteen hundred dollars thus raised for the new library building meant that the Foggies played to a full house and a very appreciative audience.

Tickets also were sold to a benefit performance at the Shepherd of the Hills farm. The weather was cold and miserable that evening,

Bringing Books to the Ozarks

but cheering the game actors on kept the audience warmed up, and the contribution was much appreciated.

Additional help came from Mildred Beck, a former library club member who had moved to Arizona but shipped back a large quantity of her handcrafted items which were sold for the benefit of the library.

In the midst of the pressures of fund-raising and preparations for beginning construction, Jane Arend learned of an original portrait of Harold Bell Wright as a young man which might be for sale. Tracking the picture down took some imaginative sleuthing, but before summer arrived she journeyed to Carbondale, Illinois, and returned to Branson with a fine portrait of the writer whose book continued to play an important role in the support and growth of the library. The previous owner of the portrait, when told the story of the Taneyhills Library, had sold it to Jane for fifty dollars.

That spring, many local workmen, plumbers and carpenters offered their services in the construction of the library. The building site had been cleared, without charge, by Epps Sanitation Company, and Rozell Engineering surveyed and staked the building site and provided blueprints at no charge as well. On May 25, without a great deal of fanfare, ground was broken, and Leon and Walter Wagner began excavating the hillside to provide a flat foundation, donating their equipment and time. But they were digging in an Ozark hill. With all the dirt removed, they were

The Fever Mounts

faced with sloping layers of hard rock and could go no further.

June rains turned the half-completed, rock-bound hole into a swimming pool. Then Robert Youngblood brought in a larger bulldozer, broke up and cleared away a lot of rock, and opened the downhill end to establish some drainage, but still the hole was not large nor deep enough. Finally a blasting specialist was paid to complete the excavation, which along with the added expense of insurance, was not planned for in the building budget. Fortunately, thanks to a sizable gift, cash was on hand to get that phase completed.

Meantime, at the June club meeting, with the building still only a hole in the ground, Betty Yates was installed as the 1976-77 president; Norma Root, vice president; Jinx Rives, treasurer, and Irene Lewis, recording secretary.

The cornerstone ceremonies were held on Flag Day, June 14th, during a city-wide bicentennial celebration. The day's events were coordinated by Dr. Everett Hendricks, who was master of ceremonies that day. A band made up of local school children marched in the preceding parade and played for the ceremonies. Those youngsters and many actors from the Shepherd of the Hills pageant wore costumes depicting some book for the parade and ceremonies.

For days visitors to the Security Bank and the Peoples Bank had signed parchment copies of the Declaration of Independence which would be placed in the library's cornerstone. The enthusi-

Bringing Books to the Ozarks

Jane Arend, Betty Yates, Josephine Madry, Bill Ellen Hall, and Jeannette Street (left to right) admire the cornerstone during the June 1976 dedication ceremonies.

asm of civic and church leaders, representatives of The School of the Ozarks, and the many library patrons and club members also on hand for the ceremonies at the building site left little doubt concerning local feelings about the prospects of a new library building.

During the ceremony, contractors Richard Townsend and Gerald Oney, who had agreed to erect the library at cost, were introduced. Another big boost came from the Branson Civic League, whose president, Juanita Thompson, presented the library club with a check for $10,000. Local school children, who had filled their decorated coffee cans with pennies, dimes

The Fever Mounts

and dollars during Library Week, brought forward a hundred and twelve dollars for their new library, and junior high students brought a hundred dollars, the proceeds from their benefit basketball game. Also the generous woman whose donation had made possible the purchase of the building site handed over a second check for $14,000!

In fact, so many people were giving so much in donated services as well as money, that Jane Arend commented that it would be difficult to ever establish when the $100,000 goal was reached.

The applause was loud and long when Miss Martha Washington of Neosho, Missouri, stepped up to unveil the time capsule which would go into the building's cornerstone.

And before Dr. John Moad, vice president for public relations at The School of the Ozarks, gave the benediction, he declared, "This dedication today is a symbol of American freedom. This library assures those who come in the years ahead freedom of learning."

In the following weeks, action was intense at the building site. Cement trucks poured foundations and the ground floor, steel girders and beams were locked in place, close set to support the heavily reinforced second story floor which would have to bear the load of rank after rank of heavily laden book shelves. Small children and their parents often gathered to watch the giant "erector set" pieces bolted and buckled in place, and fascinated citizens volunteered their help,

Bringing Books to the Ozarks

hoping to learn how such a building was put together.

The summer was at its height on July 4th, when Hollister's firemen shot off a brilliant fireworks display at the school yard atop Candy Mountain. That afternoon there had been a boat regatta on Lake Taneycomo, a floating parade to make even the most diffident person fill with pride in his nation. The status of the ancient oak tree on the Branson waterfront, a "200 year old monument of our nation's history," was recognized with a plaque placed at its base.

Through the rest of the summer and fall, as the library roof went on and metal walls were fitted with windows and bricked to the eaves, the two hundred or more members of the club continued their "season of fund raisers" into a second year, repeating the events of the previous fall and planning a Halloween carnival, including an old-fashioned box supper and a cakewalk. Before the day of the carnival, the exterior of the building was completed, and though the interior walls and plumbing were yet to be installed, Delores German quickly organized a giant rummage sale, soliciting clothing, dishes, furniture, and bric-a-brac from attics all over western Taney County.

The sale netted the building fund twelve hundred and thirty-seven dollars and promises of enough donated materials and volunteer help to finish much of the interior of the library. The building committee was greatly relieved, for the cost of the basic building exceeded that initial goal of $50,000 by ten percent.

The Fever Mounts

Shortly after the rummage sale, a full page advertisement was placed in the *Branson Beacon* listing the fittings and equipment still needed, thanking everyone for making this "impossible dream" a reality, and asking,

> Will you be a friend of the new community library -- or an "associate member" of the Taneyhills Library club? Construction of the beautiful home of the Taneyhills Community Library is now complete ... But unfortunately building funds are also depleted!

Area residents were offered their first look inside the completed library on Friday and Saturday, December 10th and 11th, during an open house featuring three fashion show performances.

Twenty-two models showed holiday fashions from local stores: the Band-Box, Brite's Clothing, Corner One, Jeri's Glad Rags, and Man's Land. Footwear came from Reish's and Mark III, and hairstyling was done by Mr. Lyle's Beauty Lounge and Gary's Coiffures. The professional presentation was chaired by Pat Shue, with Delores German heading the luncheon committee and Karol Hunter handling ticket sales.

The following Wednesday, December 15, with much help from members of the Branson Downtown Business and Professional Association and other volunteers, the books, shelves and other library equipment were moved the three uphill blocks from Highway 65 and Pacific

Bringing Books to the Ozarks

to the new library at Fourth and Pacific.

An article titled "Library opens in Branson, 18-month funds job goes on," written by new library club member Kathleen Van Buskirk, appeared in the *Springfield Leader-Press* the day of the move. The story began,

> There are 200 homes in western Taney County that may be decorated a bit late this Christmas. Members of the Taneyhills Community Library club in Branson have been moving the public library ...(to) its new home today.

The story went on to tell of the library's 43-year history and on-going efforts to get the new building completed and paid for.

Indeed, Christmas of 1976 found many library club members utterly exhausted after months of fast-paced activities. Especially so was Jane Arend. That year, in addition to chairing the building and planning committee, she was serving on the library board and head of the corporate board. She had held office in the club since shortly after she first paid dues in 1970. Now that the building was finished, the new year would bring new expenses and the challenge of training volunteers to help in day to day operations.

In early January, Merle Brooks reported to the executive board that the old library room was properly scrubbed and left in good condition. A letter of heartfelt thanks had been sent to the

The Fever Mounts

The New Library Building was Completed in 1977.

American Legion Post, for their patience and generosity as hosts to Branson's library over the past forty years.

On a bright day in April, 1977, the gentle ramp leading to the library doors was bathed in sunlight; red, white and blue bunting hung from the railing and eaves. The main entry doors and sidelights, the focal point of planned dedication ceremonies, were decorated with colorful drawings in a book and springtime theme.

Seventh District Congressman Gene Taylor, the featured speaker, praised the successful completion of the library building, declaring, "The historic independence and resourcefulness of the people of the Ozarks still lives and is perfectly illustrated in the completion of this new library."

Bringing Books to the Ozarks

Returning to Washington, Taylor submitted for publication in the *Congressional Record* a story written for the March, 1977, issue of The *Ozarks Mountaineer* magazine by Kathleen Van Buskirk, titled "The Library Built by Sharing."

In the record of the House of Representatives, Tuesday, April 26, 1977, Mr. Taylor states,

> Mr. Speaker, while more and more of our citizens seem to be looking to the Federal Government to solve more and more of their problems, I am proud to state that we still have those rugged individuals down in the Ozark Hills who firmly believe in themselves and their ability to care for their own needs without calling on the Government for assistance.
>
> On Sunday Afternoon, April 24, it was my privilege to participate in the results of such an endeavor, the dedication of the new Taneyhills Community Library located in Branson, Mo.
>
> The new $100,000 library building was financed by club funds, donations, and financial aid from many groups. In addition, volunteer services and materials, plus a low interest loan were added in.
>
> Mr. Speaker, the Taneyhills Community Library was built with the same spirit that created this nation. It is an outstanding example of what people can do for themselves and their community when they work together to reach a common goal.
>
> Kathleen Van Buskirk recently reviewed the history of the library in an article that was published in The Ozarks Mountaineer. I would like to

The Fever Mounts

submit that story so that my colleagues might also share in this rewarding endeavor.

The entire article, a brief history of the library, its supporting club, and the successful completion of the new building, is thus recorded forever in the annals of our country's history.

CHAPTER XX

PROPERTY OWNERS ANONYMOUS
(1977 - 1992)

With the dedication festivities ended, the responsibilities and challenges of owning, planning for, operating and supporting the Taneyhills Community Library did not permit the members of the library club to rest on their laurels.

The library's eighteen thousand books were shelved in their spacious new home. Well into the spring of 1977, however, work crews, both professionals and volunteers, still were installing lights and plumbing fixtures, finishing the inside walls and ceilings, and laying carpets. Suggestions for equipping and furnishing the rest of the library abounded. Patrons, young and old, looked to the library for much anticipated activities as well as more new books, and, with the building fund depleted, and the interior finishing still being paid for, every bill loomed large.

And then there was that contract to buy the small house and lot just east of the new library. A special donation had covered the thousand dollar down payment. The other five thousand

Property Owners Anonymous

was to be paid off at fifty dollars a month.

Before those payments could become a problem, an answer came which probably was a surprise only to newcomers to Branson. Betty Yates had not yet passed the president's gavel on to Florence Camp that spring when the library board received a request from the Skaggs Hospital Auxiliary to rent the little house for the Auxiliary's thrift shop, The Pink Door. Proceeds from sales would cover the rent. Any further profits would be used in support of the Auxiliary's hospital projects. Quickly the library board consulted the club board, then set about arranging for a business use permit for the house, which had, in the past, been a family home.

During Florence Camp's two years as president, the library benefited also from several other profitable ventures and some unexpected gifts.

When Grace Hart joined the library club in March, 1977, her enthusiasm was very apparent, and quickly came to the clubwomen's minds when she died only two months later. Her name was etched permanently in the memories of the members involved in the 1977 building project, for from her estate came the five thousand dollars which paid off the last of the building debt!

That final payment was presented to bank president Foster Plummer at the guest night dinner in September, 1978. Plummer, accepting the check from Florence Camp and the club treasurer, Kathy Hartel, turned to the microphone and said, "Ladies, I never thought you could do it!"

Bringing Books to the Ozarks

A permanent fund, established by the family of Eve and Jack Griffith as a memorial honoring their late parents, paid for landscaping the library grounds. Mayme Boren chaired the committee to plan and oversee the landscaping. Her assistants included a long list of helpers, both members and friends of the library. Twenty years later that memorial continues to fund the library's landscaping projects.

For several years, the upper level of the new building, more than twice the size of the room in the Community Building, was quite adequate for all of the library's book collection. The lower level included two side rooms, rest rooms, kitchen and serving area, and a large room that extended the length of the building. In 1977, that seventy-five foot long room was used for the children's summer story hours and library club events. It also was rented part time to various groups, which helped pay utility bills.

The children's story hour, long a popular feature of the Taneyhills Library program, was inaugurated in the new building by Marjorie Gilbert and Vena Anderson as soon as the doors were opened for business. Those story hours continue in the juvenile library today, encouraging lively, giggling youngsters to share their exuberance among the books, thus developing a kinship with the library and with reading.

In 1978, with the club still in high gear from the building campaign, Carol Bingham, head of the ways and means committee pushed sales of *The Shepherd of the Hills* books. Before that year

Property Owners Anonymous

ended she was forced to ask for help in making deliveries, orders having soared to almost eleven thousand books. Success followed success. In May, 1979, Adelyn Valett planned a house tour which attracted crowds of members, friends, and strangers, all anxious to view the interiors of six of the area's most elegant homes and willing to pay two dollars and fifty cents for the privilege.

The following month, Adelyn was installed as club president, and through the 1979-1980 year, her stage trained demeanor lent grace and charm to the group's regular meetings. While she was president, the library and club leaders, concerned by problems related to renting the lower level of the library for other organizations' meetings, decided to lease the space, on a part-time basis, to one responsible church or club group. The Church of Jesus Christ of Latter Day Saints was the first and only such lessee.

That year and through the 1980s the library club, leaning heavily on Adelyn's experience in directing plays and professional fashion shows, produced a style show each spring, usually presented in cooperation with local clothing stores. The profits, of course, all went to maintain and operate the library.

The 1979 promenade of styles, held downstairs in the library, was chaired by Rose Merritt, who operated a fine clothing store in the Civic League's building downtown. On her committee were Betty Stewart and Sherry Gerard. The club's style show the following year, co-chaired by Sherry Gerard and Anne Cox, with Mary

Bringing Books to the Ozarks

Elizabeth Cox as commentator, was a stage production, "Parade Pastel," presented before an appreciative audience which filled Jones Auditorium at The School of the Ozarks.

In June, 1980, after a very successful year as president, Adelyn turned over the gavel to her neighbor and friend, Nadine Miller. That annual meeting was truly a gala occasion. The lower level of the library was being named Denham Hall, and invitations were sent to all past presidents of the library club with a special invitation to the group's first president, Pearl Denham.

It was a heart-warming afternoon, with twelve of the twenty-two living past presidents on hand to admire the spacious building and share their most memorable experiences as library club president.

The incoming president, Nadine Miller spoke of her membership in the club during the early 1940s, her long absence during World War II, and of renewing her membership in 1966 when her children were grown. In the 1980s, she was living beside Table Rock Lake ten miles south of Branson. Widowed, she devoted many active years to the Taneyhills Library. In the year of her presidency, more than seven hundred new books were added to the library's collection, seven hundred and sixty-seven new borrowers were added to the patrons' list, and circulation increased to twenty-seven thousand eight hundred.

Before Nadine's year as president ended, the members were treated to another private fashion show. All the outfits that day were homemade

Property Owners Anonymous

Funny Fashion Show. After the Laughter had Died Down, (left to right) Rosemary Rose, Cathy Hunt, Mayme Boren, Ruth Mulroe, Edith Felix, and Lorraine Humphrey pose in their comedic costumes at the October 1980 Funny Fashion Show.

creations. Norma Root wore a ball gown featuring several tennis, pingpong and basketballs hung from shoulders to shins, and Lorraine Humphrey, creator of many publicity releases about the library, modeled a print dress, newsprint, that is.

Of course, the women also shared a more formal fashion show that year. "An Ozarks Spring Fling," again held in the Jones Auditorium, featured several square dance groups and was organized by Adelyn Valett and Florence Camp. The president of the college, Dr. M. Graham Clark, participated in the program, and his many contributions to the community and the library were

Bringing Books to the Ozarks

Library Club Officers 1981-82.
(left to right) standing. Sherry Gerard, Mary Thompson, Carol Defebaugh, Marie Tammay, Virginia Martin, Nadine Miller, and Lois Moran; seated. president Arden Cargin, Shirley Mizell, Florence Camp, and Adelyn Valett.

recognized with an honorary membership in the Taneyhills Library Club, the first man to be thus honored.

In 1976, the club had, in the midst of their building drive, adopted a fourth category of membership, so that active members could choose to pay a sum which was then equal to ten year's dues and become an active "Life Member," an option which several dedicated library workers had elected by 1980.

Arden Cargin, installed as president that June, provided the club enthusiastic leadership in the year when the group's budget first exceed-

Property Owners Anonymous

ed twenty thousand dollars. An avid fisherman, her favorite sport brought humorous boating and fishing tales into the monthly club meetings and social conversations. Her artistic nature was reflected in the library, where old mismatched shelves were replaced with standard sized metal ones and Denham Hall got a new coat of paint. A copy machine, installed in the upstairs workroom, offered new services to library patrons and simplified many tasks for the librarian, her volunteer assistants, and the club.

Marie Gibson Tammay was elected president for the club's Golden Anniversary year. The shy young winner in the 1935 essay contest presided in 1982-83 with poise and confidence, an outgoing woman recently retired after a long successful career in New York City.

Soon after Marie took office, Norma Root was hired as librarian. Norma joined the club in 1971, when she and her husband, Floyd, retired from their jobs in Kansas City and moved to Hollister. As librarian, her friendly, outgoing personality, wry humor, and dedication to the library endeared her to the volunteer assistants and library patrons.

The spring of 1983 was a time of great celebration in the Taneyhills Library. That April the club would enter its fiftieth year, and the entire community was invited to an open house and reception in the library.

The day of the open house, patrons, club members, and many neighbors who had not previously visited the new building, wandered

Bringing Books to the Ozarks

Golden Anniversary Tree.
Each fruit bears the description of a fund-raising project which contributed to the support of the library between 1933 & 1983.

among the books on the upper level, then went downstairs to enjoy punch and homemade cookies. There they were greeted by a huge colorful tree, painted floor to ceiling across the windowless west wall of Denham Hall, laden with fruits, each globe bearing information about one of the scores of fund-raisers which had supported the library since 1933.

When the celebration ended, several members wanted the Library Tree left on the wall. Instead it was painted over and bookshelves were installed along the walls of Denham Hall. By early 1984, the juvenile books were moved downstairs amid furnishings to fit the needs of pre-school through high school boys and girls.

Property Owners Anonymous

Soon many youngsters were rushing into the library after school and heading straight for the stairs and their own special library.

The juvenile library was developed during the 1983-85 presidency of Barbara Boone. Conditioned to volunteering and club work by many years as wife of a navy pilot, Barbara accepted the job of vice president of finance just months after becoming a member in 1980. While she held that position, *Treasured Recipes Book II* went on sale, *Shepherd of the Hills* book sales flourished, a lake cruise was organized, and several fund-raising card parties, bake sales, and a holiday home tour were held. Barbara also was responsible for the library's float "Book Worms Have More Fun," which won third place in the Branson Adoration Parade's "non-religious category" on December 5, 1982.

In her first year as president, Barbara helped establish a "development fund" with a goal of $250,000, or half the projected cost of enlarging the library building. The bylaws were up-dated, and monthly newsletters brought club and library news and information to everyone present at each luncheon.

Through that year, more than a third of the budgeted $21,576 was covered by the annual four thousand dollars interest on the Civic League's Shepherd of the Hills Farm note and rents from Denham Hall and the Pink Door. The rent on Denham Hall also was anticipated in the 1984-85 budget which, reflecting current rampant inflation and the expense of reshaping and

Bringing Books to the Ozarks

furnishing the juvenile library rooms, jumped to fifty thousand dollars.

Soon after the juvenile library opened in Denham Hall, however, the eighteen hundred dollars annual rent from the Mormon congregation disappeared from the club's monthly receipts. Rearranging furniture two times a week for church services caused too many problems, and the lease was not renewed.

The coming year definitely was going to be a challenge. Library supporters would simply have to work harder at fund-raising.

On April 25, 1985, as Barbara Boone's presidency drew to an end, the library supporters received a welcome morale booster when the Tri-Lakes Council of the International Reading Association presented its annual Literacy Award to the Taneyhills Community Library.

When Florene Stilwell assumed the presidency in June, she reviewed the club's projected expenses and quietly set to work. Before that year ended, the Pink Door was moved to a new building in Hollister, and she found herself working even more diligently.

In the crucial days after the Pink Door's removal, library club members and their husbands refurbished the old house for a shop of their own which, at Norma Root's suggestion, was immediately dubbed the 2nd Edition Thrift Shop. The club also arranged to purchase a small, much abused house on a lot across the alley, facing on College Street, and several of the men began its reconstruction. The damaged old

Property Owners Anonymous

house was transformed into a charming Consignment Shop where people put their unwanted goods on display for sale, and shared their profits with the library.

Florene's husband, Bill, who helped rejuvenate the consignment shop, also created a fine ink drawing of the library building, for use on a brochure advertising the library and its many services.

With the active support of her husband, Florene led the organization through that year and the next, managing the club, encouraging the library and thrift shop volunteers, solidly behind each money-raising event, and helping engineer the purchase of the College Street property.

The annual "Library Associates" and "Friends of the Library" fund drives were expanded. An audio-visual room was established after Barbara Boone and her husband George installed shelves in a conveniently located closet near the front desk. And finally, after taking stock of the area's growth rate, the club members reluctantly voted to reinvigorate the long dormant expansion fund, which had stalled at $40,000.

Renewed interest in the expansion fund came hard on the heels of another financial decision made that spring, the establishment of a Perpetual Trust Fund which, club leaders hoped, would one day assure support of the Taneyhills Library. It was a step which the two surviving members of Branson's Civic League had been hoping for. A few weeks before Rose Merritt's

Bringing Books to the Ozarks

death in August, 1987, Juanita Thompson arranged to donate the $34,000 remaining in the League's account and the Shepherd of the Hills Farm note to the library's newly established perpetual trust fund, and officially disbanded the Civic League.

Norma Root brought further excitement to the library's supporters in the spring of 1987, when she was selected by the Missouri Library Association to receive its "Outstanding New Librarian Award." Having completed the college courses required for a librarian's certificate, Norma had for some time been encouraging reading and use of the library through an engaging weekly newspaper column written under the byline "Dusty Shelf." Her friendly, knowledgeable presence in the library won the hearts of patrons and volunteer librarians alike. Now she was invited to St. Louis to receive this very special award. When family obligations made it impossible for her to be at the award ceremony, Ruth and Truman Benson made the trip and accepted the award in Norma's behalf.

That June, Ruth Benson was installed as president of the library club, and had the pleasure of presenting the librarian her award at the club's September meeting.

Ruth had served in several offices since joining the club in 1981. Most recently, as vice president of membership, she spent much time recruiting new members and actively encouraging volunteer participation.

Through two terms as president, Ruth kept in

Property Owners Anonymous

close contact with the 2nd Edition Thrift Shop and the Consignment shop, and participated actively in the Friends of the Library campaign. She also monitored an "Improved Reading Center of Missouri" program for local high school seniors. And she donated a beautiful handmade afghan which brought more funds for the library.

In the spring of 1989, with the library facilities in full use and planners looking at expansion within five years, the building fund showed little increase. The president and the club board faced a frustrating situation. Many of the club women were serving as officers, chairmen or committee members and at least half the members were working from a half day to virtually full time each month staffing the library and the two shops. On the other hand, with several of the older members moving elsewhere, or in ill health, in the past three years the club's membership had dropped from two hundred and twenty-eight to a hundred and eighty-three.

In the years following the completion of the library building, the monthly meetings themselves had changed. From the earliest days of the club, a committee of three to five women had made meeting plans, deciding on the menu and meeting place, and calling on other members to help plan and carry out special events.

When the building drive began in the mid-1970s, monthly luncheons were being held at the Branson Inn's White Frog Restaurant, north of town on U.S. 65. That restaurant ceased operation a short time after the library was completed. The clubwomen, who had been pooling their S & H Green stamps to exchange for folding tables and chairs for library readers, increased their goals to include sufficient tables and chairs to serve refreshments to all who attended the club's meetings. Through much of the 1980s, a rotating "hostess committee" of twelve members planned and served a dessert or salad luncheon in Denham Hall each month.

After that space was restructured for the ever-expanding juvenile library, rearranging and setting up tables and chairs for each meeting gradually became too disruptive for the library and too much of a burden for the women who were providing the food. In 1988, arrangements were made to use a large meeting room in the Branson Methodist Church for the club's luncheons. Each month's hostesses provided the dessert or salad, prepared in their own homes and served from the church kitchen.

When the club gathered at the Methodist Church for their election meeting in June, 1989, Florene Stilwell was again being installed as president, and Ruth Eastman, just completing a term as vice president of programs, was about to take on the role of vice president of finance. Ruth was pleased with the substantial surplus from the previous year, and determined to improve on it. After hearing the report that the building fund had grown to $64,000, but was a long way from the $250,000 needed to start the addition, Ruth made an impassioned plea for support in actively seeking funds to expand the library building.

Property Owners Anonymous

As soon as such a resolution was passed, she challenged the women to each make an extended pledge, a hundred dollars per year for five years, if possible. Ruth knew she had strong allies in the new president, and in Barbara Boone, who was efficiently managing both shops at that time. Through the summer, as pledges trickled in, plans were roughed out for doubling the size of the library.

Before the first fall meeting however, Barbara's husband George died. To allow her freedom to sort out her personal affairs, management and oversight of the shops was simplified and taken on by daily chairmen.

At year's end, the consignment shop, its profits lagging far behind those of the thrift shop, was closed just long enough to allow all consigners to claim their unsold goods. The donated stock was divided between the two thrift shops and both re-opened in early 1990.

The loss of George Boone, who had for ten years actively assisted wherever he was needed in the library and shops, helped bring the question of accepting men to full library club membership up for active debate. Certainly, for many years, and especially since the construction of the library building, the women of the club frequently had looked to men of the community for assistance.

Late that fall, the board proposed that membership be opened to men and, with little dissent, the club agreed that the bylaws should be edited to remove all gender specific wording.

Bringing Books to the Ozarks

That editing, which sounded simple, had to be repeated several times before the process was deemed complete.

The first man who applied for membership was Allen Brackin, who had been a library volunteer since the early 1970s, when he was a student at The School of the Ozarks. After graduating from college, he found employment on the evening shift at the White River Valley Electric Cooperative, Inc., and continued to devote many of his daytime hours to helping in the library.

Men did not rush to become members, but several already staunch supporters quietly joined over the next two or three years: Max Hromek, Bill Stilwell, honorary member Dr. M. Graham Clark, and retired educators John Mizell and Ralph Sellmeyer. Others, including many longtime "Friends of the Library," elected not to become active members, but continued their quiet assistance.

When the question of opening membership to men was being considered, many of the women had the same "building" problem on their minds. During the years when the lower floor was being used for library club meetings as well as for the juvenile library, a folding door had been installed closing off the back twenty-five feet of the main room so club equipment could be stored there. However, by late 1990 the small room being used for juvenile non-fiction books was filled to overflowing, and the folding door was moved to open up that potential shelf space for the young people's reference section and close off the serving

Property Owners Anonymous

room behind the kitchen for use as a board room.

In the spring of 1991, bookcases were installed along the back walls, similar to those already in place, and the three rows of free-standing stacks, one shelf shorter than those used upstairs, were moved from the small room to fill the center of the new area. Later, the large, heavily illustrated "Q" books, which the young people loved, were moved to those stacks as well, relieving overcrowding upstairs. To complete the improvements, the small room which had held the reference section, was refitted as an "easy reader" room.

Upstairs there now was room for readers to truly enjoy the handsome, sturdy reading table and four upholstered armchairs Carmen Cole Gerard had donated in 1988, dedicated to the memory of her parents, James and Blanche Cole, and the similar set donated by Ruth and Truman Benson the following year.

As the library board prepared for the annual Children's Summer Story Hour, the club re-elected Florene Stilwell for another year as president, her fourth term in the past six years, and nominated Barbara Boone for honorary membership.

After her mother died early that spring, Barbara had traveled to California to deal with her grief and sort out plans for her future among long time friends. Her leadership abilities and willingness to take on complicated projects would be missed.

Meanwhile, the library's copy machine, one of

Bringing Books to the Ozarks

the staff's most used tools, was developing serious problems.

At the beginning of 1991, Norma Root accepted delivery of several boxes of income tax forms and instructions, and notebooks filled with master copies of forms, as she had every winter for eight years. With practiced speed she made a place for them in the library work room near the front desk.

Since 1983, the Internal Revenue Service had relied on the nation's county and town libraries to make available in each community the materials citizens might need in preparing to pay their income taxes. Librarians were directed to give out the various materials, but never to provide any help or advice.

Even with that restriction, January through April 15th became the busiest time of the year in the Taneyhills Community Library. In April, 1991, the librarian breathed a sigh of relief that the frequently complaining copier had survived another tax season. Through the spring, visits from the repairman were more and more frequent.

That summer, as the weary machine groaned through the copying of the yearbook pages and the first monthly newsletter of the fall season, the library board, with the approval of the club board, appointed a committee to evaluate and purchase a new copier. The committee members, all of whom were frequent users of the old machine, lost no time in following those instructions, and a new copier was in place before the

Property Owners Anonymous

club's September meeting.

While the aging copier was struggling to survive the 1991 tax season, Adelyn Valett was organizing the library's first Annual Art Competition and Exhibition for Branson and Hollister high school students.

For a week the students' art projects were displayed on the walls and along the tops of the bookcases in Denham Hall, and club members were invited to study them and vote for their choice of best entries from each high school.

At an open house and reception held at the end of the week, the two first place winners each received a fifty dollar scholarship to assist with their continuing art education.

That year's weekly Summer Story Hours for four to eight-year-olds drew an average of fifty per session, and more than a hundred youngsters ages six through twelve registered for the reading program and enjoyed a record number of books through the summer months.

In early August Marie Buck passed away. A dedicated library club member since 1973, who had served two three-year terms on the library board, and worked many hours in the thrift shop, she left a thousand dollars to the library's Perpetual Trust Fund. When her family also donated much of her household furnishings to the library, the new club president, Arden Cargin, and her husband, Clad, emptied Marie's house as requested and, on August 28th, everything was sold in the parking area at the south end of the library.

Bringing Books to the Ozarks

A few days later the club met for its the first meeting being held in the student cafeteria at the College of the Ozarks (the name of The School of the Ozarks having been changed in the summer of 1990). As the members sat down to a delicious luncheon, prepared and served by the professional staff assisted by students working their way through college, everyone was talking about the parking lot sale, which had netted over a thousand dollars. That money also went into the Perpetual Trust Fund, a fitting memorial for Marie Buck.

Later that fall, after six months of observing the harried thrift shop "chairmen of the day" trying to round up helpers on a day by day basis, Arden established a permanent thrift shop committee with Dolly Hromek and Virginia Bell as co-chairmen. Their first major decision, carried out by the beginning of 1992, was to consolidate both shops in the Pacific Street house and use the house on College for sorting and marking.

Early in the new year, furniture and stacks on the library's upper level were rearranged to make room for a third library table and four chairs, the second set offered by Carmen Cole Gerard. The Library Board authorized the acceptance of the third set despite the fact that the upstairs, so recently freed from congestion by moving books to the lower floor, would again be losing precious "moving around room."

In April the juvenile library was spruced up for the art show, being planned this year by Darlene Rea. Publicity about the event pro-

Property Owners Anonymous

claimed the juried contest the "Adelyn Valett Art Competition and Exhibition," in honor of its organizer. Just three months later, Adelyn passed away, and the annual event became her memorial.

That spring, as Arden prepared to turn over the president's gavel to Darlene Rea, the library club members voted to award honorary memberships to Norma Root and five other hard working, long-time volunteers: Ruth Benson, Eleanor Goltz, Lois Moran, Marie Tammay and Annie Wheeler. In making those awards, it was noted that the six honorees had served a total of sixty-nine years in various club offices, spent uncounted hours raising money for the library, and worked regularly as library volunteers and in the thrift shops. Barbara Boone, the most recent honoree already on the club's list, was on hand in June to offer her congratulations, having returned that spring to her lakeside home in Hollister.

The retiring president was experiencing health problems, and later that year, after the death of her husband, Arden wound up her affairs in Branson and moved to her former home in Mallard, Iowa, to be near other family members.

Darlene Rea, wife of Peter Rea, a prominent Branson lawyer, had been an active member since 1989. As president of the library club she was taking on the responsibility for a sizable business. The budget approved for the library and club in 1992-93 exceeded $53,000. There

Bringing Books to the Ozarks

was $142,000 in the building fund. Darlene looked forward to her responsibilities with a youthful vigor and enthusiasm which was to bolster the members through two years in which the pressures of overcrowding in the library steadily increased.

CHAPTER XXI

MOVING INTO THE COMPUTER AGE
(1992 - 1998)

In 1992, after years of moderate but constant growth, of reaping the fruits of friendliness and cooperative advertising, of getting acquainted with new attractions a few at a time, Branson's entertainment world became the focus for a "Sixty-Minutes" segment on national television. Overnight the stampede was underway to build more theaters for more shows, and provide more motels and restaurants to house and feed the ballooning crowds of fans already arriving.

Many young families, drawn by the promise of jobs, swelled the permanent population and brought new challenges to local housing, schools, and public services, including the Taneyhills Community Library.

The growth and excitement which gripped Branson and surrounding communities in 1992 as famous musical stars and groups took up residence in the area, brought many new demands to librarian Norma Root and her volunteers.

High school students rushing in after school to find materials for reports, which seemed

Bringing Books to the Ozarks

always to be due "tomorrow" and often involved the newest events in Branson, found themselves competing with reporters from local newspapers and national magazines. The library staff issued cards to families of well known stars and sometimes to the stars themselves, with the same neighborly friendliness extended to all the library's patrons.

At first musicians and actors seeking information about their trade found the library woefully lacking, but the librarians always tried to help in any way possible. Longtime patrons and Branson's new arrivals alike were thrilled that year, when the Branson Arts Council donated for check out whole shelves-full of cultural videos on ballet, the classics, museums, and arts and crafts. Norma was delighted with these donations despite the lack of an adequate place to shelve them. And installation of new touch-tone telephones reopened the door to interlibrary loans and many other services for all the library's patrons.

Checkouts in 1992 reached a record 50,600, and the librarian found herself juggling the requests of newcomers and the expectations of longtime patrons as she placed her book orders. Before the year was out she blessed the many donors whose gifts of money and books stretched her ability to fill those requests.

Norma's sense of humor could usually be counted on to resolve intimidating problems and get through difficult moments in the library. One of her favorite stories, truly a triumph as a librar-

Moving into the Computer Age

ian, involved the large print books. In the 1980s, the *Reader's Digest Magazine,* as a service to the vision impaired, began publishing a large print edition. First as donations and then by regular subscription, those oversized *Reader's Digests* were made available in Branson's library. When publishers began offering popular books in large print editions, Norma ordered several novels and biographies in large print, hoping to meet the many complaints about the "tiny" type in so many new books.

"But no one checked them out," Norma remembered, wryly. "Readers who should be enjoying them were avoiding them like the plague, apparently thinking a white cane or a seeing eye dog was required as proof of need. So I did the sensible thing, and ordered several bestsellers only in large print."

By 1992, the large print collection totaled seven hundred volumes, and included general fiction, mysteries, westerns, biographies and non-fiction. Today that collection is one of the library's very popular sections, filling several stacks. But, just in case, Norma never stopped ordering some of the best new books only in large print.

That summer Darlene Rea took office as president of the library club and began coping with the problems of fund-raising and dealing with questions such as who was responsible for the upkeep of the two thrift shops and the maintenance of their surrounding yards. The library's annual book budget, including some seventeen

Bringing Books to the Ozarks

Admiring the Proceeds of Yet Another Fund-Raiser
are Darlene Rea, Glenda McCormick, and Mary Holmes,
all library club presidents in the 1990's.

hundred dollars for subscriptions and videos, was nearly $10,000, and Norma Root's annual "half-time" salary was raised to seven thousand five hundred dollars. By the following spring, with revenues through the past year exceeding the budgeted needs by almost $22,000, and the projected budget for the coming year almost $60,000, Darlene accepted a second year as president, but was firmly convinced that her successor needed to be better prepared for the responsibilities of leading the Taneyhills Library Club!

Too late to affect the 1993 election, the club

Moving into the Computer Age

Library Club Officers 1994-1995. (left to right) Eleanor Goltz, Glenda McCormick, Alice Gatchell, president Darlene Rea, Barbara Boone, Helen Williams and Shirley Mizell.

approved the addition of the office of president-elect. Glenda McCormick, who was installed as first vice president in charge of programs that June, spent the summer arranging programs for the coming year. That task accomplished, at the September meeting she agreed to accept the added role of president-elect. In that new position, she was to spend the rest of the club year learning more about Darlene's responsibilities as president, and the organization and operation of the library and club, while at the same time assisting the president and presiding in her absence. In June, 1994, she was to automatical-

Bringing Books to the Ozarks

ly succeed to the presidency.

At the September, 1993, meeting members heard reports of the summer's popular reading and story hour programs, and learned that the price of new books had risen again, so the charge on rental books had been raised to fifty cents a week. It also was announced that a committee had been established to investigate costs and draw up plans to computerize the library.

All else paled that day, before the news that the building fund now exceeded $250,000 and it was time to draw up plans for enlarging the library!

The months before Christmas were filled with consultations and committee meetings. Building plans began appearing on paper. Members who had been involved in building the present library were consulted. Advice was sought from the library's advisory board and from members, husbands, and friends whose experience included large building projects. Tentative floor plans left on the conference room table gave rise to other helpful suggestions.

Special projects for library patrons continued. In late 1993, College of the Ozarks professor Fred Pfister, backed by a grant from the Missouri Humanities Council, organized an evening book/film discussion group which met in the library twice monthly through the ensuing spring. At the first meeting each month, a modern regional classic book was discussed. The following week enthusiastic participants viewed a film based on the book and discussed the ways

Moving into the Computer Age

in which the story and its telling had been altered for better or for worse.

There was a ferment in the library as 1994 began. In mid-March, amid the daily stream of harried citizens seeking tax forms, Allen Brackin, with permission to develop a plan for a comprehensive computer system, began translating his months of study into "cable systems and computer stations." Norma Root worked overtime up-dating the library's book list to be sent away for barcoding.

In April, Dorotha Douglas, author of the library's cookbooks, returned to the area from her present home in Kansas for a visit and took time to entertain the littlest readers with a special story hour. Later that month and into May the current year's artworks by local high school students were again on display in Denham Hall. This time the entries were professionally juried and after the awards tea, the top recipient from each school was invited to attend the club's May luncheon to receive a fifty dollar scholarship.

That spring there was no let up for the finance committee, Barbara Boone or her untiring assistants Florene Stilwell and Virginia Bell, nor for the many project managers and thrift shop workers. Few will forget the day that famous author Janet Dailey, who had been enlisted to co-chair the building fund drive, opened her colonial mansion on the banks of Lake Taneycomo for a grand "cakewalk" and some fun-filled talent contests, all in support of the Taneyhills Library.

At the June, 1994 meeting, Delphine Sed-

Bringing Books to the Ozarks

wick, the club's parliamentarian for the past quarter of a century, but now in a nursing home, was recognized with an honorary membership.

The new president being installed that day was Barbara Boone. Over the past twelve months, Darlene Rea, racing to keep up with the club, the library and rapidly developing building plans, had found little time to mentor her successor. Glenda McCormick, herself deeply involved in fund-raising through the past eight months, felt ill-prepared to preside over the club, not to mention that $500,000 building project, and asked for another year as president-elect.

On the other hand, Barbara was already deeply involved in the building project and well acquainted with the president's duties. She knew she could count on much advice and expertise from Florene Stilwell, Allen Brackin (being elected to the library board), and from the library's new purchasing agent, Ralph Sellmeyer, and his wife Millie, who would be the new president of the library board.

Before any work began, members of the building committee and a representative from Branson City Hall walked the building site and the property which would be the parking lot, to identify the trees and shrubs which would have to be removed and determine how many must be in place when the project was complete.

Fieldstone Development Company's blue prints of the proposed addition, contracted for in May, were filed with the city in July. In August, Fieldstone contracted to build the two story, six

Moving into the Computer Age

thousand square foot addition which would double the size of the present library and provide a wheelchair accessible elevator, restroom, doorways and halls.

But first the thrift shop's home must come down.

Shortly after sunrise on August 16th, after the shop's stock had been moved across the alley to the sorting house and all salvageable building materials had been sold or given away, a demolition tractor pulled up to the empty house and began chewing it apart. Within moments, it seemed, forty minutes at most, the cottage was a heap of splintered wood on the ground, a load of fragments in a dumpster, then gone.

The sun was still low in the east when workmen began preparing to move the library's heat pumps forty feet east across the lot to their new location so site preparation could begin. Already someone was putting a fast coat of paint on the "new" thrift shop, and just to its west another old cottage, whose last tenants had moved out in early August, had been rented by the library club at two hundred dollars a month, for use in sorting and pricing merchandise.

On the second day of September, a hundred or more guests gathered on the building lot to take part in ground-breaking ceremonies. Those present included State Representative Doyle Childers, Dr. M. Graham Clark, Mayor Lou Schaefer, John Bowers from the Branson/Lakes Area Chamber of Commerce, and architect Ed

Bringing Books to the Ozarks

Ground-breaking Ceremonies for the Library Addition were held September 2, 1994. Wielding the golden shovels are (left to right) Melba Sorensen, Arline Patton, Barbara Boone, Edd Akers, Glenda McCormick, and Florene Stilwell.

Muckey and project manager Matt Foster, both from Fieldstone.

The ceremonies over, Fieldstone's workmen immediately began leveling the building site, excavating the elevator pit, and preparing to pour the heavily reinforced concrete foundation. Thus far the busy library had changed little, inside or out. To retain the strength of the long eastern wall, a third of which would be removed on the upper level to provide access between the main library room and its twin which was to be filled with book stacks, planners had decided to leave the remainder of the brick wall intact.

Moving into the Computer Age

That fall, through the office and workroom windows which were not being altered, Norma and library volunteers kept a close watch on progress as the steel framework of the lower and upper floors took shape, and the stressed and re-stressed concrete upper floor was poured. Bricks like those on the outside of the original building were ordered, with assurance from the 1970s supplier that a good match could be provided, keeping in mind, of course, that the bricks already on the building were twenty years old.

Construction had barely begun when the computer committee was given the go ahead to place its big order. Within days pandemonium prevailed inside the library. Throughout the fall and winter months, new wiring and cables sprouted from walls, ceilings and floors, and shelves and desktop space were filled with as yet unusable computers and monitors. Meantime shelf by shelf, volunteer crews began the gargantuan task of installing the assigned barcode in each book.

Some of the 36,000 volumes being readied for the computer age had been on the shelves of the Taneyhills Community Library for decades, kept in readable condition by repeated repairs. The job of repairing books had always been a labor of love. Eleanor Goltz, who has held some office through most of her twenty years of membership, took on the added job of book repairs very early in her volunteer librarian career. The box which holds books in need of repairs is seldom empty, but so long as the pages can be read and there are neighbors wanting to read them, Eleanor has patiently reattached pages and mended backs which seem in danger of falling completely apart. A few of those much repaired volumes were donated back in the fall of 1933!

Whatever each member's regular library projects were, in the fall of 1994 virtually every member was drawn into some fund-raising effort. As the work began, including the monies in the perpetual trust fund which could be borrowed but would have to be paid back, the club had $359,740 toward paying the construction contract of $414,731. Through that fall and winter, thanks to much help from fund-raising organizer C. Major Close and many very busy club members, every business, theater, service organization, club or previous donor in the area was offered a chance to make a donation, and no offer of free services was ignored.

For several hectic days in late November, patrons edged their way past workmen clearing and leveling a path beside Fourth and Pacific Streets, and avoided the mess while cement sidewalks were poured. It was noted that donation jars inside the library filled very quickly during those days.

On December 11, 1994, a gala tea was held at Ye English Inn in Hollister, honoring the campaign chairman, Dr. M. Graham Clark and his late wife Elizabeth for whom the library's reference collection was being named. Invited were local civic, banking, business and club leaders, faculty and administrators from the college and

Moving into the Computer Age

local schools, ministers, doctors, and lawyers.

The stage was set, the cast had been called. Confident, after several months of working from the library and watching the club members in action, Major Close joined the library club and pulled back to a minor role to watch the donations come in.

Through the last days of 1994, sidewalk superintendents stared as workmen took off the old gutters and removed the eaves to make way for the wider roof which would rise to a higher peak as it spanned both the new and old wings. There was some consternation on wintry days when unchanneled runoff from the roof turned the sloping walk to the library's front door into a sheet of ice. While the library was closed over the winter holidays, early January winds were followed by heavy rains, but no one was present to see that the plastic rain skirts protecting the east and north walls had blown off.

Water streamed down the north wall and into the book drop. At the east corners, puddles collected inside the emergency exits, and dark rings stained the ceilings and carpet as water ran down the inside walls. Alerted to the problem, Norma Root and a volunteers crew rushed to unload the endangered mystery novels from wooden shelves at the northeast corner upstairs, while workmen secured the roof again.

Through the days which followed, everyone inside the library knew that the roofers were hurrying to get the building safely under cover again. From overhead and to the east the noise

Bringing Books to the Ozarks

of tramping feet and power drills attacking wood, metal and brick invaded the usually quiet book rooms, as section by section the old roof was ripped away and its successor was installed. Frequently the librarians, struggling to appear unflappable, calmed startled patrons, then reassured themselves that the end result would be well worth it.

Once the roof was complete, and the elevator equipment installed, it seemed no time at all before the outside walls of the building were in place. However, to the building committee and those in charge of the construction it was obvious that the work would not be completed on schedule. Beside the alley at the south end of the library there were stacks of new bricks which did not match at all the color of those which had endured years of summer sun and winter snow, rain, hail, and sleet. After weeks of negotiation, when the new bricks were all in place, the brick company sent a specialist who spent days cleaning then painstakingly modifying the color of the old bricks, one by one.

No amount of building clutter dampened library patrons' enthusiasm for that year's book/film discussion series, the high school art exhibition and competition, the children's story hours and summer reading programs. And when the Branson Arts Council planned a benefit Spring Fashion Show in the Canteen at the Lawrence Welk Theater that April, in support of the library, virtually every library club member who could move attended, along with several

Moving into the Computer Age

groups from other clubs. It was a star-studded affair featuring the famous Lennon Sisters and their families. Everyone in attendance went home with one or more surprise gifts, donated by local merchants. Using the proceeds from that day, the Arts Council again made a large donation of cultural videos to the library.

By May the new building was almost completed and renovation of the original building was well underway: Needed repairs, new guttering all around, new paint inside and out, new carpet throughout the building, a larger front desk, and a long needed security system.

Elated fund raisers prepared their reports for the annual business meeting in June, 1995, secure in the fact that thanks to the generosity of Branson's citizens, professional leaders and clubs, strong support from city hall, and a $67,000 loan from the library's Perpetual Trust Fund, the last of the building costs were almost covered.

From that heady position, the library's executive board at its May 1, 1995, meeting voted to purchase, for $70,000, the property being rented for sorting and the corner lot next to it. The purchase would give the library ownership of the entire west end of the Fourth Street block between Pacific and College and allow solution of some serious run off problems in the parking lot. The two old cottages would be demolished along with the present thrift shop as soon as the completed building was accepted and the shop and sorting operations were moved to the new down-

Bringing Books to the Ozarks

stairs rooms. The parking lot would be somewhat wider than originally planned. For the present, however, about half of the newly acquired lots would be kept in grass, forming a narrow park along Fourth Street, shaded by a clump of prized old trees.

Glenda McCormick succeeded to the presidency the following month, her experiences of the past two years having provided more than adequate understanding of her new responsibilities. It was a good year to be president. The library, inside and out, emerged from all the construction and renovation a spacious, cheerful place with seemingly endless room for all the books and activities. Beyond the rows of stacks on the main floor a large new conference room, its long inside wall providing closet space for library storage needs, awaited board meetings, special programs and receptions. The facilities for handicapped patrons were easily accessed, and the thrift shop below was doing a booming business. As long as the thrift shop was downstairs, the new stairs and exit at the northeast corner of the building would serve only as an emergency exit.

At the end of her year as president, Glenda turned over the gavel and leadership of an organization which was completely free of debt, to the president-elect, Virginia Praner. The loan from the Perpetual Trust Fund and all the construction bills and property costs had been paid.

In recent years the library club's annual budget, including salaries and building expenses,

Moving into the Computer Age

have ranged from $62,000 to $70,000. More than a third of that has come from thrift shop receipts, the remainder from member and associate dues, fund-raising activities, and donations large and small. With the building project behind them, the club made the hard decision to stop wholesaling Harold Bell Wright's *Shepherd of the Hills* books. Since the copyright ran out, many competing paperback versions have appeared, and printing costs have risen, so that there was much work and smaller and smaller profits connected with that project.

In the late 1990s, the Taneyhills Library allocates a thousand dollars each month for new books, an amount which is often equaled or surpassed by donated volumes. In addition to new purchases earmarked as rentals (the fee is now ten cents per day so the computer can do the tallying) the library maintains a set of shelves labeled "New to Us," where recent donations are easy for patrons to locate.

Ten times a year, hardworking library club members, who number between a hundred and fifty and two hundred, enjoy monthly luncheons, with informative and entertaining speakers and short book reviews, but every new member is soon made aware that "This is a working club." At any given time some twenty-five are volunteer librarians, as many as seventy-five volunteer time in the thrift shop, either sorting and pricing or dealing with customers. In addition, there are those holding offices and serving on committees. Many serve in more than one capacity at a time.

Bringing Books to the Ozarks

Honorary Memberships Were Awarded
in June 1995 to staunch library supporters
Melba Sorensen, Irene Lewis, and Florene Stilwell

And then there are members like housewife and mother Helen Williams, who works in her husband's office, dances on stage in one of the music shows, and since 1994 has served as treasurer for the club and library!

Down through the years thirty-seven women and men have been recognized for their contributions to the library and club with honorary memberships. The most recent are Melba Sorensen, Irene Lewis, and Florene Stilwell in 1995; Allen Brackin in 1996, Rosemary Rose and Virginia Bell in 1997, and Ruth Eastman in 1998.

Moving into the Computer Age

The library these members are serving continues to grow, though Branson, its home town, still counts its population as less than four thousand. Due to the increasing number of theaters, motels, restaurants and other commercial enterprises within Branson's incorporated area, most of the people that the Taneyhills Community Library serves, a population which nears 20,000, are scattered over the western half of Taney County plus many neighbors in southern Stone County to the west as well. And, true to its beginnings, a visitor's card continues to be available, with the payment of a small, refundable deposit.

On May 31, 1997, Norma Root, having served as a volunteer for several years and as part-time paid librarian for fourteen years, was honored at a reception in the library. She would soon be returning to Kansas City to enter her second "retirement." Loyal library patrons and fellow club members filled the library that afternoon. She would be greatly missed.

The following Monday morning Lisa Boushehri, a vibrant young mother, went to work as the Taneyhills Community Library's full time librarian. Her challenge was obvious: to become acquainted with the library's holdings, its volunteers and patrons, and at the same time stay on top of the creeping congestion which seems inherent in every library. The challenges continue. She is handling them well.

As Lisa began her new role, Mary Holmes was installed as club president. In mid-1998, she began her second term in that office. Her vice

Bringing Books to the Ozarks

president is Ralph Sellmeyer. The office of president-elect was discontinued during Mary's first term as president, an interesting experiment which did not fit the Taneyhills Library Club.

Well over a thousand club members have shared the work, the books, the fun and fellowship for a year or ten or twenty. A few, like Juanita Thompson and Bill Ellen Hall, have stayed with it for a lifetime, keeping the books which make up the Taneyhills Community Library available to families, friends, and neighbors.

Today, as always, most new members, both men and women, join the club first, later coming to understand its mission. And often they find, as Bill Ellen has through the years since 1933, that when one starts collecting books to share with neighbors and friends, it's very hard to stop!

BIBLIOGRAPHY

BOOKS

Aly, Lucile F., *John G. Neihardt, A Critical Biography,* Univ. of Oregon, Eugene, Ore., 1977.

Godsey, Helen & Townsend, *Flight of the Phoenix,* School of the Ozarks Press, 1984.

Horine, Maude, *Memories of Rose O'Neill,* Maude M. Horine, 1950, 1954.

Horine, Maude, *Ozark Fantasy,* S & S Press, Branson, Mo. 1959.

Lyon, Marguerite, *Take to the Hills,* Bobbs Merrill, 1941.

Mahnkey, Mary Elizabeth, *Ozark Lyrics,* 1st edition, Taneyhills Library Club, Branson, Mo., 1935.

Spurlock, Pearl *Over the Ozark Trails,* 1936.

NEWSPAPERS

Branson Beacon, 1950.
Branson Beacon and Leader.
Branson Echo, Nov 1905 - Nov 1909.
Springfield News Leader, 1920 - present
St. Louis Post Dispatch, Belymer, F.A., "Golf Pro and Radio Entertainer Happy with Farm Life in the Ozarks," 1946.
Taney County Republican, Forsyth, 1930 - present
White River Leader, Branson, 1920 - present

MAGAZINES

Country Home Magazine, vol. 29, no. 8, p. 5, August 1935.
Laugeson, Alma Jones, "Old Matt's Cabin - A Club Saved it for Posterity," *The Ozarks Mountaineer,* July 1962.
New York American, July 22, 1935.
"The Press," *Time Magazine,* July 19, 1935.

Bibliography

INTERVIEWS

Arend, Jane (KVB)* 1976-77.
Asselin, Lyn (LH).*
Awbery, Iva (LH).
Beall, Mildred (KVB) 1983.
Benson, Mary Helen (LH).
Blankenship, Ruth (LH).
Boone, Barbara (LH).
Boren, Mayme (KVB) 1983.
Boren, Mayme (LH).
Brown, Bud (LH).
Camp, Florence (LH).
Dodds, Ruth (LH).
Ford, Reva (LH).
Gardner, Jill (LH).
Godsey, Townsend (KVB) 1982, 1983.
Hackett, Jessie May Kite (KVB) numerous.
Hall, Bill Ellen (KVB) 1976.
Hall, Bill Ellen (LH).
Hamilton, Florence (LH).
Holman, Lois, (KVB) numerous.
Hunt, Cathy (LH).
Ingenthron, Frieda, (KVB).
Jaenicke, Paul (KVB) 1983.
Madry, Josephine (KVB) 1976.
McMasters, Annabelle (KVB) 1983.
Merritt, Rose (LH).
Speight, Norwood (KVB) 1976.
Stark, Marion (LH).
Street, Jeannette (LH).
Thompson, Juanita and Ike, (KVB) 1983, 1984.
Valett, Adelyn (LH).

* KVB = Interviewed by Kathleen Van Buskirk
  LH = Interviewed by Lorraine Humphrey

Bibliography

TANEYHILLS LIBRARY CLUB RESOURCES
Constitutions and Bylaws File 1934 - present
Membership Records 1933 - present
Newsletters 1983 - present
Records of Officers 1933 - present
Scrapbooks 1934 - present.
Secretary's Records 1940's - present
Yearbooks 1936 - present

TANEYHILLS LIBRARY RESOURCES
Acquisition Records 1933 - present
Treasury Records 1933 - present

MISCELLANEOUS RESOURCES
Denham, Pearl. Speech to Library Club, June 7, 1980.
Hall, Bill Ellen. Speech to Library Club, June 7, 1980
Jaenicke, Paul. Unpublished letter to KVB, July 31, 1983.
Mahnkey, Mary Elizabeth. Unpublished notes, (Property of Doug Mahnkey) April 16, 1935.
Records of Maids and Matrons Sunday School Class, Branson Presbyterian Church, early 1930's.
Sansom, Mary. Unpublished letter to William Sansom, (Collection of Edith Sansom McCall) 1935.

Kathleen Van Buskirk

Kathleen Van Buskirk, writer, photographer and editor, has for the past 25 years traveled the Ozarks exploring, interviewing and researching before writing each of her feature articles which have appeared in the *Ozarks Mountaineer Magazine* and other regional publications. For two of those years she also edited the *Mountaineer*.

A graduate of the University of Missouri School of Journalism, she was a newspaper reporter before her marriage to George Van Buskirk, a career Air Force pilot. At military bases here and in Europe, along with raising four children, she wrote for and edited organizational magazines.

In the mid-1970's, she and George retired to Table Rock Lake, near Branson, where he could fish, between research jaunts about the area. In the 1980's she also assisted in development of Elmo Ingenthron's Civil War history, *Borderland Rebellion*, and in 1992 was a major contributor for White Oak Press's *In the Heart of Ozark Mountain Country*, a collection of articles about Branson's history and its growth as an entertainment mecca.

Lorraine Humphrey

Lorraine Humphrey moved to the Ozarks in 1977 with her husband, Leslie, who was retired from Civil Service. Leaving the business world of St. Louis behind, she traded her expertise in hectic office routines for the not-so-calm atmosphere of newspaper work at the *Branson Beacon*.

Her career began in the mid-1940's when years were spent as a bilingual secretary. Able to compose correspondence in Spanish and English, she developed a keen sense of efficient writing and editing in the work place.

At the *Branson Beacon* from 1978 until 1987, Lorraine was part-time typesetter, proofreader, country correspondent, wrote a craft column, and edited the endearments. Since 1987 she has been a volunteer news columnist for the now *Branson Tri-Lakes Daily News*.

Joining the Taneyhills Library Club in 1979, she has continued to write the news releases and publicity.

Other of her literary works have been published in several magazines: *America's Civil War, Springfield!, and The Ozarks Mountaineer.*

Index

A

A. A. Ball Company 48
A play in the park 105
Adoration Festivities 239
Adoration Scene 183, 192, 199, 210
A. H. Alexander Drug Store 17
air-conditioned 88
Akers, Edd 308
Alaska 213
Alcan Highway 213
Alexander Drug Store 17
Alexander, Helen 17, 131
Allen, Lee 15
Allen, Lonnie 15
Allendale Resort 15
Allman, Gary 263
Almon, Ingrid 141 (also see Ingrid Almon Russell)
Almon, Rev. Hanna 182
Aly, Lucile 18
amendments 127, 147, 162, 207
American Bicentennial (1976) 262-263, 267
American Legion 75, 77, 88-89, 214, 243, 272-273
American Library Association 138
American Red Cross 128, 132-133, 142, 144, 159, 259
Anchor Tavern 86
Anderson, Bob 242
Anderson, Sherwood 16
Anderson, Vena 265, 278
anniversary dinner 56, 94, 109

Applehans, Fran 248-249
architect 47, 88, 261, 307
Arend, Jane 250-251, 253-254, 256, 258-261, 265-266, 268-269, 272
Arend, Jim 250
Arkansas 3-4, 7, 20, 23, 33, 52, 70, 95, 160, 202, 232
Armstrong, O.K. 218
art 13, 17, 19, 33, 43, 51, 73, 79, 101, 141, 235, 295-297, 300, 313
Art Competition and Exhibition 295, 297
Asselin, Lyn 167, 177, 188, 236
Asselin, Vi 236
associate members 162, 191
astronauts 240
Augustus, Emperor 82
Aurora, Missouri 11
Austin, India v
Autumn Daze street fair 260

B

baby, having a 20
Bald Knobbers 232
Baldknobbers Show 265
Ball Company 48
Ballentine, Caroline 97, 100, 104, 109, 115, 117-118, 122, 124, 129-130, 133, 135, 137, 143, 146-149, 156, 164, 171, 177-178, 194, 197, 207-208, 213-214, 230
Band Box 222, 271

Index

Bank of Branson 6, 73
Bates, Mrs. 192
Baxter Springs, Kansas 22
Bear Creek 31-32
Beasley, Lee 261
Beaux and Belles 105-106
Beck, Mildred 266
Beimdick, Flora 164, 170, 175
Beimdick, Mrs. E.J. 150
bell, church 6, 8, 35, 111
bell toll 8, 35, 111
bell tower 6
Bell, George F. 96
Bell, Margaret 96, 125-126, 131, 137, 151
Bell, Virginia 296, 305, 316
Bennett, Dean John 16
Bennett, Mrs. John 16, 66
Benson, Mary Helen 242
Benson, Ruth v, 288, 297
Benson, Truman 288, 293
Benton, Mrs. 156
Benton, Thomas Hart 191
Betty Crocker cake mixes 215
Bible, The 2, 69, 182
Bicentennial, American (1976) 262-263, 267
Bigelow, Zamah 25
Bingham, Caleb 191
Bingham, Carol 278
Binkley, Gwen 26, 73-74, 99, 177
Birthday Calendar 208, 216, 232, 244
Bishop, Mabel 192
Blain, Rev. R. Waller 96, 151
Blain, Winnie 96, 151
Blair China 192

Blanchard, Florence 152
Bloomsberg, Pennsylvania 30
Blue Eye, Missouri 52
Blue Lantern Tea Room 47
Board of Directors 190, 256, 264
boat cruise 137
boat regatta 270
Boehm, Ruskin C. 95
Boehm, Virginia 95, 133, 142
Boehmer, Dr. Florence 103, 132, 182, 191
Boles, Mrs. E.K. 142
Bonniebrook 31, 148
Book Worms Have More Fun, 285
book/film discussion series 312
Bookworms 247
Boone, Barbara v, 285-287, 291, 293, 297, 303, 305-306, 308
Boone, George 291
Boothe, Edna 172
Borderland Rebellion 231, 322
Boren, Mayme 183-184, 192, 201, 206, 208-209, 211, 220, 234, 242, 258, 278, 281
Bowers, John 307
Brackin, Allen 292, 305-306, 316
Branson Arts Council 300, 312
Branson, Bank of 6, 73
Branson Beacon and Leader 230, 261, 319, 323
Branson Bridge 153
Branson Christian Church 113, 226

Index

Branson City Hall   306
Branson Civic League   71, 167, 204, 268
Branson Community Band   105
Branson Community Building   77
Branson Echo   319
Branson Flood of 1927   102
Branson Flood of 1945   102, 153
Branson High School   93, 117, 199, 229, 234
Branson Hotel   6, x, 26-28, 30, 38, 40, 46, 54, 165, 238
Branson Library   viii, 46, 121, 145, 172
Branson Main Street Bridge   153
Branson Methodist Church   290
Branson Post Office   141
Branson Presbyterian Church   2, viii, 15, 22, 39, 96, 321
Branson School   17, 52, 79, 210
Branson Sluggers   110
Branson Tri-Lakes Daily News   323
Breeden, Henry and Mary   5
bridge   5, 7, 11, 15, 32, 62, 74, 88, 102, 112, 131, 150, 153, 192, 225, 238
Bright Elbow   179
Brite's Clothing   271
Broiler Hatchery   12
Brookhart, Smith   253
Brooks, Merle   249-250, 253, 258, 265, 272
Brown, Marion   148
Buck, Marie   295-296
Buck, Pearl S.   226
Bull Shoals Dam   114, 159, 179, 189
Bunche, Dr. Ralph   194
Buntin, Gladys   206
Bushnell, Clara   106
Business and Professional Women's Club   262
butterflies   61-63
buy a brick or a book   261
bylaws   22, 162, 217, 238, 256, 264, 285, 291, 321

C

cabbage   1
Cahill, Louise   25, 43
cake mixes, Betty Crocker   215
Caldwell, Taylor   226
calico dress   37
Camp, Florence   277, 281-282
Campbell, Joan   135
Campana Lady   115
Canada   177
cannon, toy   262
Canote, Donna   244
Canote's Drug Store   236
Cantwell, Clay   262
Cantwell, Georgia   104
Carbondale, Illinois   266
card parties   184, 211-212, 244, 249, 263, 285
cardholders   53, 90, 100, 121
Cargin, Arden   282, 295
Cargin, Clad   295
Carter, Edith   68, 95
Catalogue system   242
Caulfield, Mrs. Henry S.   125
Chamber of Commerce   89, 112-113, 173, 307

Index

Charleston, Lola   v, 264
charter associates   85
Chase, Betty   165
Chase, Martha   170
Chase, Rev. J.E.   113
Chicago, Illinois   12, 14, 95-96, 115, 118, 126, 139, 176, 179, 203
Chick's Barber Shop   241
chickens   65, 93
chicks   12, 57
Chick's Barber Shop   241
Chigger Hollow Sewing Circle   94
Childers, Doyle   307
Children's Summer Story Hour   278, 293
Chilton, Lou   244
China   137, 155
Chinese holiday traditions 137-138
Chinese Lord's Prayer   137
Christian Church   113, 195, 207, 221, 226-227
church bells (see bell, church)
Church of Jesus Christ of Latter Day Saints   279
church tower   8
City Council   89
Civic League   x, 71-77, 79-80, 89-90, 98, 101, 132, 160, 167, 182-183, 195, 204, 207, 214, 220, 268, 279, 285, 287-288
Civic League building   x, 74, 76, 79-80
Civil War   30-31, 231-232, 322-323
Clark, Dr. M. Graham   185, 218, 281, 292, 307, 310
Clark, Elizabeth   185, 217

cleaned chickens   65
Close, C. Major   310-311
Coast-to-Coast   105
Coday, Berniece   152, 163, 168-169
Cole, Helen   207, 211, 221
Cole, James and Blanche   293
Collect, Study Club   29, 49, 144, 146, 185, 212
College of Eureka Springs   33
College of the Ozarks   296, 304
Columbia, Missouri   146, 176
Combs, Nelle   206, 210, 226, 229
Command the Morning   226
Commercial Hotel   8
communistic literature   154
Community Building   viii, x, 75-77, 79, 86-91, 94, 101, 104, 108, 157, 178, 195, 204, 207, 226, 229, 238-239, 251-252, 278
Community Hall   72-73, 88, 90
Como Craft   157, 194
compulsory military service   121-122
Congressional Record   274
Consignment Shop   287, 289, 291
constitution   22-24, 29, 40, 118, 146-148, 165, 169-170, 172, 176, 179, 207, 238, 321
cookbooks   263, 305
Cook, Daisy   139, 151, 157-158
Coolidge, Calvin   12
copier   294-295

327

Index

Corlis, Dr. E.E.   51
corn-cob pipe   37
Corner One   271
cornerstone, new library   267-268
Corps of Engineers, U.S.   114
Cotter, Arkansas   95
Couchman, Irene   129, 156, 164, 167, 170, 178, 190, 203
"Country Correspondent of the Year"   1, 58-60
Country Home Magazine   1, 319
Cox, Anne   279
Cox, Marian   212
Cox, Mary Elizabeth   279
Cram, Margaret   ix, 251-253
Crane, Missouri   171
cross-file   156
Crouch, Clifford   260
Crowell Publishing Co.   59
Cunningham, Juanita   114
Cushing, Irene   126
Cycle   18

D

Dache, Lilly   217
Dailey, Janet   305
Dallas, Texas   14, 133
dance   14, 62, 112, 210, 281, 316
dance boat   62
Davenport, Missouri   192
Davidson's   222
Davis, Jane   240, 242
Davis, Mrs.   149
Dawes, Charles G.   12
Dawes, Fanny   9, 12-17, 22-23, 29, 33, 36, 44, 64-65, 93, 111
Dawes, Frank   12
Dawes, Herbert   12
Dawson, Mildred   177, 208-209, 211, 214, 221, 241, 249, 251
Dean, Neal   209
Dear and Glorious Physician   226
DeBoard, Weldon   54
Declaration of Independence   267
Defebaugh, Carol   282
Denham Hall   285, 290, 295
Denham, Pearl   15, 17, 21, 41, 280
Denham, Pearl Booth   22
Denham, Ted   17
Development fund   285
Devil's Pool   46
Dewey Bald   37, 70-71, 113, 122, 167
Dewey Decimal System   121
Dickerson, Dorothy   178
Dillon's   222
Dooley, Dr. Thomas   226
Doubleday Mystery Book Club   213
Douglas, Dorothy   305
Douglas, Lloyd   17
Dr. Smith family   178
Drury College   16, 52, 65-66, 103, 132
Drury College President   52
Duckworth Drug Store   73
Durr, Rosabelle   247, 249
Dusty Shelf, The   288

E

East Indies   137
Eastern Star   236
Eastman, Ruth   290, 316

Index

Eckert, Grace   v, 265
Edge of Tomorrow   226
Edgewater Pavilion   113
Edwards, Delsie   133
Edwards, Jean   116, 132
Edwards, Jill   115-116
Edwards, Lyn   116, 167
Eiserman, Laura   175
Eiserman, Lloyd   88
Eiserman, Rose   175
electric power   189
electricity   6
elevator   307-308, 312
Ellie's Guided Tours   237
Ellison, Katherine   29
Ellison, Lydia   131
Encyclopaedia Britannica   221, 250
Encyclopedia   112, 188, 221
English Garden   47
Episcopal congregation   195
Epps Sanitation Company   266
Erbes, Dora   202
Estella Skaggs Hospital Auxiliary   201
Escher, Myrna   206, 217
Eureka Springs, Arkansas   52, 202
Evans, Dr. Harry   85, 213
Evans, Edna (Mann)   85, 108, 130, 176, 198, 209, 213, 220

F

Fain, Charles   236
Fain, Lenore   236
Fain, Mary Anna   210
Fairbanks, Alaska   213
Fairy Cave   38
Fairy Tree   32

Farrow, Tiera   220
fashion   ix, 132, 210, 222, 249, 258, 263, 271, 279-281, 312
Fashion show   ix, 258, 263, 271, 279-281, 312
feather   14, 65
Fechner, Effie   125
Fechner, Rose Eiserman   175
Federal Government   274
Federal Revenue Code   257
Federated Clubs of Missouri   42
Felix, Edith   281
Fibber McGee and Molly   228
fiddle string   32
Field, Mary   176
Fieldstone Development Company   306
fire   8-9, 57, 71-72, 109
first nighter   115
Flapper   14
Flautt, Mrs. J.S.   95
Fletcher, Helen   viii, 10-11, 96, 242, 247
Fletcher, Rockwell   10
Flint Hill School   69
Flood of 1927   102
Flood of 1945   102, 153
flooding   76, 102, 140, 153, 160, 189
Flying Grandma   212-213
Foggy River Boys   265
Ford, Reva   99
Forsyth   4, 6-7, 33, 62, 66, 69, 76, 82, 145, 159-160, 173, 195, 198, 248, 319
Forsyth Art Guild   248
Forsyth, Missouri.   6, 62, 145
Foster, Matt   308

329

Index

4-H club   110
Freeland, Minnie   162
Freeland, William   160
Friends of the Library   157, 278, 287, 289, 292
fund-raiser   ix, 68, 190, 244, 284, 302
fund-raising   29, 55, 68, 87, 100, 106, 119, 134, 139, 141, 144, 161, 181, 190, 192, 202-203, 205, 211-212, 217, 228, 242, 247, 254, 258, 260, 262-263, 266, 284-286, 301, 306, 310, 315
Funny Fashion Show   ix, 281

G

Galbraith, Etelka   202
Galesburg, Illinois   27, 98, 120, 149, 213
Gallon, Martin G.   243
Galsworthy, John   16
Game Parties   112, 193
Gansz, Jessie   16, 190
Gansz, Phillip   16
garden   17, 47, 61-62, 82, 120, 136, 157, 172, 191, 217
Gardner, Don   115-116, 237
Gardner's Golf Ranch 115, 151, 237
Gardner, Jill   viii, 116, 128, 132, 141, 165, 167
Garner, Dorothy   98, 104, 126, 130, 137, 148, 156, 163-164, 177, 188, 220, 241
Gary's Coiffures   271
Gatchell, Alice   303
Gay Nineties Review   210

General Mills Company   215
Geneva, Switzerland   51
genius   21
Georgia pecans   234-235
Gerard, Carmen Cole   293, 296
Gerard, Sherry   279, 282
Germany   121
German, Delores   247, 258, 263, 270-271
Gibson, Marie   v, viii, 54-55, 283
Gift shops   100, 120
Gilbert, Marjorie   278
Girl Scout Week   251
Give Of Thy Vineyard   183
Gladys Swarthout   192
goat trail   37, 70
Godsey, Helen   141, 143, 146, 199
Godsey, Townsend   140-141, 145, 198
Golden Anniversary   ix, 55, 283-284
Golden Anniversary Tree   ix, 284
Golden Wedding Anniversary   185
Golf Ranch   115, 151, 237
Goltz, Eleanor   297, 303, 309, back cover
Gone With the Wind   98
Good, Robert M.   25, 218
governor   60, 125, 234
Governor's Conference on Library Development   234
Gran, Walter C.   83
Grandview Hotel   64-65, 108
Gray, Josephine   188
Green Forest, Arkansas   23
Greenland   121

Index

Griffith, Eve   146, 163, 175, 220, 238, 278
Griffith, Jack   278
Grosset and Dunlap   122, 196
Groucho Marx and Me   226
ground-breaking ceremonies   263, 307-308
guest speakers   13, 103
gypsy basket   119, 172

H

Hackett, Jesse May (Kite)   219
Hall, Bill Ellen   v, ix, 17, 21, 23, 26, 41, 97, 99, 114, 116-117, 119, 122, 125, 134, 136, 138, 141-142, 233-234, 253, 255, 259, 262, 268, 318
Hall, Ted   18, 23
Hamilton, Florence Campbell   246
Harris, Hazel   217
Hart, Grace   277
Hart, Robert   54
Hartel, Kathy   277
hat   14, 126, 217, 227
having a baby   20
Hawaii   98, 131, 191, 226
Hayes, Edith   131, 165
Hazel Vaughn Johnston   132
Heath, Dorothy (see Jaenicke, Dorothy Heath)
Heath, Sara   viii, 20, 22, 24-25, 40-43, 45, 49, 53, 56, 64-65, 78, 109, 145-146, 161, 179, 198, 220
Heath, Willard P.   5, 57
Heer's Department Store   95
hemophilia   12, 110
Hendricks, Dr. Everett   267

Herschend, Hugo   222-223
Herschend, Jack   222-223
Herschend, Mary   222-223, 246
Herschend, Peter   222
Hess, Jerry and Martha   261
Hester, Thelma   206
Highway 65 by-pass   x, 246, 263
Hilburn, Mae Stafford   51, 65
Hillbilly Day   128
Hillbilly Luncheon   207
Hitler, Adolph   121
Hodges, Pearl   248, 265
Hollister   3-5, 7-viii, 8, x-12, 16, 20, 33, 46-47, 52, 54-57, 61, 66, 69-70, 85, 88, 95-96, 99, 102, 109-112, 139-140, 142, 144-145, 152-153, 160, 176, 179, 182, 188-189, 195, 203, 209, 215, 227, 233-234, 238, 262, 265, 270, 283, 286, 295, 297, 310
Hollister book collection   139
Hollister Grade School   234
Hollister High   110, 295
Hollister High School   110, 295
Hollister librarian   144-145
Hollister Presbyterian Church   69, 96
Hollywood   85, 122, 198
Holman, Lois   176, 191, 200
Holmes, Mary   302, 317
Holt, Bill   260
home extension agents   71
honorary members   147, 230, 245, 251
Horine, Capt. Harold   156
Horine, Maude   16, 31-32,

331

Index

40, 103, 106, 120, 142, 157, 191, 194
Hostess committee   290
hours   10, 12-13, 23, 36, 69, 76, 83, 94, 99, 104, 118, 122, 124-125, 135, 144-145, 167, 188, 190, 216, 220, 226-227, 244, 278, 292, 295, 297, 312
House of Representatives   152, 274
Howard, Mary Louise   151
Howard, Rev. Guy   151, 183
Hoyt, Mary   54
Hromek, Dolly   296
Hromek, Max   292
Humphrey, Lorraine   v, ix, 281, 320, 323
Hunt, Cathy   236, 238, 281
Hunter, Karol   271
Huntley, Jean   128, 132, 137, 151
Hush, Ruth   258
hydroelectric dam   6, 66, 224

I

Iceland   121
income tax forms   294
India   137
Indians of the Ozark Plateau   231
inflation   165, 265, 285
Ingenthron, Elmo   231, 322
Inspiration Point   71, 167, 226
Internal Revenue Service   257, 294
International Christian Fiction contest   183
International Collegiate Council   51
International Rose O'Neill Club   248
IRS   257, 294
Isle of Capri   82

J

Jabara, Majelly   101
Jaenicke, Dorothy Heath   25, 29, 36, 43, 53, 68, 80, 83, 90, 94, 99, 101, 104, 107, 109, 115-117, 119, 122, 124-126, 128, 130, 135, 138, 141, 143-144, 147, 149-150, 157, 165, 174
Jaffee, Bernice   133
James, Prof. Vernon   52
James, Sybil   79, 85, 93, 99-100, 106, 137, 151, 164-165, 185, 200, 220
Japan   155
Japanese   121, 131, 143, 212
Japanese concentration camp   212
Jefferson City, Missouri   51, 110, 122, 124, 232
jellies and jams   120
Jenkins, Fred   218
Jenkins, Virginia   192, 197, 206, 214
Jennings, Ellie   237
Jeri's Glad Rags   271
jitney dinner   87, 99-100, 112, 120 (a jitney = a nickle. Each serving costs 5 cents at a jitney dinner.)
Jones, Bill   262
Jones, Connie   265
Jones, Dr. J. Leland   219
Jones, Dr. Margaret   217, 219, 221

Index

Joplin, Missouri   4
J. T. Duckworth Drug Store   73
Judge McClary farm   115
Junior Chamber of Commerce   112
Junior Literary Guild   213
juvenile library   278, 285-286, 290, 292, 296

K

Kansas City, Missouri   12, 14, 105, 118, 156, 165, 218-219, 235, 249, 261, 283, 317
Kansas City College of Osteopathy   219
Kansas City Star   261
Kelso, Bess   223
Kennedy, Aletha   195, 200, 220
Kewpiemania   249
Kewpies   82, 148
Kewpiesta   249
Kingsport Press   124
Kite, Jesse May (see Jesse May Hackett)
Kite, Rolland B.   52, 220
Kite, Vitae   viii, 52, 61-63, 103, 115, 220
Korean War   193

L

LaGuardia, Mayor Fiorello   60
Lake Taneycomo   11, 18, 61-62, 64, 75-76, 85, 87-88, 103, 113-114, 131-132, 139, 141, 152, 155, 159, 183, 189-191, 198, 219, 227, 230, 236, 270, 305
Lamb, Janet   188

Land of Taney   231
Land Where Rivers Meet, The   227
Lane, Rose Wilder   56-57, 60
large print books   301
Latter Day Saints   279
laughter   85, 157, 163, 199, 281
Law, Dr. Gertrude   193
Lawrence Welk Theater   312
Lawyer in Petticoats   220
lectures   14, 39, 121
ledger of acquisitions   36
Lennon Sisters   313
lepidopterist   viii, 61, 63
Lewis, Irene   267, 316
Lewis, Sinclair   16
Library Associates   287
Library Board   135, 169, 180, 186, 188, 196-197, 203, 206, 213-214, 221, 229, 231, 233, 240-242, 244, 247, 250-253, 264-265, 272, 277, 293-296, 306
Library Building   ix, 130, 204, 211, 215, 233, 238, 253, 255, 265, 268, 273-274, 285, 287, 289-291
Library Built By Sharing, The   274
Library Club President   v, 146, 201, 227, 241, 280, 302
Library Committee   79, 95, 99, 104, 124, 148, 150, 156, 164, 167, 170, 179, 206
library on wheels   211
library science classes   252

333

Index

Library Tree   284
life member   282
Lincoln, Abraham   215
Lions Club   233, 244, 248, 250
Literacy Award   286
Literary Guild   213
Little House on the Prairie   56
local industry   5
London, England   65, 85
Long Creek   66
Lord's Prayer in Chinese   137
Lowe, Hazel   210
Lucas, Virginia   258
Lucia, Town of   4-5
Lyle's Beauty Lounge   271
Lyon, Marguerite "Marge" Kemp   139
lumber yards   9

M

Mabe Brothers' Baldknobbers Show   265
MacFarland, Grandfather   249
Madry, Josephine   11, 13, 16-17, 27, 31, 41, 52, 86-87, 114, 175, 186, 197, 199, 211, 220, 232, 240, 242-244, 250, 258, 268
Magnificent Obsession   17
Mahnkey, Charles P.   2
Mahnkey, Douglas   235
Mahnkey, Mary Elizabeth   viii,1-2, 20, 33-34, 41-42, 44-45, 47-48, 56, 58-62, 64-67, 124, 164, 177, 194, 235, 319, 321
Mahnkey, Preston   66
Maids and Matrons class   2, 9-11, 15, 21-22, 35

Maids and Matrons Study Club   18, 21
Main Street   7, 18, 26, 44-45, 54, 74, 78, 80, 102, 113, 131, 153, 194, 238, 245-246
Main Street Bridge   153
Major Bowes' Amateur Hour   105
Mang Field   259-260
Mann, Edna (see Edna Evans)
Mann, Etta   35, 65, 79, 85, 100-101, 149, 190, 220
Mann, Ned   85, 198-199
Man's Land   271
Mansfield, Missouri   56-57
Marble Cave   (Marvel Cave)   38
Martin, Dr. Charlotte   22
Martin, Virginia   282
Marvel Cave   34, 38, 222, 225
Masonic Order   72
Matt's cabin   167-168
May, Cora   220
mayor   44, 60, 74, 101, 140, 307
McCall, Edith   227
McCanse, Ralph Allen   33
McClure, Dee   177
McCord, May Kennedy   218
McCormick, Glenda   302-303, 306, 308, 314
McCullom, Ruth   242
McDaniel, Elizabeth "Lizzie"   71, 166-167
McDougal, Elizabeth   209-210
McGee, Edward   228
McGee, Fibber and Molly   228

Index

McGee, Molly 228
McGill building 72
McHaffie, Ella 60, 99, 111
McMasters, Annabelle 69
Mehus, Jewell Ross 235-236
memorial 110-111, 138, 159-160, 178, 213, 231, 278, 296-297
Memorial book 110, 178, 231
Memorial Tower Council 159
mental food 16
Merle, Margaret 105-106
Merritt, Rose Eiserman Fechner 175
Michel's Restaurant 229
mildew 90, 104, 107-108
milk toast 16
Miller's Family Style Restaurant 185
Miller, Gertrude 178
Miller, Nadine 165, 176, 280, 282
Miller, Ron 165
Miller, Steve 165, 176, 183, 192, 248
mills (tax) 49, 215
Mincy, Missouri 66
miracle drug 92-93
Miracle Man of special effects 85
Miracle of Milan 198
Miser, Gay 41, 220
Missouri House of Representatives 152
Missouri Humanities Council 304
Missouri Library Association 233, 288
Missouri State Library 120, 172, 203, 217

Missouri State Library Commission 120
Missouri Waltz 177
Mitchell, Betty 92
Mitchell, Dr. Guy 98
Mitchell, Ellie 92-93, 100, 105-108, 112, 114, 130, 132, 136, 146, 149, 185-186, 190, 197, 204, 206, 220-221, 261
Mitchell, Jane 104, 261
Mitchell, Margaret 98
Mizell, John 292
Mizell, Shirley 282, 303
Moad, Dr. John 269
monthly reports 42, 87, 167, 185
Montreal, Canada 177
Moore, Odelle 117
Moran, Lois 282, 297
Morgan, Mary 115
Morlan, Sue 240
Mormons 279
motels 197, 234, 237-238, 299, 317
Mottesheard, Bernice "Bunny" 211
Mount Branson 7, 101, 192, 249
Mount Como Inn 194, 209
movie theater 73, 75
Mr. Lyle's Beauty Lounge 271
Muckey, Ed 307
Mulroe, Ruth 281
music 14, 18-19, 33, 68, 93, 95, 126, 131, 141, 143, 165, 176, 182, 185, 199, 212, 265, 316
Mutton Hollow 37

Index

N

Nadal, T.W.   52
Nalle, Irene   249
nanny goat   157
National Library Week   220, 233, 241
National Register of Historic Places   148
National Rose O'Neill Club   248
Native Americans   18, 231
Nativity Parade   210
Nazis   143
Nebraska   18, 20-21, 31, 156
Neihardt, Alice   18, 21, 33, 41, 53
Neihardt, Enid   21
Neihardt, John G.   viii, 18-19, 319
Neihardt, Mona   18-19, 21, 46, 54
Nelson, Elaine   264
Neosho, Missouri   269
New Look, The   222
New York City   1, 25, 55, 58, 60-61, 65-66, 101, 109, 117, 122, 283, 319
Nightingale, Dr. Alice   191
Norway   235
not-for-profit corporation   256

O

Oak Manor Apartments   254
Oasis, Missouri   1-2, 33, 42, 46, 66
Oklahoma   95, 146
Old Matt's cabin   167-168
Old Shepherd's Book Shop   235-236
Omaha, Nebraska   31
O'Neill, Alice   30
O'Neill, Rose   viii, 84, 148, 248-249, 261, 319
O'Neill, William Patrick   30
Oney, Gerald   268
orchards   5
Oregon Trail   178
O'Reilly Military Hospital   142
Orient   137
Ottic, Major   155
Outstanding New Librarian Award   288
Over the Ozark Trails   113, 319
Owen Boat Company   74
Owen, Dr. Lyle   171, 200, 245
Owen, Frank   226
Owen, Georgia   206
Owen, Jim   viii, 73-75, 101, 117, 230
Owen, John B.   73
Owen, Stella   86, 120, 136, 138, 171, 175, 185, 191, 245
Owen Theater   viii, 80-81, 111, 113
Ozark Beach   103
Ozark Mountain Folk   34
Ozarks Book Club   118
Ozark(s) Lyrics   44-45, 47-48, 59, 62, 64, 67, 319
Ozarks Mountaineer Magazine   274, 322-323 back cover

P

Palmer, Grace   51
Paramore, Ethel   95, 101, 104, 107, 109, 115, 117-119, 124, 126, 130, 135-

336

Index

136, 142, 144, 146-149, 154, 161, 164, 170, 174, 177, 220
Parent-Teachers Association 241
Park Board 89, 106
Parks, Jessie 96, 105, 115, 135-137, 141, 144
Parks, Mrs. Jessie 96
Parnell, Agnes 175
Parnell, B. Albert 44
Parnell Building 46
Parnell, Opal 34, 40, 60, 198, 205
Parnell's 222
Patton, Arline 308
Patton, Ella viii, 27-28, 35, 37, 40, 43, 54, 72, 74, 92
Pearl Harbor 131, 191, 212
Pemberton-Jennings American Legion Post 88, 243
pencil factory 9
Pennies from Heaven 144
People's Bank and Trust 253
Perpetual Trust Fund 287-288, 295-296, 310, 313-314
Persinger, Brenda 260
Peterson's 222
Peyton, Mrs. 145
Pfister, Fred 304
Philippines 137
Phillips, Jewell 51
piano 21, 140, 146, 186, 220, 236
Pierce, Jane Mitchell 104, 261
Pink Door, The 277, 285-286
pipe-smoking lady 37, 237
Pirate Cruise and Water Pageant 236
plastic mills (for taxes) 49
Plumb Nelly Days 230, 247
Plummer, Foster 277
poetry 18-20, 33, 36, 44, 48, 52, 57, 59, 103, 176
Point Lookout 5, 7, 34, 198
Poland 121
Pollyanna 26
Portman, Mrs. Ronald 163
Post Dispatch 35, 319
postwar improvements 160
Powell, Virginia 249
Powersite Dam 62, 66
Praner, Virginia 314
Presbyterian 2, 6, viii, 8-9, 15, 22, 35, 39, 64, 69, 96, 98, 105, 182, 254, 321
Presbyterian Church 2, viii, 8-9, 15, 22, 39, 69, 96, 98, 105, 254, 321
President of the United States 12
president-elect 303, 306, 314, 318
Presleys' Mountain Music Jubilee 265
propaganda 16, 154
PTA 241
Pulliam, Wilma 202, 210

Q

Quaker Oats Company 118
quilting 202
Quistgard, Ruth "Johnnie" 247

R

Radcliff, Helen 243
radio 19, 51, 60-61, 105, 115, 131, 218, 228, 319

Index

rain   76, 90, 94, 101, 152, 238, 267, 311-312
Randolph, Vance   34
REA   5, 107, 218, 255, 297, 302-303, 306, 312
Rea, Darlene   296-297, 301-303, 306
Rea, Peter   297
Readers Digest   86, 171, 301
Red Cross   128, 132-133, 142, 144, 159, 259
red velvet   82
reference materials   188
regatta   270
remodeling   214, 238, 243-244
rental books   193, 304
Republican   12, 33-34, 59, 82, 162, 319
Republic, Missouri   254
resorts   7, 9, 100, 120, 124-125, 128, 134, 162, 238
Rhoads, Edna   29, 41, 93, 100
Richardson, Mabel   29
Ridgedale   20
Riley, Bill Ellen   23 (also see Bill Ellen Hall)
Rinehart, Harriet   208-209, 211, 217, 220-221, 227, 229
Rives, Jinx   267
Road to Hollister   33
Roark Creek   4, 15, 18, 37, 98, 190, 238
Roberts, Mary   171
Rockaway Beach   62, 69, 137, 141, 145, 195
Rodin, Auguste   46
Roosevelt, Franklin   60
Root, Norma   ix, 255, 267, 281, 283, 286, 288, 294, 297, 299, 302, 305, 311, 317
Rose, Rosemary   281, 316
Rotary Club   221, 244, 248, 250
royalties   48-49, 67
Rozell Engineering   266
Rubesam, Helen   208
rug   53, 129, 133
rummage sale   99, 165, 184, 270-271
Runyon, Evelyn   81-82, 151-152, 162, 167, 177, 182, 188, 207, 219
Runyon, Forrest   81, 155, 198
Rural Electric Association (see REA)
Russell, Ingrid   142-143, 167, 169, 176, 182, 186
Russell, Ingrid Almon   141
Russell, Ray   143
Russia   51

S

Saad, Bobby and Majelly   101
Sailor, Mrs. William A.   152
salary   83, 93, 143, 206, 220, 231, 247, 302
Sammy Lane Boat Line   62, 236
Sammy's Lookout   113
Sansom, Mary   179-180, 188, 191, 210, 227
Santa Claus   113, 262
Sarber, Mabel   243, 249
Sarcoxie, Missouri   191
sawmills   5
Schaefer, Mayor Lou   307
Schimpf, Madge   265

Index

School of the Ozarks 7, 20, 23, 25, 29, 32, 34-35, 43, 45-46, 51-52, 54, 61, 67-68, 70, 82, 95-97, 115, 131-132, 149, 152, 156, 164, 182, 184-185, 188-189, 192, 194-195, 198-199, 202, 207, 212-213, 216-219, 234, 242, 252, 268-269, 280, 292, 296
School of the Ozarks Press 45, 67
Scudder, Kate 138
Sedwick, Delphine 264
Sellmeyer, Millie 306
Sellmeyer, Ralph 292, 306, 318
senior sneak trip 110
Servicemen's Honor Roll 141, 159
Second Edition Thrift Shop 286, 289
sewers 82
Shadow Rock Park 195
Shaw, Nell 211
Shedd, Charles 240
Shepherd of the Hills, The viii, 26, 37-38, 62, 70-71, 83, 113, 122-125, 128-129, 134, 136, 138-139, 144, 149, 157-158, 161, 167-168, 196-197, 199, 204, 206, 208, 214, 217, 219, 225, 235-237, 244, 248-249, 251, 265, 267, 278, 285, 288, 315
Shepherd of the Hills Garden Club 217
Shreve, Ann 192, 200, 202
Shue, Pat 261, 271
sidewalk 90, 310-311

sidewalk superintendents 311
Silver Dollar City 34, 205, 225, 235, 246
Sixty-Minutes 299
Skaggs Community Hospital 190
Skaggs, M.B. and Estella 190
Skinner, Helen 211-212
Smith, Ann 211
Smith, Asenath Cecilia 30
Smith family 178
Smith, Florence 141
Smith, Governor Al 60
Snowden, Jewell 260
Snyder, Ruth 171
Social Security 206, 257
soggy books 90
Sorensen, Melba 308, 316
South America 228
South Pacific 185
Soviet Union 154
Spanish American War Veterans 89
Sparky Spurlock 37-38, 70, 113, 237
Springfield, Missouri 3-4, 13, 16-17, 31, 33, 41, 48, 51-52, 57, 64, 71, 95, 100, 107, 110-111, 132, 137, 142, 195, 218, 221, 272, 319, 323
Springfield Leader-Press 272
Springfield News-Leader 41, 221
Spurlock, G.F. 37
Spurlock, Lee 113
Spurlock, Pearl "Sparky" 37-38, 70, 113, 237, 319

339

Index

St. Louis, Missouri 5, 14, 20, 25, 35, 41-42, 46, 86, 101, 156, 161, 171, 176, 192, 288, 319, 323
St. Louis Post Dispatch 35, 319
St. Louis Public Library 41
staff manual 243
Stark, Marion ix, 206, 229, 231, 233, 239-241, 243, 251-252, 255
Stark, Walter 229
State of Missouri 71, 256
State Representative 307
Stephens College 146
Stephens, Elsie 200, 214, 216, 220
Stephens, Mrs. Fred 209
Steve Miller Art Association 248
Stewart, Betty 241-242, 244, 279
Stewart, Birl 241
Stewart family 254
Stewart, Mary 193
Stilwell, Bill v, ix, 292
Stilwell, Florene v, 286, 290, 293, 305-306, 308, 316
Stonewall Motor Inn 184
Stork is Dead 240
Stratte, Helen 46, 97
Street, Jeannette 256-258, 262, 264, 268
Study Club viii, 1-2, 15-16, 18, 21, 23-27, 29, 31, 34-36, 39-40, 44-46, 48-49, 51-54, 56-57, 60-62, 65-69, 71-72, 74-75, 78-83, 85-86, 89, 92-93, 95-98, 100-102, 105-107, 109-111, 113-117, 121-122, 124-125, 127-128, 130-132, 135, 137, 139-140, 142, 144, 146, 149, 179, 248
sunbonnets 129, 135, 230
Sunshine Press 48
Suttle, Harry 176
Swan Creek 160
sweaters 128
Swinney, Ila 210-211
Switzerland 51

T

Table Rock Lake & Dam 66, 223, 224, 322
Ta-Co-Mo Art Club 248
Take to the Hills. 139, 145
Talking Rocks Cave 38
Talley, Jay 55
Talley, Marion 191
Tammay, Marie Gibson v, viii, 54-55, 282-283, 297
Taney County Public Library 27, 35-36, 39, 67, 69, 81, 89, 96, 110, 117, 120, 129-130, 142, 151, 156
Taney County Republican 33, 59, 82, 162, 319
Taneycomo 7, 11, 18, 61-62, 64, 75-76, 85, 87-88, 103, 113-114, 131-132, 139, 141, 152, 155, 159, 183, 189-191, 198, 219, 226-227, 230, 236, 238, 270, 305
Taneyhills Community Library iii-iv, ix-x, 124, 220, 271-272, 274, 276, 286, 294, 299, 309, 317-318
Taneyhills Public Library 156, 170, 173, 178, 188
Taneyhills Study Club 1-2, viii, 24-25, 27, 36, 39, 53,

Index

56, 60-61, 65, 67-69, 71-72, 78, 82, 100, 102, 106-107, 114-115, 131, 140, 179
tax exemption 257
taxi driver 37, 152
tax-supported library 172-173, back cover
Taylor, Gene 273-274
Teen Age Football Stories 226
telephone 160, 181, 229, 251, 254, 300
Tennessee 124
The Land Where Rivers Meet 227
The Library Built By Sharing 274
The New Look 222
The Pink Door 277, 285-286
This is Your Life 218
Thomas, Vera Courtney 191
Thompson, Ann 126, 262
Thompson, I.M. "Ike" 114
Thompson, Juanita v, 133, 161, 170, 174-175, 177, 197, 201, 203-204, 206-207, 214, 220, 268, 288, 318
Thompson, Mary 282
Thompson, Mrs. Wilmer 17, 47
Thompson, Peggy 35
Thornhill, Eula Whelchel 11
Thrift Luncheon 132
Thrift Shop 157-158, 277, 286-287, 289, 291, 295-297, 301, 305, 307, 313-315
Thrift Shop volunteers 287
Thurmond, R.S. 176
Tiberius, Emperor 82

Tiffany, Marie 131
Todd, Kathleen 14, 17-18
Todd, Marshall 174
Todd, Minnie 53, 109
Todd, Vernon 18
tomatoes 5, 71
tourist cabins 238
Townsend, Richard 268
toy cannon 262
train depot 9, 88
Traubel, Helen 191-192
Treasured Recipies 285
treasury 15, 39, 42, 44, 49, 53, 56, 64, 67, 75, 78, 85, 87, 92, 100, 107, 111, 119-121, 124, 129-130, 134, 136, 138-139, 144, 149, 152, 161, 169, 175, 182, 184, 196-197, 200, 205, 207, 210, 214, 216, 250-251, 321
Tri-Lakes Adult center 254
Tri-Lakes Daily News 323
Tri-Lakes Press 261
Trimble, Mary 167
Turkey Creek 4-5, 61-62, 153
Turkey Creek bridge 153
Turnbeaugh, Mary Margaret 207

U

U-Haul 261
Union Pacific Railroad 178
United Nations 193-194
University of Oklahoma 146
University of Southern California 215
Upton, Lucille Morris 182
U. S. Corps of Engineers 114

Index

V

vacation resorts 9
Valett, Adelyn 279, 281-282, 295, 297
Van Buskirk, Kathleen v, ix, 272, 274, 320, 322
Vaughn, Hazel 52, 96-97, 132
Veterans of Foreign Wars 247
vice president 12, 17, 41, 100, 126, 184-185, 196, 200, 206, 241, 258, 267, 269, 285, 288, 290, 303, 317
victrola 104
Villa Narcissus 82
vineyards 5
violin 19, 21
Volkswagen buses 237
volunteer fire department 9
volunteer librarians 288, 315

W

Wagner, Walter 266
Walker Novelty Shop 192
Walking Preacher of the Ozarks 151
War 30-31, 89, 121, 127-128, 133-134, 137, 139, 142-143, 155, 157, 159-161, 165, 171, 176, 191, 193, 231-232, 240, 322-323
Warder, Elizabeth 265
War Memorial 159
Warrensburg State Teachers College 219
Washington, D.C 60, 111
Washington, Miss Martha 269
water in the library 104, 311

Wayland, Adelaide 33
Ways and Means Committee 83, 87, 108, 119-120, 130, 134, 137, 141, 157-158, 163, 168, 171, 193, 199, 201, 208, 232, 234-235, 241, 248, 278
Weaver, Juanita 142
Weaver, Sam 192
Webb Novelty factory 149
Wheeler, Annie 297
Whelchel Funeral Home 133
Whelchel, Minnie 122, 130, 133, 174, 205, 220, 245
Whelchel, Mrs. Norman 133
Whelchel's Hardware Store 107
White Frog Restaurant 249, 289
White River 3-7, 10, 17, 27, 34, 51, 68, 74, 76, 81, 88, 96, 107, 113-114, 124, 126, 128, 132, 139-140, 151-152, 155, 162, 164, 179, 189, 198, 216, 238-239, 241, 292, 319
White River Booster Club 239
White River Hotel 113, 126, 128, 132, 139, 151, 238
White River Leader 10, 17, 27, 34, 68, 81, 88, 96, 107, 124, 155, 162, 164, 198, 216, 319
White River Valley Electric Cooperative 292
Wilbur, Mary 79, 95
Wilder, Laura Ingalls 56
Wiley, "Cap" 171
Wiley, Ruth 170-171
Wilhelm, Joyce 228, 230

Index

Williams, Audrey 265
Williams, Helen 303, 316
Williams, Lena 15, 96
Williams, Marjory 126
Williams, Rev. Glen A. 15
Wing, Esther 184-185
Wise, Frank 177
Work Projects Administration 75
World War II 137, 143, 171, 191, 193, 280
Worman, Dorothy 46, 53, 98, 106
WPA 75-77, 86
Wright, Daisy Belle 185
Wright, Harold Bell viii, 26, 37, 71, 85, 122-123, 196, 198, 225, 246, 266, 315
Wynn, Mr. 171

Y

Yanet Club 69
Yates, Betty 256, 258, 267-268, 277
Ye English Inn 56-57, 79, 94-95, 109, 125, 131, 139, 142, 146, 153, 163, 192, 194, 310
Yearbook, Library Club 29, 95, 100, 147, 164-165, 176, 212, 230-231, 294, 321
Youngblood, Robert 267